Where We Live

The Residential Districts

of Minneapolis and Saint Paul

The John K. Fesler Memorial Fund provided assistance in the publication of this volume, for which the University of Minnesota Press is grateful.

Where
We Live

The
Residential Districts of
Minneapolis and Saint Paul

Judith A. Martin
and David A. Lanegran

Photographs by Henry Hall

Published by the
University of Minnesota Press, Minneapolis
in Association with the
Center for Urban and Regional Affairs,
University of Minnesota, Minneapolis

Library of Congress Cataloging in Publication Data

Martin, Judith A.
   Where We Live.

   Bibliography: p.
   Includes index.
   1. Cities and towns—Minnesota—Growth. 2. Minneapolis
(Minn.)—History. 3. Saint Paul (Minn.)—History.
I. Lanegran, David. A. II. Title.
HT371.M29 1983   307.7'64'09776579   82-11064
ISBN 0-8166-1093-2
ISBN 0-8166-1094-0 (pbk.)

For Karen and Bill

Acknowledgments

This book developed out of our experiences teaching about the Twin Cities. Our general approach to observing and writing about cities comes in large measure from our association with John R. Borchert and a group of scholars of the Twin Cities which includes Ronald Abler, John S. Adams, Hildegard Binder-Johnson, David Cooperman, Fred Lukermann, Ernest Sandeen, Warner Shippee, and Steve Trimble. It would be impossible to recognize all the individuals who have contributed to our understanding of the evolution of the Twin Cities. Years of fieldwork and library research have brought us into contact with hundreds of people whose individual contributions can never be adequately acknowledged. They each have helped us and made our research a constant source of pleasure. Our students, in Urban Studies workshops at the University of Minnesota and in Urban Geography classes at Macalester College, have aided us through their observations of particular parts of each city. Brian Blackard and Amy Tessmer served as research assistants on this project and performed many tedious chores with good cheer. Particular thanks are due to Michael Munson of the Metropolitan Council for sharing with us his data on social and economic conditions in Minneapolis and Saint Paul, derived from information gathered by the R. L. Polk Directory Company. Finally we wish to thank Thomas Scott and Thomas Anding of the University's Center for Urban and Regional Affairs; their interest and financial support through several phases of this project made the publication of this book possible.

Table of Contents

Where We Live

The Residential Districts

of Minneapolis and Saint Paul

The Ford Bridge. The bridges that link Minneapolis and Saint Paul symbolize the interplay of transportation and topography which has characterized the development of the two cities.

I

The Patterns of Residential Development

The Twin Cities of Minneapolis and Saint Paul contain a fascinating mix of places and people. The oldest residential sections date from the late nineteenth century, when Germans, Irish, and Scandinavians came to the Twin Cities. Many areas reflect the evolution of both cities throughout the twentieth century. A current phase is redevelopment, involving either post-modern architectural styles or those reminiscent of the past. The population has also changed and now includes many Hispanics, Native Americans, and Southeast Asians. Over the years, the residential areas of the Twin Cities have come to reflect in a very precise way the people who live here, their interests and their aspirations.

What types of changes have produced the present configuration of residential districts in Minneapolis and Saint Paul? Dramatic changes like highway construction, the closing of employment centers, and the arrival of new immigrant groups may have a profound effect on residential communities. But such changes occur infrequently. The set of changes that have had the greatest impact on the Twin Cities are more subtle and occur on a fairly regular basis. These include improvements in transportation technology, changes in architectural styles, in the local economic conditions, and in levels of property maintenance.

In this book, we shall explore the residential areas of the Twin Cities. We hope to heighten readers' appreciation for the special qualities of each area and to provide them with an understanding of the processes that have shaped the growth of these two cities. We begin with a brief overview of residential development in Minneapolis and Saint Paul.

THE GROWTH OF MINNEAPOLIS AND SAINT PAUL

The residential sections of the Twin Cities grew outward from the original settlements at Lowertown in Saint Paul (established in 1835) and at Saint Anthony Falls (1847) and Bridge Square (1851) in Minneapolis. The areas closest to the river were built up first. Even in the 1860s and 1870s houses ranged from small cottages (like the Stevens house, now located at Minnehaha Park) to stately mansions (Governor Ramsey's house near Irvine Park). A few adventurous souls lived away from these primary concentrations. The Desnoyers farmed east-bank bluff land on the road from Saint Paul to St. Anthony, and the Morrisons settled the Fair Oaks section of south Minneapolis, both antedating the Civil War. Eventually even these far-flung locations became residential sections of the cities. But in the period of stagecoach and rail transit between the cities and pedestrian travel within the cities, most residential development remained close to the original settlements.

By the 1880s both downtowns had expanded their commercial facilities and were becoming somewhat cramped. More and more residences were squeezed out of the central areas as land values there escalated and businesses expanded into former residential areas. Thus there was a need to build up more residential areas. The development of fashionable residential districts helped establish the high-income sectors of each city, while working-class housing competed with transportation and industry for areas disdained by the wealthy.

Fashionable areas developed to the west of downtown Saint Paul, on Saint Anthony Hill and across the top of the bluff on Summit Avenue. In Minneapolis these areas were most prominent southwest of downtown, in Loring Park and on Lowry Hill. All the fashionable areas tended to be rather inaccessible. Their hilly terrains were unsuited for anything but expensive housing. To live here one had to own a private carriage, and one's working hours had to be somewhat flexible since bad weather could impede access to downtown. Most houses in these locations were constructed of brick or stone, with many elaborate design details. All were exceptionally large, having servants' quarters as a matter of course.

Working-class residences, on the other hand, were built in areas close to industrial employment because most laborers in the 1880s walked to their jobs. Those who could afford streetcar fare had the choice of living farther from work but were limited to areas where tracks had already been laid. Working-class sections of Saint Paul were the North End (north of University and west of Jackson) and the West Seventh Street area, both of which were close to the large breweries and railroad yards. In Minneapolis these areas included the Near Northside, located close to the lumber mills on the river, and lower Northeast, Cedar-Riverside, and western Seward, all within easy walking distance of large flour mills or railroad yards. Houses in these areas were primarily small frame dwellings on cramped lots. Because many residents of these areas were foreign-born heirs to long-standing craft traditions—particularly Scandinavian woodworking—a great number of the dwellings contained features considered extremely desirable today.

Examples include natural woodwork, built-in buffets, and some intricately designed windows.

The Impact of the Streetcar

During the 1880s, 1890s, and into the first decade of the twentieth century both Minneapolis and Saint Paul gained population at startling rates. People came to both cities from abroad, from rural parts of the surrounding states, and from worn-out farming areas of the eastern United States. The residential areas of both cities expanded quickly, owing to the rapid extension of electric streetcar lines in almost every direction. The improvements in transportation coincided with the national emergence of professional, salaried white-collar workers. These people imitated the wealthy insofar as they could, copying their housing styles and moving to similar sections of each city, if not to the same blocks. In Saint Paul, the following areas were developed at this time: Macalester Park and Merriam Park, far to the west of downtown but on reliable transit lines, and the Summit-University area where blocks of duplexes and apartment buildings flanked the blocks of elite mansions. In Minneapolis, streetcar expansion led to settlement in the Wedge and Whittier areas southwest of downtown, on the periphery of the elite settlements on Lowry Hill and in Washburn-Fair Oaks. The streetcars also stimulated housing construction on the eastern edges of Lake of the Isles and Lake Calhoun. Roomy Victorian frame structures with stained glass and carved wood details were the typical housing style of the middle class settling these areas. Although none of these houses were as luxurious or spacious as contemporary elite residences, by today's standards they seem elegant fare for merchants or managers, with their occasional ballrooms and maid's bells.

Until the 1920s these patterns of development continued as the streetcar network was extended. The wealthy set the standard for residential desirability. In some cities this group moved away from downtown so continuously and so quickly that they were soon beyond the city limits. In Minneapolis and Saint Paul the wealthy did not move their permanent residences so far so fast. They remained close to established areas of high-income settlement in each city, while also building summer houses outside the city limits on Lake Minnetonka or White Bear Lake. The middle class continued to fill in areas along transit lines, moving farther west in Saint Paul and farther southwest in Minneapolis. At the same time the working class built up the landscape of small frame houses and duplexes, moving north along Rice Street and Payne Avenue in Saint Paul. In Minneapolis this group fanned out along North Lyndale, University Avenue Northeast, and Hiawatha and Cedar Avenues on the south side.

Residential Development in the 1920s through 1960s

With the widespread introduction of the automobile into American society around 1920, residential development was no longer confined to sectors served by streetcars. First the rich and then the middle class purchased their own autos. Having thus acquired independent transportation, many people were now free to live in areas that had hitherto been relatively inaccessible. New residential areas began to be developed, with much of the housing being built between and beyond the edges of prior settlements. In Saint Paul, the Groveland addition, the northern stretches of Highland Park, and most of the Midway area began to fill up with houses. In Minneapolis settlement began in earnest in places like Willard-Homewood on the north side, most of the city south of 38th Street, and up the hill in Northeast. This movement was predominantly middle-class. It created a residential landscape of two- and three-bedroom stucco homes that have come to personify single-family housing in the Twin Cities.

The 1920s also brought the first major residential redevelopments in both cities. The housing demands of young couples and downtown workers caused a construction boom in the 1920s, which led to the building of apartments close to the downtown areas. In Minneapolis this changed the landscape of those areas directly south of downtown, including Loring Park, Stevens Square, and Elliot Park. In Saint Paul, apartments appeared along Grand Avenue on the fringes of Crocus Hill and along Selby Avenue.

The pattern of gradual residential construction between and beyond established streetcar zones continued until the late 1940s when the suburban building boom started in earnest, facilitated by the development of the freeway system. Returning veterans and ill-housed families who had doubled up during the war now had access to homes of their own in both cities and their suburbs. Inside the cities post-war housing construction led people directly to the peripheral sections not yet touched by settlement. These remnants were quickly filled in with bungalows, ranch houses, and variations on the Cape Cod theme, looking for all the world just like their abutting suburban counterparts. Because the streetcar system in Saint Paul was never quite as extensive as that in Minneapolis, Saint Paul had much larger in-city areas left to develop in the postwar period. Battle Creek, Hazel Park, and most of the Lake Phalen area on the east side, along with much of Highland Park, were all built up during the 1950s and 1960s. In contrast, the only undeveloped areas of Minneapolis were the part of the city south of 54th Street, the northeast corner around Waite Park, and the Shingle Creek area, and most of these areas filled in during the fifties.

Beginning in the 1960s many older areas of the cities experienced a mini-boom of apartment construction as the older members of the postwar baby boom left their parents' homes. This construction was concentrated around the University of Minnesota and in the Whittier area of Minneapolis, and close to the northern edge of Saint Paul. Two-and-one-half-story walkup buildings appeared in all these areas. By the late 1960s this mode of construction hit the suburbs with full force; large clusters of apartment buildings appeared in suburbs like West Saint Paul, Richfield, and Saint Louis Park.

The Impact of Redevelopment

Observers have noted the beginnings of what may be an important new development pattern. Some older sections of Saint Paul and Minneapolis have recently attracted significant new investments. Most often this occurs through the preservation or renovation of deteriorated late nineteenth-century houses close to downtown. It brings with it the accoutrements of "sophisticated" living (theme restaurants, trendy clothing, plant and kitchen supply stores), and it spawns new industries or revives dying ones (stained glass manufacture and repair). In the Twin Cities today, as in cities across the country, some longtime city residents worry about being priced out of their homes by upwardly mobile newcomers. (Meanwhile, suburban dwellers are beginning to worry about declining school enrollments and aging population bases.)

The Impact of Population Shifts

Distinctive residential patterns derive from more than physical development. The people who build and live in houses make a difference as well. Their income and occupations, their educational backgrounds, their ethnicity, even the number of children they have, all help to determine the residential landscape. These factors influence both what gets built and how well such structures are maintained. It was a commonly accepted view of late nineteenth- and early twentieth-century urban life that each ethnic group sought to inhabit a distinct section of the inner city. As these groups prospered and became Americanized, they and their offspring moved out toward the edges of the city and mixed with other ethnic groups. People moved to improve their housing conditions and to raise their social status. Typically, they moved to increasingly newer and better-maintained housing. The housing that was left behind deteriorated as it continually served the newest groups arriving on the urban scene. Thus the processes of social and economic achievement have been closely linked to the process of residential "filtering," whereby older, denser, and close-in housing was abandoned in favor of newer and more spacious housing located farther from the city center.

Population shifts affect the commercial well-being of a residential area in addition to the quality of its housing. For example, when the central Twin Cities began losing population to the suburbs in the 1950s, they also suffered a commercial decline. Shopping malls, constructed to serve the new suburban residents, quickly drew retail dollars away from both downtowns, while industries took thousands of job opportunities with them when they relocated to the suburbs.

Finally, population shifts have an impact on the overall quality of life in a residential area. The presence of local schools, the provision of social services and public services ranging from police protection to garbage collection—all are dependent on the number and types of people living in an area at a given time.

THE RESIDENTIAL ZONES OF MINNEAPOLIS AND SAINT PAUL

In Minneapolis and Saint Paul, these development patterns have produced eight types of residential areas, or zones. (See map 1.) Each zone is discussed in a separate chapter of this book. The zones can be subdivided into smaller areas, which we refer to as residential districts. We have made no attempt to describe every district within a zone. Instead, we have used a set of districts to illustrate the range of conditions within the larger zone.

We have included a map of each residential zone. The maps do not show all the place-names mentioned in the text, for the high cost of cartographic assistance made it impractical to provide details of every residential district. Our maps can easily be interpolated to city street maps to locate precise references.

The geographic area of the zones is variable, and some

Lake Calhoun. Despite the highly urbanized character of both cities, many areas retain an almost pastoral look.

6

Map 1: Twin Cities Zones of Residential Development. There are eight residential zones within the Twin Cities. These zones have resulted from the interplay of population dispersal, economic activities, transportation, topography, and architectural style.

zones contain no more than a handful of districts. The largest zone in each city may be as much as four or five times bigger than the smallest in total area. It is important to remember that the eight zones are not continuous areas and that their parts may be found widely separated from one another in both Saint Paul and Minneapolis. But no matter where the individual parts of the zone may be located, they share a similar physical appearance and are occupied by similar people.

Our descriptions and analyses are predominantly based on the environmental/architectural/aesthetic characteristics of particular zones and districts, correlated with available demographic data. In devising the classifications, we have taken into consideration when an area was developed and the median age of most housing there, as well as evidence of rehabilitation and renewal. There are some variations within each category. For example, the level of home maintenance may vary slightly within a zone—all blocks are not necessarily interchangeable. We do believe, however, that each portion of every zone more closely resembles the rest of that zone than it does any other part of the city.

The residents of any given zone have similar hopes and experiences. In most districts they share social and economic characteristics as well, including such things as similar incomes, occupations, or ethnic ties. Many residents have developed strong emotional ties to their district. In some districts it is not unusual to find people in their seventies who have lived their entire lives in the same locale. Fortunately, the younger people who now share their districts seem to have the same attachment to their homes and neighbors.

The eight residential zones of the Twin Cities are as follows:

1. *Aging Inner Ring*. This zone encompasses the pre-1900 streetcar landscape that rings the core of each city. It contains large amounts of older housing, primarily built between 1880 and 1910. Types of residence include small frame houses, frame or stucco duplexes, occasional fourplexes, and highrises for senior citizens. Some portions of the aging inner ring originally housed clerical workers and others with white-collar aspirations. But in recent years these districts have been the home of the stable working class. Levels of home maintenance vary greatly. Most houses have decayed somewhat, but on any given block one can find properties that are extremely well maintained right next to some that are severely deteriorated.

2. *Protected Genteel Zone*. Located quite close to the downtowns, these districts were built up around 1900. They originally housed the upper and upper middle classes, the sons and daughters of the "first families." For the most part, they have been able to retain or attract residents who are financially secure or well educated, or both. Large dwellings, many of them architecturally interesting, are commonplace here. These houses have been and continue to be well maintained. Perhaps the hallmark of these districts is an element of style associated with the leisure activities of residents, who tend to patronize cultural and artistic events en masse.

3. *Rebuilt Zone*. This zone contains some of the oldest parts of each city, built up before 1900 and bordering the downtowns. At first, the zone housed industrial workers, day laborers, and some clerical workers, but it began to suffer both social and physical decline as early as the 1920s. Small frame houses originally covered the landscape in most of these districts. With few exceptions, these are long gone. The distinguishing trait of the rebuilt zone is the substantial amount of clearance and new construction or reconstruction. Whether the rebuilding process was initiated privately or publicly, these districts were at one time the most severely deteriorated parts of each city. The rebuilding process yielded both single-family homes and large highrise buildings. The population of these areas now ranges from the very poor to the financially secure.

4. *Turnaround Zone*. Like the rebuilt districts, the turnaround zone has experienced serious decline since first being settled around the turn of the century. But unlike the rebuilt zone, these districts were originally middle class in character and housing stock, and did not receive very much public or private attention until quite recently. The first residents of these districts were managers, entrepreneurs, and upwardly mobile young people. More recently, some of the turnaround districts have sheltered a number of the cities' poorest residents. The predominant characteristics of the turnaround zone include the very recent evidence of Victorian restorations, expensive townhouse or condominium construction, or substantial housing rehabilitation on block after block. Although some current residents of these districts fear a wholesale invasion of well-off home buyers,

it is still too early to tell whether this will come to pass. These are clearly the places in each city where some of the most interesting things are happening now, and where, some feel, the future of the city will be decided.

5. *Settled Mid-City Zone*. Most of the housing in this zone was built between 1900 and 1920. It consists primarily of medium-sized to very large single-family frame structures, with some duplexes and older brick apartment buildings as well. This zone was built for the middle class and has continued to serve this group, though stable working-class families have always lived there too. There are now signs of deterioration in these areas; some houses need repainting or a new roof. These symptoms are not widespread, tending to be concentrated along the edges of the aging inner ring. In general, levels of home maintenance are very high throughout this zone. If one were to describe the ideal "older urban neighborhood," the odds are very high that in Minneapolis and Saint Paul the description would fit major portions of the settled mid-city.

6. *Prewar Grid Zone*. This zone was on the fringe of regular streetcar service in 1920. It includes some of the first sections of either city that catered to residents owning automobiles, as well as some of the first houses built with garages. Most of the housing in this zone dates from after 1920, forming block after block of tidy stucco bungalows. Residents of the prewar grid zone have been and continue to be blue-collar workers with stable jobs, clerical workers, and some lower-level managers. Levels of home maintenance are very high, with few homes being in need of even minor repairs. Nothing about these areas is pretentious; they form a comfortable middle-class landscape.

7. *Prewar Amenity Zone*. Districts in this category resemble the prewar grid zone in age of housing and demographic characteristics, with minor modifications. The distinction between these two zones is topographic and stylistic. The prewar amenity districts contain within them, or border on, a major source of visual relief from the standard grid pattern of streets. These amenities may be lakes, large parks, creeks, or extremely hilly terrain. The prewar amenity zone was also built up during the post-1920 recreational auto period. In some sections the housing tends to be large and expensive. It contains Midwestern versions of Period Revival architecture and betrays the influence, if not the handiwork, of important early twentieth-century de-

signers. Residents of this zone have above-average incomes, and their occupations are predominantly professional and managerial. As in the prewar grid zone, homes here are extremely well maintained. The attractive qualities of the physical environment in the prewar amenity zone make living here a goal for upwardly mobile families who want to live in the city.

8. *Suburban-in-City Zone*. Located at the edges of the cities, these parts of Saint Paul and Minneapolis were left open and undeveloped until after World War II. This zone filled in during the late 1940s, 1950s, and 1960s when freeway construction began to make suburbs accessible for mass residential construction. The housing here is typical of inner-ring suburbs: ranch houses, ramblers, brick and stucco bungalows, and Cape Cods. The population of this zone is predominantly middle-class and white-collar. The suburban-in-city districts of both cities are extremely stable. There are many areas where one can find original owners occupying houses they bought twenty-five to thirty years ago. Needless to say, there is little need for repair in these homes. They have, for the most part, been well cared for, and the immediate surroundings have gradually become quite attractive as vegetation has matured.

A NOTE ON THE USE OF THE TERM "RESIDENTIAL DISTRICTS"

We have chosen to refer to the smaller portions of the zones as *residential districts* rather than *neighborhoods* for a variety of reasons. First, the boundaries and names of neighborhoods are not as hard-and-fast as they might appear to be. In Minneapolis, for example, there are official neighborhoods—duly certified by a city agency. But such designated areas do not necessarily have any special significance for local residents, who routinely alter boundaries to include things they like, or to exclude things they do not like. Even official boundaries are not always stable. Officially designated neighborhoods in Minneapolis have disappeared, while others have come into being. Name changes also occur more often than one might think. Newly discovered historical connections can elicit a name change, as can the loss of a school whose presence has defined an area for generations.

Second, there are discrepancies between the historic role of the neighborhood as a social unit and current human behavior. During the heyday of migration to American cities, foreign migrants settled near their countrymen because it was the place where they could live with the least amount of anxiety. Some people had to live in certain neighborhoods simply to carry on their daily existence — they had to live where their language could be understood. In cities today, many people are less likely to choose to live among others of their own ethnic or religious background. People are, in general, less attached to institutions like churches, whose locations used to guide residential choices. These choices are now made on the basis of an area's physical attributes or perceived social status.

These localized social groupings of the past were possible because most women were at home for most of the day, helping to create a sense of neighborhood through their daily activities. As more and more women move into the labor force, the networks that form and support a neighborhood's identity change dramatically. They become self-conscious and purposeful. Declines in household size and increases in the number of households have also distorted traditional neighboring behavior. Children were once the element that bonded a neighborhood; as the proportion of children in any area declines, and as local schools close, the perceptions of neighborhood diminish as well.

As we can see, "neighborhood" has become a perplexing concept. Many of our ideas about neighborhoods are based on romantic historical notions, and are rooted in obsolete economic situations. Thus we have chosen to focus on broadly conceived residential districts as the building blocks of the eight zones in Minneapolis and Saint Paul.

CHAPTER
II

The Aging Inner Ring

The aging inner ring encompasses the older, unreno-
vated portions of Minneapolis and Saint Paul. It is
an area that, in the public mind, may be associated with deteriorated housing, crime, poor people and minorities, and
other "troublesome" aspects of urban life. It is, in short, an
area that many people with other housing options often
ignore. Yet the aging inner ring is home to many people—
even many who could afford to live elsewhere. There is a
vitality here that is unmatched anywhere else in the Twin
Cities. Though a disproportionate share of poor people live
in this zone, residents use their limited resources to display
their pride in their homes and in their communities. Many
residents have painstakingly organized their areas in order
to actively participate in decision making that might affect
them. They no longer defer to outsiders with quick-fix solutions to their problems. Instead they are gaining a voice in
planning the future of their districts.

The landscape of the aging inner ring is, for the most
part, composed of unremarkable small old houses on small
lots, utilitarian duplexes and apartment buildings, and a few
newer highrise buildings. Houses are crowded together and
close to the street, producing a cramped and closed-in feeling. There is little or no visual relief. No lakes are in or near
this zone, and the few good-sized parks seem woefully
inadequate for the population they must serve. There are
trees, but they seem almost an afterthought. Here vegetation
must compete for space with houses, cars, and people.

Although the aging inner ring may lack standard amenities, residents compensate for this by creating their own
personal landscapes. Nowhere else in the entire metropolitan area can such exotic backyards be found. Some residents
of this zone have constructed worlds of their own on these
small plots, building everything from complex mechanical
gadgets or whimsical playthings to oversized objects d'art.
There are also wonderful gardens with almost every kind of
flower imaginable. These personal landscapes, in a seemingly
impersonal environment, perhaps best indicate the residents'
resourcefulness.

GEOGRAPHY AND LAND-USE PATTERN

In Minneapolis the aging inner ring forms nearly a full
circle around downtown, separated from it by portions of
the rebuilt and turnaround zones. (See map 2.) This circular
pattern is broken only in the southwest sector of the city.
That area consistently attracted high-income residents, so
inexpensive housing was never built there. The areal spread
of the aging inner ring is extensive. It is the single largest

zone in Minneapolis, comprising nearly a quarter of all the residential land in the city.

In Saint Paul the aging inner ring forms a band surrounding downtown that is broken in several locations. In general, these are the places where scenic attractions spurred more expensive development in the past, places like Crocus Hill, Cherokee Heights, and the portion of Dayton's Bluff adjacent to Mounds Park. The two rebuilt areas in Saint Paul and a pair of turnaround districts also intrude into the aging inner ring. After the suburban-in-city zone, this is the largest of the residential zones in Saint Paul.

The land-use pattern of the aging inner ring is quite mixed. Blocks of housing are interrupted every mile or so by a major commercial artery. About every four blocks there is a store, like a small grocery, on the streetcorner. The large swaths of railroad tracks and associated shops impart a special atmosphere. In fact, most of the districts in this zone were developed to house workers employed by the railroads, or by industries dependent upon rail transit. The industrial character of this zone has diminished in the last two decades. Still, what remains of railroad-oriented industry in both cities is surrounded by aging inner ring districts. In Minneapolis industrial concentrations are found along the river north of downtown, and along Hiawatha Avenue; in Saint Paul, along University Avenue and around the railroad rights-of-way.

HISTORICAL DEVELOPMENT

Since about 1950, the aging inner ring has undergone many changes. Housing has deteriorated, population has declined, and a rapid influx of minority groups has occurred. Before 1950, this zone had a more uniform quality. Living here was not automatically associated with poverty, crime, or other adverse qualities of urban life, and less attractive parts of the zone did not necessarily inspire despair. The story of how these changing attitudes came about, and how parts of this zone declined so severely in public estimation, is the story of inner-city areas throughout the United States.

Initial settlement of this zone followed on the heels of industrial developments in the 1870s and 1880s, sometimes predating an area's incorporation into the city. Lumber mills and brickyards developed rapidly in the northern portion of this zone in Minneapolis. Railroad assembly yards

and repair shops appeared throughout both cities in the 1880s. All these enterprises needed many workers, and the workers needed to live close to their jobs. So housing was constructed in the vicinity of these industries even before the streetcars reached out from either downtown. The blocks of small houses built for industrial laborers in the aging inner ring were the same age, quality and often the same design as their counterparts in the rebuilt districts. The only difference was the rate at which they declined and disappeared.

In the late nineteenth century, the aging inner ring was a complete microcosm of the city, housing both rich and poor and every level of society in between. The small working-class settlements of the 1880s continued to expand during the 1890s, and middle-class residents appeared in other parts of the zone. The Pillsburys and other "first families" had been proud occupants of some districts since the late 1850s. The mansions still standing on Park Avenue are eloquent remnants of the past community and the individuals who once made extravagant investments here. (The Turnblad house—now the Swedish Institute—is probably the most notable example.) The problems that developed in the aging inner ring can be linked to the increasing affluence and changing consumer tastes of society. The middle and upper classes lived and worked here until better opportunities appeared; then they left these districts and showed little concern for their future.

The parts of the zone closest to industrial employment, the river, and both downtowns were densely settled during the 1880s and 1890s. Most of the rest of the zone was still prairie during those decades, but there were some isolated residential outposts along railroad and streetcar lines. In the 1890s, more streetcar lines were built in the aging inner ring, and the previously settled areas were quickly joined to settlements spreading outward from both downtowns. Streetcar expansion triggered an explosion of population growth and new construction between 1900 and 1920, phenomena detailed in Chapter VI on the settled mid-city zone.

Both these zones grew very quickly between 1890 and 1920. The differences between them were (and still are) both social and physical. The settled mid-city zone attracted a larger proportion of middle-class residents than did the aging inner ring. This was because the middle class tended to move to the newest houses being built throughout this

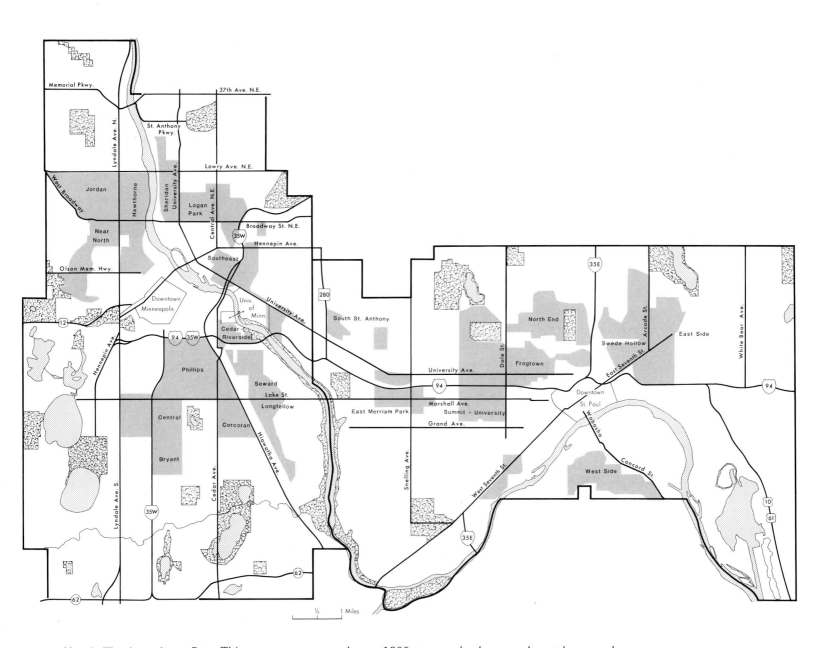

Map 2: The Aging Inner Ring. This zone encompasses the pre-1900 streetcar landscape and contains many houses built between 1880 and 1910.

13

period, and the edge of new construction by 1910 was already out in what would become the settled mid-city districts. Shop proprietors moved to the new areas, while their clerks remained within the aging inner ring.

The physical differences between these zones can be seen in the kinds of dwellings constructed and in the varying levels of housing density. The settled mid-city zone was almost completely filled with single-family houses, whereas the aging inner ring acquired more duplexes and apartment buildings. Many of the individual units in a duplex in the aging inner ring were more spacious than some of the single-family dwellings in the outer zone, but the former still lacked the privacy and independence commonly associated with living in a house with a yard.

Living in the aging inner ring during the first years of the twentieth century was not greatly different from living in most other parts of Minneapolis or Saint Paul. If some residents of this zone had to scrimp a bit more than most, they were not looked down upon for doing so. Indeed, parts of this zone exemplified the "bootstraps" theory of self-improvement at its most efficient. Some immigrants lived here only long enough to acquire a stable job and a down payment for a house in what they perceived to be a better area. But not everyone was eager to leave these districts. Churches of every denomination could be found here, as could every conceivable kind of fraternal organization and benevolent association. Foreign-born newcomers to the Twin Cities found their countrymen here, and made their way alongside earlier migrants. By 1920 the aging inner ring contained far more immigrants than did the rest of either city, as native-born residents continued to move to the outer edges of settlement.

Everyday life in this zone was typical of urban living in the early twentieth century. Men went out to work, children went to school, and most women worked at home. It was not uncommon in the early years to find chickens and cows in most backyards, though after about 1910 this practice was officially discouraged. People worked six days a week and went to church on Sunday. On warm Sundays and holidays residents took the streetcars out to the lakes, cemetaries, and larger parks, where they relaxed and picnicked. Certain lines had to employ extra cars on these occasions just to accommodate the crowds of riders. Many of the laboring men in this zone continued to work near their homes, particularly in the older industrial districts. By 1910 a commute to either downtown from anywhere in the aging inner ring was simple and quick. As the newer sections of this zone filled in, more people took advantage of rapid transportation and worked downtown. Shopping for everyday items could be done within a few blocks of any location. Even major purchases could be made without leaving the zone. In each of the major divisions of this zone in Minneapolis, for example, at least one of the streetcar routes grew into a major commercial strip long before 1920.

The aging inner ring peaked and started to decline after the first World War. Sections of the zone began to show dramatic population losses in the 1920s. A residence in these districts was no longer as desirable as it had once been. Other parts of both cities seemed to have more to offer. In a very real sense the widespread acceptance of automobiles signaled the end for this zone. Here was a large part of each city scaled for pedestrians and with a density of population sufficient to support effective mass transit. But once people bought automobiles, they did not need or want these features anymore. When the aging inner ring could no longer attract the middle class, most of its problems began in earnest.

THE ROLE OF LARGE PUBLIC INSTITUTIONS

There are some characteristics that distinguish the aging inner ring. Most interesting, perhaps, are the links that many institutions have to this zone. For example, many churches that still exist in both cities were originally located in these districts. At one time, denominations of all kinds were represented here, and church buildings were visible every few blocks. Many of these were large, imposing, vaguely Gothic structures. In recent years, numerous church buildings have been torn down to facilitate highway construction, or have been converted to day care centers, community centers, and other nonreligious facilities. At first the area churches attracted new residents to the zone. But eventually many of the congregants left the area, so a good number of churches lost their reason to exist. Some religious institutions abandoned their facilities in the city and followed their people to the suburbs. For example, a few synagogues relocated from Near North Minneapolis to suburban Saint Louis Park. Other congregations remained in existing structures, but were greatly diminished in both numbers and economic strength. Ministers and priests in these places labor diligently to serve groups of people who are vastly different from those they used to serve. In some parts of the zone, particularly Northeast Minneapolis and the North End of Saint Paul, the congregations and churches remain strong. Some are even able to lure members back from the suburbs or from other parts of the city. Incarnation Parish, the old Roman Catholic flagship church of south Minneapolis, is an example of a church with a large physical plant, including a school, that still functions in the way it always has.

The aging inner ring has the highest concentration of large hospital complexes in the entire metropolitan area, though the very largest medical complexes remain in both downtowns. In Minneapolis, for example, many hospitals are located in the southern portion of the aging inner ring, particularly in the Phillips and Riverside areas. Abbott-Northwestern, Fairview, Saint Mary's, Lutheran Deaconess, Mount Sinai, and Minneapolis Children's Hospital, and the Sister Kenny Institute are all found here. On the northern edge of this zone is the North Memorial Medical Center, and the mammoth University of Minnesota medical complex is bordered by the aging inner ring in southeast Minneapolis.

These institutions all have historical and economic ties to the aging inner ring. Most, if not all, of these hospitals are comparatively old. Like the churches, they have strong links to the original ethnic communities of this zone. These hospitals were built at a time when the centers of population in both cities were close to the downtowns, and their founders chose locations that would be closest to most people. They also chose to build on relatively inexpensive land—which may explain the hospital concentration in this zone rather than in the protected genteel districts.

The hospitals eventually became important institutions with larger physical plants. As people began to leave the aging inner ring, economic constraints forced the hospitals to remain behind. When the medical industry began expanding in the 1960s, substantial new investments were made in each of these older facilities. These investments have in turn had profound effects on nearby districts. Some areas have had to accommodate the rapid construction of new hospital buildings and of new apartment buildings for

staff to live in. Traffic has increased and local travel has become difficult owing to the daily influx of hospital visitors. In some districts hospitals are so large and their influence is so pervasive that routine community decisions cannot be made without involving their administrative staffs.

An institution that profoundly influences part of the aging inner ring in Minneapolis is the University of Minnesota. Sprawling on two sides of the Mississippi with sections of this zone almost completely surrounding it, the University affects transportation, housing, and commercial facilities on every side. The parking needs of students, staff, and visitors have progressively expanded. The usual "solution" to this problem has been to tear down nearby housing and create more lots or ramps. Students and staff who wish to live close to campus have poured into surrounding areas in such numbers that it is difficult to find traditional families not affiliated with the University still here. Conversion of single-family houses to rooming houses has been rampant. Many older homes in Southeast Minneapolis have simply been torn down in recent years, usually to be replaced by the ubiquitous two-and-a-half-story walkup apartment buildings that dot the area. Neighborhood relations and activities are confounded by the highly transient population moving in and out of this area. And at times bookstores and record shops have been more evident than grocery or hardware stores. Since the mid-1960s, as more students have chosen to live away from home and off-campus, problems of this kind have increased.

The effects of the University on surrounding areas are clearly demonstrated in census data: in 1970, the nearby portions of the aging inner ring had the highest educational levels in the city, and some of the lowest income levels. Because of the University's proximity, these districts are considered more activist, more radical, and more tolerant of what might be considered "deviant" behavior in other parts of the city. It is not always true that people living here conform to this image, but the image does indicate the strength of the University's passive influence.

COMMERCIAL DEVELOPMENT

The commercial facilities within the aging inner ring were the best in the city, outside of downtown, well into the 1950s. In Minneapolis, the streetcar shopping strips along

Remnant of streetcar commercial landscape. Lake Street looking east from Chicago Avenue.

*Commercial redevelopment. Minnehaha Mall,
Lake Street and 27th Avenue.*

West Broadway, East Lake, and Central Avenue Northeast had all the range and diversity of services now found in suburban shopping centers. The only thing they lacked were multiple major department stores, though Lake Street did have the largest Sears outlet in the metropolitan area. Each of these commercial areas was large, extending eight to ten blocks or more, and each served an extremely large residential area. For example, until Brookdale Center opened northwest of Minneapolis in the early 1960s, people from every part of north Minneapolis made most major purchases in the Broadway Avenue stores. Similarly, the Lake Street and Central Avenue centers remained prosperous until the mid-sixties, when Southdale, Rosedale, and other smaller centers that ringed both cities cut into their trade areas.

During the fifties and sixties the older commercial strips began to suffer because they did not have enough parking, and could not offer amenities as the shopping centers could. A shopper might have to walk several blocks to accomplish all of his or her errands on one of these streets. Although the same distance might be covered in a center, being inside a temperature-controlled environment with places to sit and rest was a temptation that few could resist. Shoppers no longer had to dodge traffic or get wet or cold dashing between stores. They deserted the old strips in great numbers. Only those who had to rely on public transit for their shopping remained loyal to the old strips.

The Lake Street shopping district, running from Lyndale east to the river and lying just south of the 29th Street industrial corridor, was solidly built up by about 1920. The Sears store, which anchored the entire strip, was built in 1927, clearly underscoring the economic strength and potential of this zone. At one time, Lake Street offered every conceivable kind of product or service. It had pharmacies, ice cream parlors, doctors' offices, bakeries, five and dimes, groceries, clothing stores, art deco dancehalls, and movie theaters. It even had, for a while, a large amusement park at East 36th Avenue (Wonderland) and the Nicollet stadium where the Minneapolis Millers played baseball. What it did not have, and still lacks, was sufficient parking. By the 1950s many people were routinely driving their cars to shop, and there simply wasn't space for them. The difficulty of parking, combined with the loss of population in surrounding areas, sealed the fate of Lake Street as a second-rate shopping facility. Businesses closed down or changed hands. Fast-food chain restaurants began to appear in increasing numbers over the years. And in the 1960s many of the movie theaters began showing pornographic films or went out of business.

The decline of Lake Street seemed irreversible, until two major developments were planned in the early 1970s: the K-Mart discount store at Nicollet and Lake, and Minnehaha Mall on the old Minneapolis Moline site at 27th Avenue South. The latter, in particular, has been quite successful. Anchored on either end by a Target discount store and a Super Valu grocery, the Mall contains a wide variety of specialty and service shops, including two banks. Both of these projects have generous parking facilities and have generated a strong customer response. They indicate that there is a market for suburban-style shopping facilities in the city, accommodating not only mass-transit riders, but motorists as well.

The Broadway and Central Avenue shopping strips in Minneapolis suffered from similar problems. In the early twentieth century West Broadway had several groceries, meat markets, and drug stores, a laundry, a blacksmith

Remnant of streetcar commercial strip on Central Avenue in Northeast Minneapolis.

shop, a paint and wallpaper store, a furniture store, a shoe company, a photographer's shop, a Swedish restaurant, and even a mortuary. It was an active business center, but suffered a decline in the 1950s similar to Lake Street's. Economic deterioration was gradual but widely acknowledged; by the mid-1970s it was so pronounced that plans for the comeback of Broadway Avenue were commonplace. A shopping center proposed for the area just west of the Interstate-94 extension broke ground late in 1981, anchored, like Lake Street's improvements, by a Target store. West Broadway merchants believe that their new neighbor will inspire store owners to improve their properties and will generate improved cash flow up and down the strip.

Across the river in Northeast Minneapolis, Central Avenue had a slightly different experience. It never reached so pronounced a state of economic decline as some other shopping strips in the aging inner ring. This was partly due to the many ethnic specialty shops that lined the street and catered to specific groups. Nevertheless, the Central Avenue Commercial Association worked to maintain business along the street. An example was the group's successful efforts to prevent the installation of parking meters along Central Avenue, so that customers would feel as few constraints as possible.

In the early twentieth century, University Avenue in Saint Paul offered the same range of commercial facilities as its Minneapolis counterparts. The Montgomery Ward's store and warehouse dominated the retailing sections of the street. The Lexington Baseball Park was home to the Saint Paul Saints, the Triple A League rivals of the Lake-Street-based Minneapolis Millers. Nearby rail lines brought heavy industry and warehouse activity to the immediate vicinity. Long the home of large car and truck sales facilities, University was a street where a shopper could buy anything if he or she was willing to pay the price. No wonder a local columnist, Oliver Towne, called it the "street of city slickers."

In the late 1970s local business leaders and city government attempted to breathe new life into University Avenue. A development corporation was established to help area merchants and landlords secure financing to redevelop buildings and expand their operations. A local bank initiated a series of activities designed to enhance the low-income residential districts adjacent to the street. And public development money combined with private management in an effort to create a regional shopping center for inner-city residents, namely, the Uni-Dale center at University and Dale. In many respects this shopping center resembles the developments around Nicollet and Lake.

POPULATION AND HOUSING

Most people who live in the aging inner ring are at the lower end of the socioeconomic scale. Residents have little money, limited resources, and few opportunities to advance themselves economically. They are people who invest, if at all, in property and who trust what savings they may have to insured bank accounts. Many residents of this zone are fiercely proud. One resident of Northeast Minneapolis claimed that no one in the area received food stamps and that "people would rather starve than not pay their bills on time." Income levels in this zone do vary, but are almost uniformly lower than the Minneapolis average ($15,246). As might be expected, few highly paid white-collar workers live in the aging inner ring. (See table 1, p. 144.) This zone is not a place where people tend to live alone, except around the University and where highrises for the elderly are located. Households with children are more typical of this zone.

The aging inner ring contains a broad range of population groups. There is probably greater ethnic and racial diversity in this zone than in any other. Most of Minneapolis' black and Native American residents live here, though in somewhat different areas. In Saint Paul these groups are outnumbered by large Hispanic and Southeast Asian populations. The aging inner ring also houses many senior citizens and many students who live away from their families; the foreign-born and those with strong ethnic ties are readily visible too.

It is common wisdom that the inner areas of American cities are losing both households and people. But parts of the aging inner ring in Minneapolis have recently gained households, while still losing population. Most of the poorer people of both cities are being forced into the aging inner ring, since it is the only area where a large supply of relatively inexpensive housing can still be found. In the rebuilt zone, most of the deteriorated housing has been removed through public efforts, and access to subsidized housing is strictly controlled. In the turnaround zone, low-cost hous-

The growth of the University of Minnesota has transformed surrounding areas within the aging inner ring, increasing population density and altering the residential landscape.

ing is being assaulted on two fronts: by publicly sponsored rehabilitation efforts and by privately funded new construction. So the aging inner ring is left to house those who have nowhere else to go. And as the process of change in the turnaround districts accelerates, the pressures on the aging inner ring are likely to increase.

In most parts of any city the housing supply is thought to be relatively constant. This is not the case in this zone. Here houses disappear in a day or two without explanation. When single-family houses are demolished, they are usually replaced by multifamily dwellings. Nor is the condition of the existing housing particularly good. Most structures, including both single-family homes and apartment buildings, are in "fair" to "poor" condition. This means that most houses either need numerous major repairs or need to be

rehabilitated. There is less single-family housing in the aging inner ring than in other zones. The proportion of owner-occupants is also relatively low. In districts near the University, for example, homeowners comprise only about 10 percent of all residents. Recently, both public and private rehabilitation efforts have increased the numbers of home-owners in this zone. Not surprisingly, areas having more single-family houses are in slightly better condition. Marke values of property throughout the aging inner ring tend be lower than average, though even here they are increasi

We conducted a study of random blocks in this zone our findings further underscore some of the traits al mentioned. The Near North and Phillips districts of apolis demonstrate one dimension of the range wi aging inner ring. Levels of stability and home owne

19

*The aging inner ring continues to provide housing
for the newest immigrant groups to the Twin Cities.
In recent years Phillips, for example, has gained
a substantial concentration of Southeast Asians.*

tion of the North Side area seems to be of French, German, and Scandinavian descent. Residents of the Northeast district are predominantly of Eastern European stock, particularly Poles. Each district includes a large contingent of retired persons. As in the rest of the aging inner ring, the working population comprises skilled workers, laborers, and operatives (machinists, painters).

This zone, then, has a population that earns less than most people in the Twin Cities, and housing that needs more repair than most other units. We found that in districts bordering on parts of the settled mid-city zone, conditions tend to be better than elsewhere: there are more single-family houses, somewhat higher incomes, and more owner-occupants. Districts of this zone located closer to either downtown tend to be more densely settled, more deteriorated, and their residents tend to be slightly poorer.

DISTRICTS OF THE AGING INNER RING

The aging inner ring in Minneapolis is large and some of its districts are distinct. On the north side are four separate districts with a population that is predominantly white ethnic or black. Across the Mississippi, districts in Northeast and Southeast Minneapolis are populated by white ethnic families and single students. The South Minneapolis portion of this zone shelters blacks, American Indians, and working-class whites.

Minneapolis—North Side

The north side extension of the aging inner ring reaches from the Great Northern railroad swath on the south up to Lowry Avenue North. (See map 2.) The eastern border is the Mississippi, and portions of these districts approach the western city limits. The housing nearer the river is older and more dilapidated; somewhat newer and better units appear to the west. Industry in the area is now confined to the river corridor. The lumber mills that once lined this area were gone by about 1920. Since then, the land has been used by salvage yards, storage industries, and railroads. In recent years construction of the Interstate-94 extension has rendered this scattered industrial area even more barren in appearance.

These northside districts were first settled in the early

relatively low in both areas. Residents of the two areas work at both skilled and unskilled jobs. There are a good number of assemblers, drivers, factory workers, waitresses, and a few nurses and teachers. Both areas house a large proportion of elderly widows as well. The Bryant district in South Minneapolis is somewhat less transient and has higher rates of home ownership. No ethnic group stands out here, but blacks are relatively numerous. The area has a large percentage of retired residents.

At the other end of the spectrum are two districts in North and Northeast Minneapolis. Over half of the people in each area have lived there more than five years. Home ownership rates in one district are 71-73 percent, higher than anyplace else in the entire zone. Both districts are more ethnic than most other parts of Minneapolis. The popula-

Representative example of housing stock in the aging inner ring. This block typifies some of the continuous attempts to improve the older housing in this zone. Note the different siding materials on houses of similar ages. Here one also sees front-yard fences, which rarely appear in other zones.

1870s near Plymouth and Washington Avenues. German settlers expanded into this area from an earlier enclave immediately north of downtown. Within a few years a group of French immigrants were living around 14th Avenue North and Girard. Blocks of small homes were quickly constructed between these two early outposts, meeting the needs of workers pouring in for jobs in the sawmills, lumberyards, and brickyards. As workers' wages and prospects increased, both foreign colonies dispersed throughout the north side of Minneapolis. Most of the area east of Lyndale was completely built up by 1885.

Away from the riverfront, transit expansion contributed to residential development. The 1883 horsecar on West Broadway led to the platting of the Forest Heights Addition (roughly James Avenue North). This "suburban" development, with its winding streets and small parks, was intended for upper-income residents. Forest Heights never achieved the status its promoters desired; its isolation ended abruptly and its stylish nature was lost when electric streetcar lines opened the area for mass settlement. Still, this area's large homes and hilly winding streets are a clear reminder of its former aspirations. Streetcars on Emerson and Penn Avenues North made it possible for one to live as far north as Lowry Avenue by the 1890s. The southern edge of these districts, near the Great Northern tracks, was almost fully developed in the same period, spurred on by streetcar lines on Glenwood and 6th Avenues. One particular ethnic group—the Finns—occupied this area well into the twentieth century.

Most of the central and northern portions of these districts were filled with houses after 1900. Many of the new residents were middle-class clerks, office workers, and skilled laborers who worked in and around downtown. Commuting was easy and housing affordable. There were clear lines of social demarcation within this set of districts. The area east of Lyndale housed working-class residents, whereas the area between Penn and Lyndale was middle-class. By 1915 this landscape was crowded with stucco cubes, both single-family dwellings and duplexes, and along the streetcar routes one could see occasional apartment buildings.

This section of the aging inner ring began to show signs of strain by the mid-1920s. The older industrial area along the river was in decline. Houses east of Lyndale were occupied by a mixed group of blacks, poor whites, and a variety of Slavic immigrants, all of whom were dependent on day labor and seasonal work. The houses were small and overcrowded. Landlords did not repair their property, and larger single-family homes and duplexes progressively deteriorated into rooming houses. Problems engendered by poverty and unemployment took a heavy toll in this area. One early social worker cited the evil effects of prostitution, moonshine production, pool halls, and "vile resorts" on the children who lived here.

The area surrounding North Commons Park was still middle-class in the 1920s. The population comprised native-born Americans, assimilated Scandinavians, and prosperous Jews. Homes here were large and well landscaped, and their owners lived contentedly. Similar conditions existed in the area south of Lowry Avenue, though the Jewish population did not extend into this area. This group was already moving west to the newer housing of Willard-Homewood, rather than moving northward.

Through the Depression the economic and social problems of these districts intensified. The deterioration typical of the Glenwood area to the south began spreading into surrounding parts of Near North Minneapolis. By the late 1940s much of the eastern portion of this zone was being considered for public renewal. Population had declined precipitously, even though the proportion of blacks in the district increased dramatically. Between 1950 and 1960 this district lost people at about twice the rate of the city as a whole.

During the 1960s a major renewal plan was enacted for much of Near North Minneapolis. It included most of the area south of Broadway and east of Penn Avenue, except for a small section near North Commons. The plan emphasized rehabilitation and spot clearance. Most structures were to be saved and brought up to code. Single-family homes and apartments would be built on sites where existing structures were beyond repair. And new housing would be built for elderly residents—to free up existing housing for families.

It is difficult to measure the impact of these improvement efforts. Although many of the stated goals were met, parts of this district required continuing economic assistance and are still in need of physical improvement. Plans were affected in part by the racial turmoil of the mid-1960s. The Plymouth Avenue riots hastened the exodus of Near North's

Northern Phillips district exemplifies the mix of housing types and ages within the aging inner ring. As older single-family houses and duplexes are replaced by higher-density structures, including highrises for the elderly, the density of these areas increases dramatically.

Jewish population, driving out the area's most stable and affluent residents. Blacks have continued to move to this district. Some observers have noted that more affluent blacks move from this district to south Minneapolis, leaving behind those less able to carry out improvements. Since Near North today has one of the largest concentrations of subsidized public housing in the city, the public tends to see only its drab multiunit buildings, neglecting everything else that is here.

Residents of Near North have mixed emotions about the attention public agencies pay to them. Some are grateful for the subsidized units and the improved housing opportunities. Others dislike the concentration of "projects" and resent being relocated when their dwellings are declared unfit. Residual racial feelings surface occasionally. White working-class Jordan residents have lobbied for federal housing assistance funds after watching money go to predominantly black areas for years.

The potential of the aging inner ring is evident here too. Residents of Hawthorne, for example, claim that their area is very livable and is continually improving. Block clubs are working to raise and resolve issues. Many residents are proud of the racial mix of whites, blacks, and Indians in the area. Pride in and identification with Hawthorne are important elements of life here. Pessimists may look at the vacant lots in the north district as a problem. But optimists see them as an opportunity. If a genuine "back-to-the-city" movement ever materializes in Minneapolis, it could well benefit this area.

Minneapolis—South Side

The southern portion of the aging inner ring in Minneapolis is a variation on the theme of development and decline. These districts sprawl from the older part of Cedar-Riverside to Interstate-35W and about 40th Street. Another arm extends out Hiawatha Avenue toward Minnehaha Park. This pattern is interrupted by a section of the settled mid-city zone around Powderhorn Park.

The oldest part, northern Phillips, was settled in the 1870s, soon after being annexed to the city. Although settlement tended to spread southward from downtown, several outlying areas were built up in an isolated fashion during this period. One of these was on Lake Street between Lyndale and Nicollet, along the route of an interurban railroad to the lakes. A sizable settlement was in place south of here long before expansion from the city encompassed it. Similarly, jobs in the Milwaukee Railroad shops along Hiawatha spurred housing construction in eastern Phillips in the 1880s. These southern districts were better served by transit lines than any other part of the city. When electric street car lines appeared during the 1890s, rapid development followed. The most concentrated building occurred along streetcar routes and close to terminals such as the one at 35th and Chicago.

All the districts north of 35th Street had at least some housing by the time of the 1893 depression, but it was after the turn of the century that the most rapid growth occurred. Industries continued to attract new residents. The Honeywell Corporation (then the Minneapolis Heat Regulator Company) began here as a small shop in 1906, and the gigantic Minneapolis Moline plant (then the Minneapolis Threshing Machine Company) was built around the same time at Hiawatha and Lake. New houses were being constructed everywhere but in some low-lying areas that were too difficult to drain. The usual forms of construction were small single-family frame houses, often covered with stucco, and good-sized duplexes. Substantial frame houses equivalent to some in the settled mid-city zone were quite prevalent on the far southern edges. Elsewhere the housing was compact and tidy. West of Park Avenue large apartment buildings rose in substantial numbers, creating much higher population densities than in the rest of the city.

Portions of these districts close to industrial concentrations were always attractive to the working class. Many of these districts also drew middle-class residents, and continued to do so for quite awhile. Ethnically and racially these districts were a thorough mix. The area east of Chicago Avenue housed low-income immigrants, especially Swedes. This heritage is still visible today in the churches and associations that remain. Park Avenue and much of the area south of Lake between Lyndale and Nicollet were upper-class and middle-class WASP strongholds. Blacks settled in several parts of this zone, but especially along 4th Avenue, south of Lake Street.

Change came to this part of the aging inner ring soon after it was initially settled. Well before the 1920s, apartment construction began to predominate, increasing the population of renters. Consequently, the number of families with children started to decline. Areas to the south had a more abundant supply of single-family houses and were more attractive to families. Population decline was well under way in Phillips by 1930; it was a trait of the entire zone by 1950. The southern portion of the zone, like the northern one, continued to attract minority residents. Immigration to the small nodes of early black settlement accelerated during the 1920s, and again from the 1950s on. Areas of minority residence have expanded continuously to the south, led by more affluent and better-educated blacks. Native Americans have also moved here in recent years, particularly to Phillips. Southeast Asian immigrants are the most recent in a series of relatively disadvantaged people to seek out the inexpensive housing of the aging inner ring.

The elite and comfortable areas of the south side districts soon lost their appeal for those with money. Not even the working-class areas could hold residents once they had acquired a steady income. Since 1960 these patterns have intensified, as population levels have continued to decline. More elderly and young people have moved in to take advantage of low rents. New construction has occurred—predominantly highrises for the elderly. The overall condition of housing has remained relatively poor, however. Many single-family houses have been subdivided or converted to rooming houses. Recently the Minneapolis Community Development Agency and nonprofit corporations have attempted to rehabilitate houses in this area. This has alarmed residents who worry that people with more money or more resources will buy up their housing and displace them.

During the 1950s and 1960s many of the industries in this portion of the aging inner ring were rendered obsolete. Warehouse and storage facilities along the 29th Street rail corridor were abandoned as trucks and containers took over long-distance hauling. The railroad business in general declined, and the Minneapolis Moline Plant, a longtime major employer, closed down in the late sixties.

Despite problems in these districts, many residents have positive and enthusiastic attitudes. Longtime residents of the portion of the zone on both sides of Hiawatha Avenue are heartened by a recent influx of young families. They believe that their areas are stabilizing and that the fixing up of older homes is a good sign. The major issue in these areas has been the loss of local elementary schools. Many people dislike the fact that their children must attend one of the large magnet schools (i.e., Andersen or Wilder). There are fewer complaints about busing in parts of the zone that have not had a local school for many years.

The largest "neighborhood" in Minneapolis—Phillips—is the most ambiguous part of this zone. It contains some of the most interesting architecture in the aging inner ring, both old (the Park Avenue mansions) and new (the Native American Center on Franklin Avenue, and Hans Christian Andersen school at 27th Street and 11th Avenue South.) Phillips is an area with some difficult problems, including unemployment, vandalism, and financial institutions' reluctance to invest here. In addition, some tension exists among the Native American, Southeast Asians, and white residents. This is one part of the Twin Cities where three or more cultures and ways of life can come into conflict everyday, for these cultures are not always compatible. Nevertheless, the Phillips area offers many opportunities. It is among the best organized sections of Minneapolis, with committed residents and political clout. For example, in 1981-82, residents of Phillips initiated and completed an effort to

purchase and move about fifteen houses from nearby areas into Phillips. These houses would have been destroyed had the Phillips residents not acted when they did. Now these houses are being renovated. They will be sold to low- and moderate-income people, with preference given to current Phillips residents who qualify as buyers.

Minneapolis—East Side

The east side portion of the aging inner ring in Minneapolis differs from other parts of the zone primarily in ethnic composition. More people with an Eastern European heritage live here than in any other part of the Twin Cities. The numerous ethnic and national churches still define the cultural distinctions of these districts. The other distinguishing feature is the way industry intrudes into the residential landscape. The portion of the district located in Northeast Minneapolis is crisscrossed by railroads, and a great amount of space is used by industries that require fast, reliable rail service. Residential portions of this district are cut up into separate islands. Contact between and among neighboring areas is prevented by the lack of bridges over or tunnels under the numerous rail lines.

Hans Christian Andersen School in South Minneapolis. This "magnet" school contains four distinctive schools and programs. Large schools of this type have increasingly replaced the local schools which served smaller areas.

Settlement on the east side began at the town of St. Anthony in the 1850s. The "Southeast" portion of this zone, in which the Minneapolis branch of the University of Minnesota is located, assumed an air of prosperity quite early. The patriarch of the Pillsbury clan settled here near the family mill, surrounded by other entrepreneurs. As the University grew, this area attracted many faculty members. Professionals were drawn to the area because of its easy access to downtown. In contrast, the "Northeast" section began as a working-class residential area. The riverfront here was lined with lumber mills, providing jobs for local residents. In the early years this part of Northeast was no more ethnic than the rest of the city. Not until the 1880s, when large numbers of Poles first appeared, did a strong ethnic identity emerge. By the turn of the century Germans were concentrated along Broadway (near the Grain Belt brewery), and Scandinavians filled the central portion of the district. Poles, Slovaks, Russians, and Ukranians lived close to the river and throughout old St. Anthony. The foreign-born population of Minneapolis was declining, but in this portion of this zone it continued to increase.

Like the rest of the aging inner ring, these areas grew steadily as the streetcar network expanded. Decline did not set in until the 1920s or 1930s. In Northeast, housing began to deteriorate as new immigrant groups moved in. When people could afford to "move up the hill," they quickly left the old small houses behind. Housing in the Northeast district has improved but has not changed significantly over the years. Some new houses were constructed on scattered sites during the 1970s, many homes were brought up to code, and several highrises for the elderly were built around the same time. The housing today consists primarily of older units still in good condition; most have been modernized, re-sided, or substantially rehabilitated.

In the Southeast district, middle-class families began leaving during the sixties as the University expanded and the number of students increased. In response to student demand for housing near the University, many older houses were torn down and replaced, or converted to rooming houses. Others were sold to fraternities and sororities. Two-and-a-half-story apartment buildings soon filled the landscape, especially along University Avenue and 4th Street. Unlike other parts of the aging inner ring, this area gained population during these years. The stable middle-class nature of Southeast did not evaporate, but it certainly diminished, and has continued to do so up to the present.

Today the Southeast district is dominated by students. Even local shopping areas reflect this change. Dinkytown, centered at 4th Street S.E. and 14th Avenue, had both Dayton's and Rothchild's department stores during the 1930s, but is now characterized by fast-food outlets, boutiques of various kinds, and specialty stores. There are a few major issues in this area. Some homeowners are concerned about housing conditions, and everywhere the lack of parking is a problem. Unfortunately, most of the students in Southeast, who represent a sizable proportion of its population, are transients who do not pay attention to local problems.

Northeast remains the most ethnic part of the city. Poles, Ukranians, and Italians can still be found here. Northeast is a blue-collar area, and residents consider it very stable. They are fiercely proud of their small, neatly kept houses. As one resident described the flavor of this area, "we're all Archie Bunkers here." Homes and families are the center of life for most people. For example, a Ukranian woman, a U.S. resident for over thirty years, has eaten in a restaurant only twice. Churches remain strong and influential. Local associations and bars provide most of the nightlife that residents enjoy.

DISTRICTS OF THE AGING INNER RING IN SAINT PAUL

From the 1850s to 1956, Swede Hollow on the east side of downtown Saint Paul housed a series of immigrant groups. First Scandinavians, then Irish, followed by Italians, and finally Mexicans made their homes in the lower valley of Phalen Creek. For the most part, the various immigrant groups were too engrossed in making their way in America to pay much attention to each other, but there were persistent difficulties. The younger men and boys were fond of taunting each other, and ethnic jokes and slurs were universally popular. Most of the trouble took the form of pranks, as when the Irish boys threw stones at the drum carried by the largely Scandinavian Salvation Army band.

During the century it was inhabited, Swede Hollow was a special place because it was really a squatter settlement.

There were no official building lots, streets, or sidewalks. Residents did not own their houses and only occasionally paid rent. The only sewer was Phalen Creek, richly polluted by overhanging outhouses. The water supply came from a spring in the valley wall. The sheriff came through on occasion to collect rents, even though he did not own any property there. Otherwise the official presence of civic authority was rare indeed.

In the 1890s Italians became the majority in the Hollow, and by 1905 there were very few non-Italians living there. Nonetheless, the district never lost its original name. During these years Gentile Yurosso was one of the area's most prominent figures. He found homes for many newcomers and constantly provided them with encouragement. Soon this area became the center of Saint Paul's wine-making industry, with the product being consumed entirely within the immediate vicinity. In the fall the smell of grapes was in the area and prompted long, nostalgic stories about Italy and serious discussions of color, taste, and the high cost of grapes.

Little change occurred in the Hollow during the Depression, but during World War II, Mexican immigrants moved into the area. By the early 1950s, they dominated the Hollow. The great era of urban renewal brought an end to the community in 1956, when the spring that had served the community as its sole source of water was declared unfit for human consumption and the fire department burned down the jerry-built immigrant housing. Today the Hollow is empty, a monument to the hundreds of immigrants who used it as a stepping stone to the middle-class districts farther away from the city core and railroad tracks.

No one from Saint Paul will refute the notion that hockey in the Twin Cities got its start on the pond near the railroad shops on the East Side. Today the Shop Pond Gang continues the chilly recreation of the railroad workers and their families, although with a good deal more equipment.

Most visitors to Saint Paul are totally befuddled by the fact that the area known as the West Side is located on the southern border of the city. This does not phase the citizenry because they know that rivers can only have two sides, an east and west in this case. No matter how the river twists and snarls its way along, the sides are still the same. One of the very oldest of the residential districts, the West Side is home to conservative blue-collar families who alternatively

glory in their isolation or complain because no one pays much attention to their needs and hopes.

The remaining sections of the aging inner ring lie to the west and northeast of downtown. The Summit-University area is home to the city's largest concentration of minority groups. Here live blacks, Native Americans, and Hispanic families, and to this volatile mixture have been added a large number of recent immigrants from Southeast Asia. Once the home of the city's elite, Summit-University has filtered down to lower-income groups. In the process many of the fine older houses have been subdivided or fallen into disrepair because of the lack of maintenance. The history of Summit-University is quite similar to that of north Minneapolis.

The North End, on either side of Rice Street and separated from the Thomas-Dale (or Frogtown) area by Como Avenue, has remained a rather unobtrusive blue-collar residential community throughout its history. At one time home to the cities' Romanian community, today it contains Saint Paul's only Romanian Orthodox Church even though the congregation has spread into other areas. The Romanians apparently settled in this area because the housing was cheap and because they felt comfortable with the nearby immigrant neighbors, 40 percent of whom were Austrian or German. The social and economic history of this district is really a continuation of that of its older neighbor to the south, Frogtown.

One of the city's most distinctive residential districts, Frogtown is generally considered to take in the area north of University Avenue, east of Dale, south of Minnehaha, and west of Como and Rice Streets. However, some residents extend its western edge to Victoria, and others believe that Como Park is the northern limit. All agree that the area is centered on Saint Agnes, an imposing Roman Catholic Church in the Central European Baroque style on the corner of Lafond and Thomas.

As with most place-names in the folk geography of the city, the origin and meaning of *Frogtown* are obscure. Some residents believe the area was called Frogtown because it was the home of French Canadian immigrants, *frog* being an ethnic slur for *French*. This explanation ignores the fact that the insult for French Canadians was Canucks and that the use of *frog* for *French* was not widespread until after World War I, years after Frogtown was settled. Other residents, who know that the district had many German-speaking as well as French-speaking residents, believe the name is a reference to the low and swampy ground in the district. When the area was first settled, houses were scattered among the mud holes and choruses of frogs were quite remarkable. Whatever its origin, it is clear that the term was not intended to compliment the locals. Today, however, its use by the residents of the district has become a symbol of their pride and strong sense of place.

In the 1870s and early 1880s, several speculators and developers subdivided this part of Saint Paul into narrow residential lots. The working class crowded into the area because they could build cheap houses on the lots and could find employment in Frogtown's large railroad shops and other manufacturing plants.

The high population density in Frogtown created a strong local demand for butcher shops, grocery stores, taverns, and churches. Because the area was developed a quarter of a century before sophisticated concepts of land-use zoning became fashionable, no one objected to the establishment of commercial activities within residential areas. Hardly a block existed without a structure that was at one time or another used for business.

The area was so highly regarded by members of the working class that people built houses on every lot, even though some lots were unsuitable (houses built on them began to sink). Certain buildings resembled the famous leaning tower of Pisa. On some lots two houses were built: the main residence and the so-called alley houses. Although they may have been built to house relatives, the alley houses were soon rented out to strangers, often to single-person households. By modern standards they were tiny; some were smaller than a single-car garage. A concerted effort to remove these structures was launched in the early 1970s, and they are now rather rare. The few that remain remind us of a time when everyone walked and alleys were social spaces instead of parking lots.

Some homeowners converted the upper stories of their houses into apartments. The modifications were usually made by local amateurs or moonlighting carpenters. The result of all this custom or jackknife carpentry is an area full of wonderfully idiosyncratic houses, many with outdoor stairways on stilts, that provide slippery access to cramped apartments under the roofs of small houses.

Much of the local culture and folklore demonstrates the intense pride that residents take in their area. Two very different examples come to mind: people relish telling stories about the local boxers who flourished a half-century and more ago, and they take special pleasure in listening to the Twin Cities Catholic Chorale.

In the late nineteenth century many factories paid their employees in cash at noon on Saturday, after the customary half-day of work. The local taverns prepared huge lunches for the thirsty men, many of whom would spend most of the afternoon and evening in one or more of the local establishments. Their entertainments were rather primitive, and fighting was common. Sometimes during the evenings a few men would box for a small purse in a makeshift ring. Most of the local toughs got little more for their efforts than lumps, sore hands, a few drinks, and a moment of fleeting fame. A few, however, had real talent and were genuine contenders for a world championship. Although they are no longer well known, their fame lives on in Frogtown where their exploits are frequently recounted in local social gatherings late on weekend evenings when the talk turns to sports and other serious matters. The exploits of these boxers have helped to establish the area's reputation for toughness.

Whether Frogtown was any tougher than other working-class districts will never be known. We do know, however, that the local churches were important in everyone's life. Many people left the vicinity of their homes only when they attended a church picnic at Wildwood amusement park on the shore of White Bear Lake. For others, the several organizations of their congregation provided opportunities for socializing and an excuse to leave their crowded houses for a few hours.

The grand church of Saint Agnes and its adjacent school complex testify to the continued importance of the church in the local culture. In an era when Catholic secondary schools in the older neighborhoods have either closed or relocated to suburbs, Saint Agnes continues to provide an alternative education mainly for inner-city Catholic families. The Twin Cities Catholic Chorale at Saint Agnes best illustrates the continuity of the local culture. When the area's original Roman Catholic inhabitants left their homes in the Austro-Hungarian Empire nearly a century ago, they were accustomed to the Latin Mass accompanied by music written by Europe's greatest composers, Beethoven, Mozart, Schumann, and others. Their descendants have endeavored to maintain that music as a part of their lives despite the replacement of the Latin Mass. At Saint Agnes one can still hear the magnificent music of Central Europe sung by professional soloists and a local choir accompanied by instrumentalists from the Minnesota Orchestra.

Pleasant as the culture of the area may be, residents have severe problems. The poor drainage of the area has been a constant concern in the district. Heavy rains bring wet basements and backed-up sewers. Even a brief summer shower can cause problems. The city of Saint Paul is committed to rectifying this problem, but the project will be costly and funds are in short supply.

One cannot help wondering why Frogtown persists. The local industries that once provided employment for the residents have lost their importance. The houses are small, elderly, and for the most part devoid of ornamentation. Other areas of the city have finer views, more open space, and do not suffer from the noise and pollution of the nearby manufacturing plants and heavily trafficked streets. Yet these places have disintegrated while Frogtown remains. Perhaps it is the deep sense of place that characterizes this part of the city which is the critical factor in Frogtown's continued survival. The many miles of fences surrounding small lots clearly tell strangers that this is an area where private property is greatly prized and where owners are expected to maintain their property.

CONCLUSION

The aging inner ring is a somewhat deteriorated, though not uniformly depressed, set of districts. They have problems, but are not beyond redemption. In fact today we witness many improvement activities, both public and private, in this zone. These efforts are as varied as their effects. Overall they point out many reasons to view the aging inner ring's prospects in a positive light.

Public assistance has been used liberally to upgrade the housing of this zone. In Minneapolis the former Housing Authority had programs for new housing and urban home-

steading. Home improvement or rehabilitation programs were funded by the federal government, by the state, and by the city. These took the form of both loans and grants to homeowners. The use of these programs in some parts of the aging inner ring has been substantial. In the North district of Minneapolis, for example, loan and grant programs have been actively sought out, and the proportion of dwellings improved with public assistance is higher here than in the rest of the city. Fewer publicly assisted improvements occur in the east side or south districts. Judging from the recent rise in the number of building permits being issued, owners throughout this zone clearly intend to improve their housing and their environment. But nearly all parts of the aging inner ring still have houses in need of some repair.

The most difficult housing problem in this zone is the deterioration of multifamily units. Since most improvement money goes to owners of single-family homes, rental housing continues to deteriorate further. In recent years both federal and city agencies have tried to rehabilitate these units. Perhaps the most substantial program in this zone has been the concerted effort to send federal money directly into it. The seventeen "Neighborhood Strategy Areas" in Minneapolis and the six "Identified Treatment Areas" in Saint Paul have been so designated because they have high proportions of low- and moderate-income residents, large amounts of deteriorated housing, and as such qualify for special funding. In Minneapolis fourteen of these "NSAs" fall almost entirely within the aging inner ring. All are places where physical improvements, private investment, and citizen participation have already had a positive effect. Obviously both cities' governments believe the physical and social problems of this zone cannot be ignored. They have also recognized, and are rewarding, locally initiated improvement efforts.

The aging inner ring, then, presents both the positive and negative aspects of urban life. It shelters many people who have few alternatives, as well as those who live here by choice and intend to improve conditions. There is no denying the problems that exist here, but the hidden potential should be recognized too.

29

III

The Protected Genteel Zone

A Crocus Hill hostess and her caterer were panic stricken when an afternoon thunderstorm threatened to wash out that evening's lawn party. As they fretted and hoped for a change in the weather, their neighbors called, one by one, and suggested that the white tables and their yellow umbrellas be moved from the hostess's lawn on to several of the neighbors' large front porches. The move was made, the storm broke and passed over, the festivities went on as planned.

A unique combination of upper middle-class families, Victorian and Edwardian architecture, and local pride distinguishes the protected genteel zone. The population is financially secure and well educated. The architecture includes large single-family detached houses, plus a seasoning of apartment buildings mixed in large enough numbers to alter the tone of some districts within the zone. The buildings are generally well maintained, and many have interesting architectural details. In some parts of each district there are a few buildings of exceptional design, but most are well-constructed examples of styles popular when they were built. Residents generously support the local cultural activities with money and enthusiasm. However, only well-established artists and intellectuals can afford to own a home in this zone.

Several pieces of fiction written about the Twin Cities contain extensive descriptions of these areas, and their plots incorporate features of the local life-styles. The short stories by F. Scott Fitzgerald depict the Crocus Hill and Summit Avenue section of Saint Paul, and the recent mysteries by Thomas Gifford capture the excitement of the Lowry Hill and Kenwood districts of Minneapolis.

Five distinctive and widely separated districts comprise the protected genteel zone. (See map 3.) Two, Kenwood, and Lowry Hill, are adjacent to each other but nonetheless are separate districts. Although they all enjoy excellent access to the central business districts of both Minneapolis and Saint Paul, all but one occupy positions on or near the limits of their city. Kenwood and Lowry Hill are on the west-central edge of Minneapolis, whereas Prospect Park is on the eastern border, cut off from the rest of the City of Lakes by the Mississippi River and a broad band of industrial, institutional, and railroad land. Likewise, Saint Anthony Park comprises the northwestern most section of Saint Paul and is surrounded by three other municipalities. Only Crocus Hill lies snugly within the central city's corporate limits.

Each of the districts is quite isolated. Few arterial streets lead into these places, and Saint Anthony Park is the only protected genteel district through which a major traffic

Maintenance levels along East River Road represent the investment that succeeding generations of occupants have made in this upper-middle-class housing built a half-century ago. This zone continues to attract striving members of the middle class.

corridor passes. This isolation is more apparent than real because major streets pass by each of the districts. Hennepin Avenue, Lake Street, and Interstate 94 serve the districts of Kenwood and Lowry Hill. University Avenue forms the northern edge of Prospect Park and the great ditch of Interstate 94 lies near its southern limit. Saint Anthony Park is bounded by Highway 280, and Como Avenue bisects the area. Grand Avenue forms an edge for Crocus Hill and provides quick access to the major arterials of Saint Paul. Thus the districts are both accessible and isolated at the same time—accessible because they are adjacent to major streets, isolated because almost all traffic is discouraged from passing through them.

The proximity of the districts to white-collar employment centers in both central business districts, the State Capitol complex, and the campuses of the University of Minnesota is significant. These institutions provide employment for many of the zone's wage earners. High-level bureaucrats and technicians tend to live in Crocus Hill, which is close to their jobs at the Capitol. Much of the population in Saint Anthony Park and Prospect Park works at the University of Minnesota; the Saint Paul campus lies across the street from Saint Anthony Park, whereas the main Minneapolis campus is two miles from Prospect Park.

Thus the five protected genteel districts have many features in common. They are near centers of white-collar employment; they are accessible but without large volumes of through traffic; and four of the five were developed at the city limits of their respective central city. In addition, the physical landscapes of the districts are handsome.

THE LOOK OF THE LANDSCAPES

The attractiveness of the protected genteel districts is enhanced by the presence of striking features in the physical landscape. Each district is built on a hill. Prospect Park and Saint Anthony Park are both built on kames, isolated hills formed by the melting glaciers at the end of the Pleistocene era. Their slopes are gentle and the tops rounded. Each hill was well suited to building techniques employed at the end of the nineteenth century. Crocus Hill is located on the brow of the highest terrace above the Mississippi and looks over the natural amphitheater that contains the oldest part of Saint Paul. The cliff was cut by small streams, and these

ravines provide some local relief in the area. Lowry Hill and Kenwood occupy another piece of the landscape formed by glacial activity, a large moraine called the Devil's Backbone by the early map makers.

The topography in all these locations was covered with mixed hardwood forests when settlement began. Thus the areas combined a view with pleasant pastoral surroundings. The wild vegetation was gradually replaced by lawns and plantings. The lakes near Kenwood and Lowry Hill were improved by dredging and shoreline stabilization programs, but this resulted in a loss of the pastoral atmosphere. The park managers and residents substituted a sense of mature urban forest by planting hardwoods and an understory of flowering shrubs and flowerbeds.

Large houses, mostly of frame construction, dominate all the protected genteel districts, yet the housing styles vary from district to district. Those along Mount Curve and Lake of the Isles Boulevard in Minneapolis' Lowry Hill and Kenwood districts are constructed of stone and brick. Styles almost defy description because each house was intended to be distinctive. Nonetheless, the fact that the buildings were constructed at specific times produces some regularity. Along Mount Curve one finds late nineteenth-century villas, houses greatly influenced by the prairie school of Chicago, tudor revivals of the twenties and thirties, super-ramblers of the early 1960s, and examples of individualistic modern architecture of the middle and late 1960s. This hodgepodge of styles is the result of infilling. The first homes were surrounded by extensive grounds which were subdivided when the original residents moved or died.

The scene is quite different along Irving Avenue, which forms an intersection with Mount Curve. This street was completely built up within a twenty-year period beginning in 1890. Houses along the street are quite similar, although most have distinctive decorating motifs. The style of house is frequently referred to as the large eclectic cube. Houses were built with front porches, a living room, dining room, and kitchen on the first floor, three or more bedrooms on the second floor, and were usually covered with shake siding. At the street intersections, houses are somewhat larger and tend to be constructed of masonry or stone. A few have giant columns on the front of the house that stretch from the ground level to the roof line. The delightful shore of Lake of the Isles was built up somewhat later and is dom-

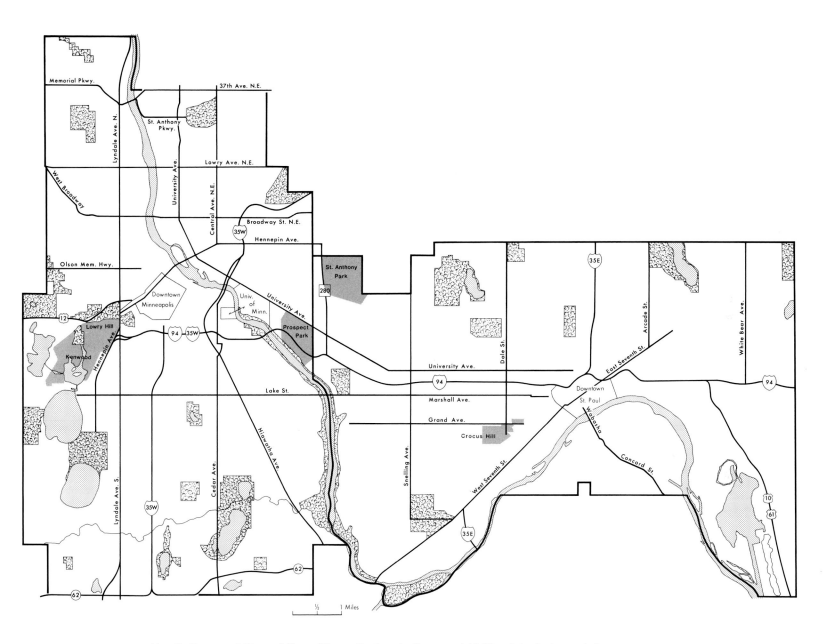

Map 3: Protected Genteel Zone. These districts, built around 1900, originally housed the upper and upper-middle classes. They continue to attract financially secure households.

inated by masonry and stucco houses from the twenties. Tudor, colonial, and period revival styles are dominant.

The other districts were built up with less grandiose houses, but they are in the same styles. Saint Anthony Park and Prospect Park have some modest structures mixed in that date from the 1920s and the 1960s. Both these districts have been greatly affected by the demand for housing created by the expanding student and faculty populations at the University. This demand led to the building of apartments and the conversion of larger single-family detached houses into multiple units. The most dramatic examples of this are the several fraternity and sorority houses along Cleveland Avenue in Saint Paul.

Residential construction in Crocus Hill dates from the final years of the nineteenth century. All but one of the half-dozen mansions built before the 1890s were razed prior to the turn of the twentieth century to make room for new structures. The district was built up gradually, one or two lots at a time during the first three decades of this century. The dominant style is the eclectic cube, but a local architect named Clarence Johnson had a tremendous impact on the styles. Johnson was active around the First World War and built several significant houses in the early 1920s. He was very fond of masonry and red tile roofs. Although there was infill building during the twenties and thirties, the street-scapes in Crocus Hill are quite uniform. Over the years the housing has remained unchanged to a remarkable degree.

The protected genteel districts were planted with boulevard trees, usually elms. On blocks where elms still live, the branches form the high arched canopy over the streets that locals are quick to compare to the beams in the ceilings of ancient cathedrals. Yet the roots of these elms clog sewer pipes and break up sidewalk blocks, and the trees attract armies of worms during the spring. On the positive side, the elms provide deep shade for the houses and lawns, and shield the slowly decaying houses from the prying eyes of passersby. Now that the trees are dying, residents have begun to landscape their property. Flowers and low shrubbery give color to the areas, and grass is becoming popular. As more trees die, the districts will look more and more as they did when they were young.

Another striking feature of the landscape is the relationship between the size of the houses and the area of the lots. Although the large homes along Mount Curve on Lowry Hill were once surrounded by extensive grounds, today these districts have a somewhat crowded feeling. Large houses in each district are sited on standard city lots. There may be only ten to fifteen feet between most houses in Crocus Hill. Kenwood, Lowry Hill, and parts of Saint Anthony Park have a little more space, but the openness that is the hallmark of upper-income districts developed in the modern era is notably absent from the protected genteel zone.

The crowded houses, large trees, and mature gardens combine to give the districts a cozy feeling. The sense of security is greatly enhanced by the street patterns. A part of each district was laid out on what can only be referred to as the tangle town plan, characterized by curved streets, complex corners, and irregularly shaped blocks that are difficult to navigate. One-way streets pose additional problems for strangers traveling through these areas. The net result of this plan is to diminish greatly the through traffic in each district and to increase the residents' sense of privacy.

The protected genteel districts' sense of separateness is increased by the presence of sharp boundaries around each area. As mentioned previously, some of the districts are bounded by heavily trafficked arterial roads. Nearly every resident of the Twin Cities uses the commercial land associated with arterial streets to demarcate residential districts. The abrupt change from residential structures to commercial buildings gives even the most casual observer a visible sign that he or she is entering a new kind of place. There are also topographic changes at the borders of these districts. Residents of the districts travel to the edges to shop or to enjoy the vistas or to participate in recreational activities in the open spaces. The edge of the Lowry Hill district is the north-facing slope of Lowry Hill. This place is the site of two of the most recognizable Minneapolis landmarks, the Walker Art Institute and the Guthrie Theater. Thousands of people come to this portion of the district each year but do not enter the residential district because of the lack of through streets, the steep hill, and the obvious fact that neither Lowry Hill nor Kenwood is on the way to anyplace.

POPULATION

The residents of the protected genteel districts include some of the most influential members of Minneapolis and

Fairmount Avenue in Saint Paul, indicating the pattern of large houses on small lots that is common to this zone.

Saint Paul's political, financial, and artistic communities. The influence of residents is not based on personal wealth, but on the positions they hold in the institutions that structure the economic and political life of the metropolitan area. Although nearly one-third of the households in the zone are classified as managerial or professional, some districts in other zones have a higher proportion of such households. Incomes are among the highest in the city within these districts, but not all the residents are among the wealthiest in either city. (See table 2, p. 144.)

The protected genteel zone does not experience great population shifts. Movement into and out of this zone is continuous, but not substantial. All parts of the zone exude a sense of stability, no doubt owing to their historic character. Except for corporate transfers, turnover in single-family housing seems limited to the death or institutionalization of elderly residents. Voluntary movement from this zone seems particularly difficult, especially for longtime residents. One observer cited the stubborn refusal of many elderly Lowry Hill homeowners to consider living in retirement homes or going into nursing homes. If stairs pose a problem, they install elevators, and if frequent medical attention is required, they hire private nurses. But because turnover in the many apartment buildings along the edges of these districts is high, none of the districts qualify as being the most stable in either city. Only 50-60 percent of the residents have been in their homes or apartments five to ten years.

Households in this zone are somewhat larger than average. Professional families with children, especially those who can afford private schooling, often choose to live here. The proportion of households with children is well above the city average in both Kenwood and Lowry Hill, for example. Since houses in this zone are large and are not usually subdivided, few single-person households are found here. Female-headed households with children are also relatively uncommon. Although some may think of the zone as made up primarily of senior citizens living in oversize dwellings, the actual percentage of retired residents is well below average. The proportion of lower-income and jobless residents is close to the lowest in either city, yet there are fewer homeowners than might be expected. Although home ownership figures are above average, they fall below the levels in the prewar amenity and suburban-in-city zones. This reflects the higher incidence of multifamily construc-

tion along the edges of the protected genteel zone, some of it dating from the 1920s.

Perhaps the most common characteristic of people in this zone is a shared sense of cultural sophistication. Residents think of themselves as well-informed citizens and are active patrons of cultural events. Most subscriptions in the metro area to the *New York Times* and the *New Yorker* magazine probably originate from the protected genteel zone. Despite the differences in income and social circles among residents of these districts, there are essential similarities. As someone observed, all the residents go to the opera when it comes to town. Some dress formally for the occasion and have seats on the main floor, others wear street clothes and sit in the balcony; but they are all there.

HISTORICAL DEVELOPMENT

The protected genteel districts were first settled in the last quarter of the nineteenth century. Kenwood and Saint Anthony Park then enjoyed excellent commuter train service to downtown, though the zone's primary form of transportation was the horse-and-carriage. As soon as the electrification of the streetcar system was complete, horses vanished from the districts and men began commuting by streetcar. Promoters advertised the convenience of these districts as well as the attractive physical settings. In Saint Anthony and Prospect Parks, their appeals were directed at academics, clergy, and retired business and political leaders, who were offered a quiet intellectual community protected from the hubbub of the other high-status districts. In Crocus Hill, Lowry Hill, and Kenwood, promoters addressed active businessmen and their families, focusing on the prestige of the areas and their accessibility to downtown. As a result of this subtle difference in advertising, the districts developed distinct subcultures.

The development pattern of this zone was the same as that in the settled mid-city zone and the other older residential areas. When the available building lots in the protected genteel districts were taken, generally around the beginning of the second quarter of the twentieth century, households began to seek similar social spaces in new districts at the edge of the city. Established families remained in their homes, but the population stabilized and perhaps stagnated. Little happened in the housing market between

1929 and 1945, so these districts were not greatly threatened by either the migration to new suburbs or the spread of urban blight. When the war ended, the situation changed dramatically. The two protected genteel districts near the University underwent a reevaluation as the population of faculty exploded and the professors and administrators looked for housing close to their work. College and university faculty are a most interesting subset of the housing market. By and large, these households have a high opinion of themselves and wish to live like upper middle-class families on a rather middle-class income. Thus they are attracted to used housing designed for upper-income families. Saint Anthony and Prospect Parks were both considered perfect residential areas by this population, and housing prices in these districts increased accordingly as early as 1960. Thus the areas could attract new residents without being a part of the historic preservation or neighborhood conservation movement of the 1970s which has affected other older sections of the Twin Cities.

These districts were so isolated from other residential areas that small-scale investors felt secure in the special market conditions that seemed to prevail. Although they were isolated to some degree, Kenwood, Lowry Hill, and Crocus Hill were not described as special subsets of the housing market during the 1950s and 1960s. These three districts were once part of a large swath of middle- and upper middle-class housing that stretched from the downtowns to the limits of both cities. In both Minneapolis and Saint Paul the filtering process worked to transform housing in these areas into homes for lower-income families. Mansions were torn down, converted into office buildings, or carved up into several rental units. Large frame houses, many decaying from lack of maintenance, were also subdivided to provide shelter for several households. The presence of strong barriers such as bluffs and amenities such as lakes slowed down and partly deflected the advancing wave of urban blight away from certain places. But the conventional wisdom of the Eisenhower and Kennedy eras was that housing was handed down from group to group within the city and that government renewal programs eventually cleared away the battered structures to make room for new and better communities. Realtors expected the districts we refer to as protected genteel to be the last of the old neighborhoods to go. Residents were already

complaining about crime, conditions in schools, and the high costs of keeping up the large houses.

The area immediately north of Crocus Hill illustrates the conditions that characterized the areas bordering on the other protected genteel districts. By the mid-1960s, the population of this area had changed from high-income white to middle-income Jewish to low-income black and other racial minorities. The area attracted the attention and concern of planners, insurance agents, lending institutions, and residents alike. In the late 1960s white urban pioneers moved in and began to purchase housing on the fringe of the black community. One segment of this group consisted of young professionals, in some cases just out of school. Filled with enthusiasm for the architectural quality of the area's buildings, they moved into houses along Summit Avenue or in the immediate vicinity and began the long process of renovation. The second segment comprised basically middle-class dropouts who lived in group quarters located in "higher risk" blocks where they sought to form an alliance with their low-income neighbors. The most visible aspect of their efforts was the establishment of a food co-op. These people provoked a response from the established communities, and new political alliances were forged. The Summit-University Model Cities Program began in 1969. Although the young radicals resented the middle-class professionals who were following them into the area in ever-increasing numbers, they could do nothing to stop the trend. Because Crocus Hill had not decayed, middle-class households could see the potential of the older homes. Because few homes in Crocus Hill came on the market at any time, buyers in search of similar structures went into the adjacent district, where they purchased property and began restoration and renovation activities. In so doing, they increased the value of not only their own area but adjacent Crocus Hill as well, since they were building a buffer zone against the spread of urban blight. They became the vanguard of a new population that would eventually occupy the area. These trends will be discussed in greater detail in the chapter dealing with the turnaround zone.

Each of the protected genteel districts borders on districts where similar conditions prevail. In the Lowry Hill East or Wedge district of Minneapolis, the conversion of single-family detached buildings into apartment units, and the erection of large numbers of apartment buildings in the

Extremely decorative architectural details distinguish the landscape of the protected genteel zone.

1960s, greatly increased the area's population density, prompting many observers to conclude that it would no longer serve the middle class. In the past few years, however, many homes have been restored by young adults interested in conserving some of the historic flavor of the district. The reemergence of local confidence in Lowry Hill East has increased the attraction of Lowry Hill and Kenwood.

The situation around Saint Anthony Park is somewhat different. This district is totally separated from other residential areas by strong barriers, among them Highway 280 and the University of Minnesota golf course. Its closest neighbor, south Saint Anthony, lies across a wide belt of railroad tracks and is connected to the Park by a single bridge. Nonetheless, a recent improvement in housing conditions in south Saint Anthony Park brought about by large-scale public investment has removed the threat of urban decay for the southern flank of Saint Anthony Park.

Not all threats to the integrity of the protected genteel zone come from outside. Most homeowners are able to protect their property against changes that might decrease its value, but internal threats do exist. These usually take the form of developers who want to capitalize on the high-status/high-value nature of the zone. Lowry Hill is one area that has withstood such a threat. As many of its long-time residents died or moved away in the forties and fifties, those remaining feared that decline was imminent. By the 1960s, as freeway planners nibbled away at the edges and tunneled under the hill, there was widespread apprehension about the future of Lowry Hill. Plans to deal with increasing traffic and to discourage massive apartment construction were drawn up.

The rally to save Lowry Hill really focused on the issue of highrise construction. In the mid-1960s a developer proposed to build a highrise apartment building on the crest of the hill, with terraced housing down the north slope. All of this was planned for the vacant Dunwoody property. Apartment construction was one thing. Even high-density development could be tolerated, as in the buildings on the slope of the hill just west of the Guthrie Theater. But a highrise tower breaking the wooded skyline of the hilltop was deemed an insult. Area residents mobilized at once. After a prolonged battle that seemed to pit the entire force of the city's might against the developer, the plans were first modified and then abandoned. Lowry Hill residents had clearly demonstrated their attachment to the area and their political muscle. The final resolution of this conflict has been the construction of Mount Curve Place, a luxury condominium development that does not intrude on the skyline.

Threats to this zone continue to be taken quite seriously. Residents are now quite accustomed to defending their environment. Any change, even a benevolent change, is critically examined. For example, the Minneapolis Park Board had planned to build a community center in Kenwood Park. But residents of Kenwood and Lowry Hill fought this proposal. They argued that a community center would increase traffic and exacerbate existing parking problems. They were willing to accept a small neighborhood center, but nothing large enough to draw in people from other parts of the Loring—Isles community. As a result of this resistance, no community center has been constructed in the park yet.

DISTRICTS OF THE PROTECTED GENTEEL ZONE

Crocus Hill

By *Crocus Hill*, we mean the core area as well as a small section known as Grand Hill which lies south of Summit Avenue and east of Dale. Grand Hill is topographically part of Crocus Hill, although Grand Avenue separates the two residential districts. The district is really a plateau rather than a hill. Houses were first posed near the edge of the cliff to maximize the view. Later the area took the name of the face of the cliff. Today Crocus Hill is a strip of residences stretched along the edge of the cliff from Ramsey to Victoria and reaching back several blocks to Grand and Summit Avenues. It is ironic that when you are in Crocus Hill you cannot see anything of a hill.

The lack of through streets isolates the area from the rest of the city's population. If early developers and landscape planners had had their way, this isolation would not have been possible, because at one time it was proposed to extend Summit Avenue all along the edge of the bluff through what is now Highland Park and to a connection with the Mississippi River Boulevard. Edgecumbe Road follows this general alignment south of Jefferson Avenue today. The complete story behind the alignment of Summit is not known; however, there is some reason to believe the cost of bridging the ravines was considered prohibitive. Secondarily, the prime developers of the Summit Park addition did not control all the bluff land, and yet they wished to capitalize on the image of Summit Avenue. They are the people who caused it to run due west, along the edge of their subdivision. The present alignment of Summit Avenue is largely responsible for the isolation of Crocus Hill. Had that grand boulevard followed the crest, hundreds of cars would be moving through the district daily, and the associated noise and pollution would surely have decreased the area's appeal.

Crocus Hill was platted in the 1880s and was totally built up by the 1930s. Fifty years were needed to complete this district because it was at first considered to be too remote. Wealthy households were building in the areas north of Summit because it was significantly closer to services. Little development occurred until the Grand Avenue streetcar line was electrified in the early 1890s. Most of the houses here were built by individuals working with a contractor and occasionally an architect. Even though each house was custom built, there were similarities. Homes are large, mostly frame buildings that conform to the basic eclectic cube style. They all include prefabricated decorative details like stained glass windows, gingerbread trim, and fancy brick work on chimneys. The interiors are frequently graced with intricately carved woodwork.

Until the First World War the area was quite pastoral. The streets and vacant lots served as playgrounds for the local children. In the summer people sat on their large front porches and chatted with passersby, most of whom they knew personally. Many longtime residents fondly recall the frequent trips to the western edge of the district to picnic and pick wildflowers.

The decade of the twenties brought great changes to the district. The improvement and widespread acceptance of the automobile brought about a quickening of the pace of the life. The area west of Victoria was built up, and Crocus Hill was cut off from the countryside. At the end of the decade young families with growing children were frequently disappointed in their search for housing here, and they began to look with favor on the more distant suburbs. These new suburbs possessed all the amenities that had first attracted settlers to Crocus Hill.

Little building occurred anywhere in the Twin Cities during the Depression and World War II, so there was not a great outmigration from Crocus Hill. On the contrary, housing was in short supply and many houses were modified so as to accommodate an additional household or two. When the postwar building boom began, four new suburbs replaced Crocus Hill as the ideal community for upper middle-class families: Sun Fish Lake, Mendota Heights, North Oaks, and Pinetree Springs-Dellwood. Each new district drew people out of Crocus Hill and attracted those newcomers to Saint Paul who might hitherto have settled in the older area. As a result of the shift in status, some houses were made into duplexes and along Lincoln Avenue, the district's northern edge, delapidation was visible. Despite this trend, many of the original families still resided in the area. In the mid-1960s these people were joined by a handful of younger professional households who were attracted to the area by the fine homes. The new people were interested in buying the old-fashioned homes because they could have ample living space for a modest cost. In addition, they were able to see the potential the houses possessed. Soon remodeling and rehabilitation became a favorite topic of conversation in the area. The continued presence of the Linwood Elementary School maintained the livability of the district because all the local children could walk to it.

In the mid-1960s Visitation School, which occupied a half-block site on lower Fairmont Avenue, relocated in the suburbs. The vacant site attracted the attention of developers who wished to build a highrise. The neighborhood rallied in opposition, and the plan was aborted. In 1967 the residents formed the Summit Hill Association, which has continued to articulate the concerns of the local population. The group has been particularly concerned with traffic problems, especially the proposed freeway in the Pleasant Avenue corridor. The continued efforts of the local organization and the widespread popularity of older homes have combined to make Crocus Hill one of the most sought-after residential areas in the city of Saint Paul. The most telling fact about the district is that it was one of the few areas in the city to experience a real increase in average annual household income during the 1970s.

There is an extremely interesting relationship between Crocus Hill and Grand Avenue, the commercial strip that forms its northern edge. The mixture of houses and commercial properties along Grand dates from the 1920s, when apartment developers and speculators in commercial prop-

erty were attracted to the avenue by its excellent streetcar service. Several large apartment complexes were built, and the small businesses prospered. At the beginning of the 1950s the declining population of the older parts of the city, the low buying power of the groups that were moving into the Summit-University area to the north of Grand Avenue, and the increased popularity of suburban shopping centers caused many of the old-time Grand Avenue merchants to go out of business or relocate. Many observers concluded that the avenue was about to experience severe blight.

In the turbulent years of the late 1960s a series of disturbances and burnings on Selby Avenue essentially destroyed the commercial viability of Grand's nearest competitor. Nonetheless, many business leaders and loan officers did not expect an increase of activity on Grand in the early 1970s. Instead they looked upon the amortized and obsolete buildings as an obstacle to further development.

Even though shoppers commonly complained about the lack of parking in front of stores and expressed a deep fear of street crime, by 1974 so many higher-income families wrere living in Crocus Hill that Grand Avenue was profitable despite the gloomy predictions of the old guard. As the decade came to a close, new merchants were attracted to the avenue in such numbers that there was not enough room for them. As a result, several houses were converted into stores. The new merchants, many of whom were female, came to take advantage of low rents and to exploit the decorative potential of the buildings. The old buildings have been shown to be an asset rather than a liability, and they now hold a wide variety of distinctive shops and restaurants that are doing a thriving business. Thousands of new customers have been attracted to the avenue through promotion efforts like Grand Old Days.

Today Grand Avenue exerts a positive influence on Crocus Hill by increasing the area's stylish image. Although the many antique stores, art shops, and boutiques give the avenue a special character, it continues to provide the basic necessities for both the high- and low-income residents of the surrounding areas. Crocus Hill is one of the few high-income districts with a complete shopping area within walking distance.

The household size in Crocus Hill is quite large. Nearly 16 percent of all households contain five or more members. The average household size is somewhat larger than that for

Saint Paul and significantly larger than that found on the district's northern border. It is not as high as the average household size for the suburban-in-city zone, but it does come close to that for other newer residential areas. This is a reflection of the area's attraction for families as well as childless households. Although children are important in the district, the percentage of households with them is about equal to the average for Saint Paul. The number of households with children has declined slightly in recent years, a trend which may indicate that the area is not considered as good a place to raise a family as it once was.

An interesting comparison can be made between Crocus Hill and the area to the northeast. In the latter area household size is considerably smaller and 75 percent of the population live in rental quarters. Crocus Hill, on the other hand, is dominated by homeowners; nearly 80 percent of the households owned their homes in 1978. This rate approaches that found in the suburban-in-city zone and in the familial areas of the settled mid-city.

There is more turnover in Crocus Hill than in the other areas dominated by homeowners. This is because of the high social mobility of the population and the presence of several large apartment buildings along Lincoln Avenue.

Of all the statistics that could be used to describe Crocus Hill, nothing reveals more than the percentage of professional or managerial households, 37.7 percent in 1978. Only two other districts in Saint Paul—Highland Park and the River Boulevard area—have a larger concentration of such households. This population continued to grow during the 1970s and shows no sign of slowing down. As a result, the average annual income for each household in the district is high, and it is increasing.

Crocus Hill is not without its share of problems, however. The streets are now shaded by lovely elms, most of which will eventually succumb to the ravages of dutch elm disease. Without the elms, the appearance of the streets will be changed significantly, but most observers believe the residents will respond with a greater amount of landscaping. Other problems are related to traffic. The future of the planned roadway in the nearby Pleasant Avenue corridor is

Victoria Crossing east and west. The market potential of this zone makes possible dramatic commercial reuse of property. These buildings, formerly automobile dealerships and other commercial facilities, were converted to mini-malls offering a variety of quality-service shops and restaurants.

not yet totally resolved, although a true freeway will not be constructed. The impact of the roadway on the district is unknown.

Perhaps a more serious question is whether the large, detached, single-family houses will continue to be popular. Some people consider them hopelessly old-fashioned and much too costly to maintain. With the high cost of heating fuels, more and more owners may be forced to seek other living arrangements.

Saint Anthony Park

In 1887 the City of Saint Paul annexed the City of Saint Anthony Park. The Park had been founded in 1884 as a proudly independent suburb on the railroad line, six and one-half miles from Saint Paul and one and one-half miles from Minneapolis. It was designed by Horace Cleveland, a well-known landscape architect from Chicago. Cleveland's plan depicted a pastoral landscape with large villas sited on curving streets with ample open space. The hoped-for large estates were not built, and the suburb grew slowly. In 1885, railroad tracks were laid through the village, dividing it into distinctive districts. The northern section was platted by a group of land speculators from Virginia. Their plans were given a boost by the University regents, who in 1881 purchased the Bass farm which was adjacent to the village. By the time of annexation the University was well established.

Development of the district was controlled by the Saint Anthony Park Company during the last years of the nineteenth century. The company's abstemious president, Charles Pratt, forbade the sale of liquor in the Park. Over the years the company sold lots to individuals who built their own house working with contractors. Other educational institutions were attracted to the area, most significantly Luther Seminary, and reinforced the intellectual atmosphere of the district. As the University continued to expand, the population of Saint Anthony Park became increasingly dominated by academic personnel.

Although students did not have a great influence on the Park before World War II, the student population of returning GI's with their families created a demand for married student housing in addition to putting pressure on all the traditional forms of student accommodations. As a result, large student housing communities were established on the fringe of the area. The students became an issue in the Park in the late 1950s and early 1960s. By the mid-1960s citizens were expressing a fear that the character of Saint Anthony Park was being altered by the construction of apartment buildings, the conversion of single-family homes into rental units, and the mere existence of fraternity and sorority houses. They interpreted the increasing density in the residential area as an indication of declining status and a harbinger of urban blight. The community organization, always one of the most articulate in the Twin Cities, commissioned a study of the Park and came forth with a variety of suggestions for maintaining the essential aspects of the residential districts. It seems to have been quite successful, for the area continues to draw in professional and academic households searching for a place to sink roots.

The presence of the University has attracted to Saint Anthony Park a large number of higher-status households, largely employees of the school. In 1978 only four other districts in Saint Paul had a percentage of professional and managerial households that was higher than Saint Anthony Park's 30 percent. This is particularly interesting when one considers the large number of students living in the district. It would seem that nearly all the nonstudent households in Saint Anthony Park must be in one of the higher-status occupations. The number of such households continues to increase.

Despite the high status of the district, the average income in the area is not great. Incomes are higher in the suburban-in-city zone, Crocus Hill, and parts of the settled mid-city and prewar amenity zones. There are two reasons for the lower income in Saint Anthony Park: first, the large number of students brings down the average income; and second, although the academic profession is generally classified as a higher-status occupation, it is not well paid.

In 1978 Saint Anthony Park had one of the lowest vacancy rates in Saint Paul, .87 percent. This rate is extraordinary because only 55 percent of the households in the district own their own home. Those areas of the Twin Cities with lower vacancy rates are upper-income districts, made up of owner-occupied, single-family detached homes. Clearly Saint Anthony Park is an appealing place for homeowners and tenants alike. The excellent access to both campuses of the University makes the rental units attractive to both students and staff.

Milton Square in Saint Anthony Park caters to a high-income academic community and others who enjoy the privacy of this relatively inaccessible part of Saint Paul.

43

The strong rental market has put pressure on the landscape because some developers try to squeeze units into whatever space is available. The efforts of these small-scale developers have been successful because between 1976 and 1978 the population of the district increased by approximately 135 persons.

The mix of families and students gives the district an average household size equal to that for the city as a whole. Households here are somewhat smaller than in Crocus Hill and significantly smaller than in the suburban-in-city districts, which are dominated by families. This mixture of various-sized households makes Saint Anthony Park an interesting model for other residential communities. Conventional wisdom argues that stable, family-oriented households and transitory tenants cannot survive in the same restricted community. Yet in Saint Anthony Park that seems to be exactly what is happening.

Although most residents believe that Saint Anthony is considered a great place to rear children, barely 30 percent of the district's households had children in 1978. This is below the average for the city of Saint Paul.

Competition for housing in the district seems to make it difficult for single-person households to find space here. Only 23 percent of the households in 1978 consisted of a single person, which is well below the figures for Crocus Hill and other middle-class sections of the city. This percentage is of course higher than that for the suburban-in-city zone.

Despite the image of age and stability that residents and visitors ascribe to Saint Anthony Park, it is a community of young people. Only 16 percent of its households are headed by retired persons. This is 10 percent lower than the rate for all of Saint Paul and well below the rate in all but a handful of other districts in the city. The only places with a smaller fraction of the population retired are the newest of the suburban-in-city districts and some of the inner-city areas dominated by minority populations. In Saint Anthony Park, the number of households headed by retired individuals has declined over the past few years. Clearly this area is not a retirement community dominated by elderly University professors.

Saint Anthony Park, then, is a part of the protected genteel zone that has been preserved because of its unique associations with a gigantic academic institution. The convenience of the houses in the Park to people working at the University has maintained their value. The growth of the University has brought an increasing number of professionals to Saint Anthony in search of a congenial community. The result has been the development of an isolated community of rather young people in old housing. The landscape amenities of the district, though important, are secondary to the social conditions within these intellectual communities. Saint Anthony Park is physically so removed from other residential areas in the Twin Cities that it resembles a small college town.

Prospect Park

Prospect Park is perhaps the most topographically interesting of the protected genteel districts, though each occupies some kind of slope. Prospect Park winds up, down, and around a very impressive hill: Tower Hill. With its "witches hat" water tower, the hill is a landmark recognized throughout the city. There used to be another hill in Prospect Park, but it was leveled years ago.

Like other protected genteel districts, Prospect Park was built up around the turn of the century. By 1884 enough people lived here for Minneapolis officials to have it platted. Local legend holds that the English surveyors platted streets to follow existing cowpaths, and gave them their own names (Malcolm, Seymour, Cecil, etc.). The prospective boundaries of Prospect Park were already established by this time. The Milwaukee Road tracks were laid along the bottom of Tower Hill in 1881, cutting off the Tower Hill area from the river. This separation of the northeastern and southwestern portions of Prospect Park was further dramatized some eighty years later when the interstate freeway was routed through this area parallel to the railroad tracks at the base of the hill.

From its earliest days Prospect Park exuded a sense of isolation from the city. Middle-class professionals in particular seemed to find this attractive. Isolation was a reality during the 1880s and 1890s, when one had to have a horse and carriage in order to live here. By 1896 the streetcar reached Prospect Park along University Avenue. As a result, the district's isolated atmosphere diminished, and a major building boom began. Most houses in the area date from this period of construction.

Business people, doctors, and University professors found

Prospect Park a convenient and pleasant place to live then, and many still do today. In the early twentieth century more academics lived there than do now. It was the most accessible residential area away from the University that offered direct transportation to it. One elderly woman who grew up in Prospect Park recalled that in her youth all but two homes on her block were owned by University professors. Over the years, Prospect Park has come to resemble other middle-class areas of the city.

The secluded residential character of Prospect Park seems to have withstood some formidable assaults throughout the twentieth century. One need only observe its position at one end of the largest industrial corridor through the Twin Cities to appreciate residents' strong attachments to the area. Even before World War I industry began to crowd the edges of Prospect Park. This area's exceptional railroad access was the drawing card. Industrial development north of University Avenue and along the city limits in Saint Paul eventually surrounded Prospect Park. Whereas other middle-class areas in this corridor began to decline, Prospect Park resisted. Later, highway encroachments and University expansion were similarly rebuffed. The middle-class residents of Prospect Park are tenacious and seem determined to maintain their eccentric little community. The residents' first response to the proposal to build a freeway was to ensure that it be built south of Prospect Park, rather than through the center as originally planned. After it was done, they continually lobbied for noise barriers.

But not all innovations are resisted. When the Twin Cities' first low-rent housing project was built in 1949 on the edge of Prospect Park, there was no outcry. Residents, who traditionally were liberals, saw the need for such housing and endorsed the project. Community spirit was visible in other ways as well. For example, a successful co-op store did business here for thirty years. It closed in 1967, just before other co-ops in Minneapolis got organized. Competition from large chain stores was to blame, but the women who had traditionally run it were also beginning to work at paid jobs.

The most serious challenge to the secure life-style of Prospect Park came in the early 1960s when almost one-third of the housing was torn down so that Interstate 94 could be constructed through the area. Even many residents whose homes were not threatened moved away during this period. Ironically, the freeway seems not to have adversely affected Prospect Park. Because many newer houses were removed, the district's historic character became more evident; and the large interchange west of Prospect Park gave the area a highly visible boundary. Prospect Park is now almost completely separated from the segment of the aging inner ring to its west that continually suffers University expansion.

Prospect Park's lovely old homes have aged in a graceful manner. Occasionally a new house has been tucked up onto the hill, demonstrating the continued vitality of the area. If Kenwood and Lowry Hill are the best-dressed adults in the Minneapolis family, Prospect Park might be considered a dowager aunt—a bit tattered, but cultured and full of life.

CONCLUSION

All the districts in the protected genteel zone are confronted with the same issue: will their status continue to be protected by the present configurations of amenities and attitudes? Although passing fashions in housing styles have not had a dramatic impact on these areas, they are by no means immune to change. The basic problem in each area is finding space for the increasing number of households and their cars. The districts could hold many more people than they now do if the population consisted of traditional families with children. That pattern is not common, and a continuing trend toward smaller household size dominates the housing market in all parts of the Twin Cities. A further influence on this area is the increasing cost of housing. Buildings here are expensive, and the increasing costs of mortgages combined with an economic downturn may encourage homeowners to subdivide their houses to provide space for some of the new small households that will form over the next few years.

CHAPTER

IV

The Rebuilt Zone

The oldest sections of most American cities have had similar histories. The early settlements in the central business districts were built and rebuilt through every boom period. These places quickly lost their residential character. The early settlements that remained residential faded into oblivion and decay as new housing was constructed farther from downtown. Today these portions of the city betray little or nothing of their origins; they have been fundamentally altered and rebuilt, though they remain residential in character.

The rebuilt zone of Minneapolis and Saint Paul comprises several districts that contain some land built up during each city's initial boom period. This is not precisely where the first settlers lived—those sites have largely been consumed by industry or commerce. They are instead the places that housed both American and foreign-born migrants to the Twin Cities in the 1860s and 1870s. None of these areas ever served the high society of either city. These districts provided workers with cheap housing close to places of industrial employment. The kind of work and types of people varied with each location, but the predominance of low-paying, unskilled jobs ensured that all the rebuilt districts would follow similar patterns. These areas sheltered each new wave of immigrants to the Twin Cities: the Norwegians and Swedes, then Poles and Russian Jews, and finally blacks and Mexican-Americans. People chose to leave these districts as soon as they could afford better housing. By the 1950s, all the districts in the zone had experienced severe population losses.

The hallmark of the rebuilt districts today is the near-complete removal, or substantial alteration, of their past landscapes. Reconstruction began in the 1930s and is still going on at present. In a few sections it is possible to find traces of what existed in the nineteenth century, but these areas are comparatively small and are punctuated by new construction, often highrise buildings. The largest remnants of that period's housing are in the aging inner ring. This housing consisted of small units, inexpensive to construct, that did not age gracefully.

The topography of the rebuilt areas was and is unremarkable. Some of the sites are scenic, however: St. Anthony West sits on the Mississippi River right above the falls, and part of Cedar-Riverside occupies the top of the bluff on the river gorge. Little or nothing was done to exploit the amenities of these sites during either construction or reconstruction.

Almost all of the rebuilt zone borders on one of the downtowns or an early industrial site. (See map 4.) The zone is not geographically large, but its visual impact gives it an extensive appearance. Every portion of this zone is unlike

Cedar Square West represents the most extreme form of rebuilding present in the Twin Cities.

the rest of the city that surrounds it. Cedar-Riverside, Gateway, and part of Sumner-Glenwood are characterized by tall buildings which dominate the nearby landscape. The new housing in St. Anthony West and the rehabilitated houses on Milwaukee Avenue stand out markedly in their respective environments. Similarly, the river flats in Saint Paul look spacious and empty compared to the surrounding bluff area. What links each of these districts is their extensive rebuilding activities which have been made possible by public subsidies.

THE REBUILDING PROCESS

Rebuilding each of these districts was a lengthy and complex process which can only be briefly summarized here. The driving forces behind the rebuilding efforts were public funding and public involvement. None of these areas was capable of regenerating itself. The amount of physical deterioration was so massive that individual efforts could have little impact; public money and public sponsorship were necessary if changes were to occur. In most of these districts the housing was so decrepit that even residents who were attached to the area recognized that massive clearance was necessary. Public funding took different forms in each district, but in every case city funds were supplemented by federal and state loans and grants. For example, the rebuilding of Cedar-Riverside involved federal New Communities money, city renewal funds, and large infusions of private capital as well. Private investment also figured prominently in the Gateway redevelopment and in Milwaukee Avenue's renaissance.

In the rebuilding of several districts area residents played a pivotal role by helping to determine the direction of public efforts. In areas like Milwaukee Avenue and St. Anthony in Minneapolis, residents interceded to protect structures that might otherwise have been cleared, and to advocate rehabilitation where possible. Their efforts paid off, since these are the only rebuilt areas where some trace of the former landscape is still visible.

The rebuilding process has usually been initiated by the housing authority of each city, though the Saint Paul Port Authority played a major role in starting the redevelopment of the river flats. The role of the local housing authorities, both in the rebuilt districts and elsewhere in the cities, needs

to be clarified. When these agencies were formed in the 1950s, their mission was to carry out the urban renewal mission of the federal government at the local level. In keeping with the then-current view of urban problems and solutions, each of these agencies in Minneapolis and Saint Paul was originally oriented toward large-scale total clearance. There is no doubt that residents of areas designated for renewal by the housing authorities were not always pleased to receive this service. But the housing authorities were also charged with the task of working with residents of affected areas. In some cases this collaboration resulted in residents substantially revamping the original plans of the housing authority. The Minneapolis Housing and Redevelopment Authority (MHRA), after sponsoring total clearance projects in Gateway and on the Near North side, gradually moved to the position of rehabilitating where possible, and of doing spot clearance only where absolutely necessary. As a result, a portion of the rebuilt zone in Minneapolis contains quite old housing that is completely up to code. Of course, the rehabilitated sections of these districts were in far worse shape than other parts of the city twenty years ago. The fact that these places still exist, and that they are structurally sound, is a clear tribute to the residents' persistence and to the housing authorities' willingness to be flexible and responsive.

DISTRICTS OF THE REBUILT ZONE

Unlike some of the other zones, the rebuilt zone cannot be easily understood through a recitation of statistics or a delineation of common experiences. These districts need to be described in detail in order for their similarities to unfold. The past has played an important role in this zone; for that reason the profiles of these districts contain more detailed historical descriptions than do those of other zones. The common patterns will emerge as the unique qualities of each district become apparent.

Gateway

The most central of the rebuilt areas, Gateway, has never been primarily a residential district. But it has housed many people since the west bank of the Mississippi was first opened for settlement in the early 1850s. At the center of the original "Town of Minneapolis," Gateway experienced

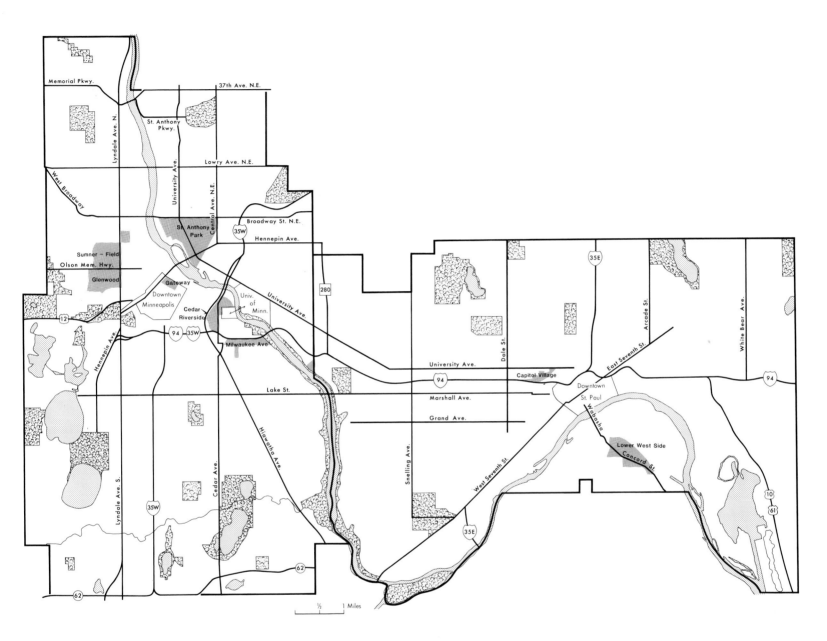

Map 4: The Rebuilt Zone. The distinctive trait of this zone is the substantial amount of clearance and new construction or reconstruction. These districts were once the most severely deteriorated parts of each city.

its first construction boom in the 1860s, consisting of small one- and two-story frame dwellings. By the 1870s, when the commercial core of Minneapolis was located at Bridge Square (where Hennepin and Nicollet Avenues converged), this area was being rebuilt with three- and four-story brick structures. Many of these were hotels which ultimately became flophouses in the 1930s and 1940s. For most of the late nineteenth and early twentieth centuries Gateway provided overnight accommodations for travelers to Minneapolis and was home for some downtown workers. It was a lively place by day and night, with its businesses, hotels, and vaudeville theaters. As the center of downtown moved south along Nicollet Avenue, this aging and declining commercial area was left behind.

The progress of Gateway's physical deterioration and commercial abandonment was well under way in the early twentieth century. The first concerted effort to improve the district was the building of Gateway Center, with its colonnades and fountains, in the teens. The second led to the creation of the main Post Office and Pioneer Square during the early 1930s. From the Depression until the late 1950s Gateway was the "skid row" of Minneapolis. To this part of the city came retired lumbermen and others who, in the past, had spent their winters and their savings in the saloons and vaudeville houses of Bridge Square. These people who had nowhere else to go formed the nucleus of a community that roved from the flophouses to the soup kitchens to the bars. By the late 1950s Gateway was such an eyesore that the public launched a drive to spruce up this entryway into downtown.

The Gateway district is perhaps the best local example of urban renewal as it has been conventionally understood. Critics of this program have charged that it was a brutal scheme to remove slums and poor people from the central city, and replace them with office towers and luxury apartments. This is exactly the process that took place in Gateway, with some slight modifications. Beginning in 1960, old office buildings, worn-out hotels and rooming houses, saloons and burlesque halls were cleared away, along with some irreplaceable structures located within the larger renewal area (e.g., the Metropolitan building, whose loss probably ignited the preservation movement in Minneapolis). The area was being made ready for new downtown expansion. Hundreds of Gateway residents were left homeless, though much of the cleared land remained vacant for almost twenty years. Rebuilding in Gateway consisted primarily of office or hotel construction: the Northwestern National Life Insurance building, the Federal Reserve Bank, the Sheraton-Ritz Hotel, and the new Public Library. The only residential construction prior to the 1970s was the Towers complex, a relatively expensive apartment building later converted to condominiums. By 1974 this residential outpost of downtown gained another highrise building; this one was designated for low- and moderate-income senior citizens. The first residents of this building enthusiastically hailed their access to cultural activities and commercial facilities. The addition of this building brought the total number of residential units in Gateway to 1,000, representing all income levels.

New office construction has started again in this district, and new residential structures, both rental and condominium, have also appeared. It seems likely that most new residential construction will continue to be geared toward people with relatively high incomes. The riverfront corridor that abuts the Gateway area has been designated for highrise apartment or condominium construction. Preliminary plans for the nearby Burlington Northern land indicate that none of this new development will be inexpensive. The residential future of downtown Minneapolis seems to hold the prospect of an office/commercial core buffered on two sides by expensive housing: Gateway on the north and Loring Park on the south.

Near North

The Near Northside rebuilt district, one mile northwest of downtown, roughly coincides with the Sumner-Glenwood area. It lay directly in the path of industries that were moving out of central Minneapolis as early as the 1890s. Listen to Harrison Salisbury describe the transformation of his childhood neighborhood bordering Sumner-Glenwood to the east:

[Our] house was set on a street of similar houses, shaded by great elms which met over the gentle curve of the avenue. . . . Every house in this little enclave set among tiny parks, two small lakes, and a rather lively creek was of a piece—broad verandas, sparkling lawns, pergolas, improbable second-floor and third-floor

balconies, mansard roofs, and copper gutters and drains.
. . . I think every detail of that house is etched indelibly
in my mind. And well it is. Not a matchstick of the
house remains. . . . All of it gone. Not only the era
but the whole milieu. . . . Gone not only our house
but all the houses. Gone the street—indeed, the whole
network of streets. Vanished as though they had never
been. As though Oak Lake Addition had never existed.
Gone from memories. Gone from maps. And in its
place acres of blacktop and concrete. Blocks of buildings,
military and rectangular. Gone the slum that grew
year by year with the days of my boyhood. . . . Oak
Lake itself—dried up, vanished, drained. I don't know
what happened to it. . . . New times, new seeds.
The area was rundown. A slum. High crime area. Un-
sanitary. Unsightly. Bring in the bulldozers and the
concrete pourers. So it was done. . . . ("The Victorian
City in the Midwest," in *Growing Up in Minnesota*,
ed. Chester Anderson [Minneapolis: University of
Minnesota Press, 1976], pp. 53-54.)

Oak Lake was once a genteel nineteenth-century neighborhood. By the second decade of the twentieth century most
of its homes were subdivided to provide shelter for the
vanguard of Russian Jews moving to Minneapolis via
Winnipeg. Even before the Depression, Oak Lake was
obliterated, and the area became an extension of the
industrial district north of downtown. Today the Farmer's
Market occupies most of the former lake site.

Sumner-Glenwood's fate paralleled but did not duplicate
that of Oak Lake. It suffered severe decline, but remained
residential instead of becoming industrialized. The Sumner-
Glenwood area was settled in the 1880s and 1890s. Homes
here were never quite as large or as elegant as those in Oak
Lake. Developers attempted to create an exclusive residential
pocket on the eastern edge of the area, similar to the Forest
Heights addition along Broadway to the north of here. This
did not materialize. Most of Sumner-Glenwood, along with
other Near North areas, developed into a solidly middle-class
residential district around the turn of the century. Throughout the early twentieth century Lyndale Avenue remained a
distinct social and physical boundary between the working-
class area to the east and Sumner-Glenwood and other
middle-class areas to the west.

Around the turn of the century and just after, two-story
frame homes, duplexes, and some small apartment buildings
were rapidly constructed in this district, spurred on by the
extension of streetcars along Glenwood Avenue and 6th
Avenue North. The impetus for all this activity was the prosperous lumber industry along the river north of Plymouth
Avenue. Its precipitous decline after 1900 spelled trouble
for Sumner-Glenwood and other Near North areas. As late
as 1916 a group studying the area and proposing street improvements called Sumner-Glenwood a district of splendid
and neglected possibilities. Citing the area's lack of connections both to downtown and to the lakes, the group charged
that the city was neglecting this area.

By the 1920s the decay of Sumner-Glenwood was well
recognized. The area was unable to maintain its middle-class
character. Consequently, it began to serve as a way station
for immigrants with limited housing options, primarily Jews
and blacks. The Jewish settlers who first lived in Salisbury's
Oak Lake demonstrated their mobility and financial achieve-
ments by progressively moving through the Near North area.
From Oak Lake they moved to Sumner-Glenwood, then on
to the Homewood area along the city's western border, and
finally to the suburbs. This is Minneapolis' counterpart to
Saint Paul's Jewish resettlement from the Lower West Side
to Highland Park. It would be difficult, if not impossible, to
find a Jewish family living in Minneapolis or its suburbs for
two or three generations which did not have some earlier
ties to Near North.

Blacks originally settled in a section of Cedar-Riverside,
but began to succeed upwardly mobile Jewish families on
the eastern edge of the Northside during World War I. They
followed exactly the same path of progress. The distinction
was that blacks were not as numerous and that it took much
longer for them to obtain the better housing to the west.
This resettlement was not accomplished until the 1950s
and 1960s, when Jewish families left Near North for the
suburbs en masse.

Sumner-Glenwood, then, became an area to move into
and out of as quickly as possible. As a highly transient area,
no one took responsibility for the upkeep of houses, and
even the most substantial dwellings soon began to decay. A
1926 study of conditions on the Northside summarized
Sumner-Glenwood as follows:

The squalor and degradation in the vicinity of Sixth
Avenue North can scarcely be realized by one who has

not lived or worked in that section. The general appearance is one of poverty and neglect. The houses are dilapidated and unpainted. Many of them are little more than shacks. Porches sag, stairs are rickety. Streets are littered with papers and rubbish. . . . Here and there alleys are almost impassable with tin cans, mud and filth. Garbage cans are rare. . . . Due to this filth and decay the neighborhood is swarming with insects, rats and mice. . . . The section is the most congested in the city. . . . In many cases whole families, father, mother and five or more children live in one room. . . . (*Study of Community Conditions—North District*. Women's Cooperative Alliance, Minneapolis, Minn., 1925.)

With the coming of the Depression the already blighted character of Sumner-Glenwood worsened. In a 1934 survey, housing in a section of this district was declared the worst in Minneapolis. Work began the following year on the city's first public renewal project—Sumner-Field. This two-story brick project substituted over 600 low-income housing units for thirty acres of decrepit houses and junk yards. Its high quality of design, construction, and maintenance made it the standard against which all other public housing would be measured. (Even today it is still a sought-after public accommodation.)

By the mid-1950s, however, it was obvious that more of this district needed to be reconstructed. Housing clearance and new construction went on for the next decade both north and south of Sumner-Field. The housing in these areas was as old and dilapidated as the housing that had been cleared originally for the Sumner-Field project. Much of it was built before 1900; all of it was built before 1920. As black migration increased during and after World War II, most of the poorest and least skilled of the newcomers sought refuge in this area. The old houses in the Glenwood area demanded a level of maintenance that a low-income renter population could not sustain. So the physical deterioration of the area continued.

The Glenwood area immediately south of Sumner-Field was the first section cleared in this round of activity. Begun in 1955 and completed in 1968, the Glenwood project included low-income family housing as well as low- and moderate-income units for the elderly. On Glenwood's 180 acres there were more than 1,000 housing units, ranging from highrises and moderately tall apartment buildings to townhouses. One serious problem area emerged in this district when the townhouses known as Girard Terrace were built in 1965. Although lacking in aesthetic appeal, these townhouses were valued by families as a more desirable location in which to raise children than the taller buildings were. Almost from the start the residents were plagued with severe maintenance problems like cracking walls. It was finally determined that these problems were not caused by residents' neglect but by poorly sited construction. The ground under Girard Terrace had once been drained by Bassett's Creek; even moderate rainfall caused flooding in this poorly drained soil. The townhouses were abandoned by 1977, and they remain a boarded-up reminder of good intentions gone wrong.

The major portion of the Northside rebuilt district lies north of Olson Highway, and north and east of Sumner-Field, in what was formerly known as the Grant neighborhood. Total clearance of this section was begun in 1964. Eventually the dilapidated housing was replaced by 1,200 units of low- and moderate-income housing. Stretching all the way to Plymouth Avenue, the Grant project continues to present some of the best opportunities for new construction in the Near North district. Many acres that were cleared are not yet rebuilt. The most recent construction has occurred at the northern edge of this area. Interestingly designed small apartment buildings have been built on portions of Plymouth Avenue that were cleared after the racial turmoil of the mid-1960s, in which most buildings were burned or abandoned. During 1980, townhouses were built at Olson Highway and Logan Avenue, and offered for sale at market rates. All of them were sold before construction was completed.

The Sumner-Glenwood area remains what it has been: a refuge for the poorer segments of the city, particularly low-income blacks. In the public mind, this district is associated with "the projects." It is perceived as run-down and blighted. It is true that most housing units in Sumner-Glenwood are subsidized housing of one form or another. It is also true that most of these units are in good condition and are fairly well maintained. With the exception of the highrise housing for the elderly that punctuates the Sumner-Glenwood landscape, the environment here is a human-scale mix of two- and three-story apartments and townhouses.

To anyone familiar with the public housing districts of Chicago and New York, Sumner-Glenwood presents a distinctly favorable impression. The most recent construction, in particular, reflects a good deal of aesthetic detail and concern. Where one might expect cinder-block buildings, one finds instead quantities of brick and stone used in a sensitive way.

East of Lyndale lies the gem of the Near North rebuilt district: Lyn Park, begun in 1973. A self-advertised "suburb in the city" with plans for an eventual 450 houses, Lyn Park has been quite successful. It has proved that middle-class housing can coexist with subsidized housing. In 1978 houses here sold for more than $50,000 in a location where land could not be given away ten years earlier. Lyn Park has attracted an integrated group of residents, who pride themselves on having the most modern of suburban housing less than ten minutes from downtown.

All this activity in the Near North district in recent years would seem to indicate a renewed vitality for an area that has been viewed only negatively for too long.

St. Anthony

While the hallmark of rebuilding in these first examples has been clearance, in northeast Minneapolis it has been conservation. This district was first settled in the 1840s and 1850s by entrepreneurs from New England and French lumbermen. St. Anthony's town center, with commercial facilities and a steamboat landing, was at Main Street and 3rd Avenue N.E. With the merger of St. Anthony and Minneapolis in 1872, this area became the east side of Minneapolis. The tie with Minneapolis was strengthened the next year when additional bridges were constructed at Plymouth Avenue and at 10th Avenue South. St. Anthony never had a chance to be simply a residential community. Lying alongside the Mississippi and adjacent to railroad yards, lumber and flour mills, this district quickly acquired an industrial character. Because so many industries were located in or near St. Anthony, it proved to be a desirable residential area for unskilled laborers who needed to be able to walk to work.

St. Anthony functioned in much the same way as Sumner-Glenwood. That is, it housed migrants to Minneapolis during the first stage of their climb up the socioeconomic ladder. Initially an area of Scandinavian settlement (primarily Swedish), the western portion of St. Anthony (west of University Avenue) had become the center of Minneapolis' Polish community by the mid-1880s. It was not unusual to find a dozen families from the same Polish town who had migrated together and lived on the same block. St. Anthony West contained a national church for its Polish Catholic residents. This institution served as a beacon, drawing other Polish immigrants to the area. It also provided a unifying element in the lives of the people.

In the early twentieth century, one proved one's social and economic mobility in Northeast by moving from the valley (Old St. Anthony and Sheridan) up to the hill (Windom Park and Audubon Park). One person we interviewed distinguished these areas as follows: valley children walked to school, while children from the hill rode to school on the streetcars. Even within the valley different social groups lived in distinct areas. The portion of St. Anthony between Marshall Street and the river, extending from Third to Eighth Avenues, was known as "the Flats." This was a section of dilapidated shacks that contrasted sharply with the tidy frame houses and duplexes east of Marshall. Interestingly, this area has recently been redeveloped with suburban-style single-family homes.

The St. Anthony district did not deteriorate as quickly as some of the other rebuilt areas. Once a family acquired the security of owning a house, they typically remained in it for a generation or more, maintaining it as best they could. The problem for this district was not pressure from commerce or industry. Nor were houses abandoned as incomes improved, or because residents feared their neighbors. The problems of St. Anthony were engendered by a very old stock of hastily constructed housing. Almost no amount of care and attention could render these houses desirable in the face of rising expectations. In addition, those who could most easily afford housing improvements most often wanted to live elsewhere. So the one- and two-story frame houses and stucco duplexes were left to the care of those who remained, for the most part, unskilled workers. The houses gradually began to reflect the residents' lack of economic progress.

Throughout the first half of the twentieth century, St. Anthony continued to serve as an initial home for newcomers to the city. Many Poles remained in the area and were joined by large numbers of Ukranians in the years

This small section of Northeast Minneapolis along the river was rebuilt with single-family homes in response to community pressure to replace deteriorated houses with something that future generations would find desirable. The Pioneer statue was moved from Pioneer Square in downtown Minneapolis during the Gateway renewal efforts.

immediately before and after World War II. The Ukranians tended to remain in St. Anthony, with its national churches and other cultural institutions, and they helped maintain the longtime ethnic flavor of this area. Until the late 1950s, life in St. Anthony went on in much the same way as in any other urban area whose residents were primarily industrial laborers. Schools, churches, and voluntary associations formed an all-encompassing social network. Working conditions were hard, hours were long. The family and traditional values lay at the center of community life. It probably occurred to few people in St. Anthony that they were living in a "slum."

By the late 1950s St. Anthony had experienced a process of decline and deterioration similar to that in other older parts of both cities. The old housing needed many repairs, and many of the residents were low-income senior citizens who could not afford this work. Like other communities surrounding downtown, St. Anthony lost population during the 1950s. The children of longtime residents were moving

to Columbia Heights and other northern suburbs. It was clear that something had to be done to salvage the area.

Urban renewal began in the western section of St. Anthony (west of 5th St N.E.) in 1964. Instead of whole-sale clearance, the program here used substantial rehabilitation and spot clearance. Houses in this area needed new roofs, new paint, new plumbing and wiring, and new furnaces. They were well worn, but they were not yet slum dwellings. Those that could be saved were identified, and over 1,000 houses (or 94 percent of the total number) were brought up to code. About 300 structures were deemed beyond repair, and these were removed. Meanwhile, new construction began. This took several forms: infill housing on blocks of older structures, apartments designated for the elderly, and blocks of new single-family homes. The portions of St. Anthony that were the most deteriorated, along the river west of Main Street, got most of the new homes. One resident remembered this area as being filled with shacks inhabited by "bums." It has since been transformed into a prototypical suburban landscape. The split-levels and ranch houses built here stand out in marked contrast to the older housing in St. Anthony. But there is some amount of continuity too. Many residents of the newer housing had been displaced from other houses in the St. Anthony renewal area. Their desire to remain in the area underscores the attachment residents have for this area.

The renewal activities in the eastern section of St. Anthony began in 1968. Here over 500 dwelling units were rehabilitated, and nearly 300 substandard dwellings were removed. Again infill housing was constructed, and several structures for moderate-income elderly were built.

Both sections of St. Anthony exemplify perfectly one of the qualities that Northeast is known for: the maintenance and improvement of the landscape. Now that these areas have been put back in order, it is impossible to find signs of their former condition. Windows sparkle, lawns are trim, flowers are everywhere—it is not unusual to find sidewalks being swept daily!

Both areas also present some of the most interesting incongruities in the Twin Cities landscape. Most of the older houses have acquired new siding or new stucco exteriors, but they still retain the characteristics of their age. Oddly shaped windows and interesting carved wooden details are sometimes visible. One can occasionally find one of these rescued oldsters right next door to something that appears to have been imported from the California coast. The juxtaposition of old houses with new homes featuring cedar decks and skylights makes for an occasionally surprising, but delightful, landscape.

Data from the R. L. Polk directories help illustrate a few of the recent changes in St. Anthony. Block samples from 1967 to 1977 indicated that few of the residents had been in the same dwelling over the ten-year period. The data did indicate that much of the housing was removed and replaced in that time period. About one-third of the people in residence in 1977 had been there since 1972, and there were five new houses on a short two-block stretch. There were changes in the type of people living in the area as well. Most of the 1967 residents had been laborers, but by 1977 professionals and managers were commonly represented. There seemed not to be a particularly strong ethnic cast to the area in the later period. Various Slavic names appeared, but so did many Anglo-Saxon names. The strong ethnic ties of this section of St. Anthony seem to have diminished somewhat in recent years.

Because of its location on the riverfront and adjacent to the economically booming historic district there, St. Anthony is bound to be subjected to renewed development pressures. Plans already exist for two office/condominium towers (Riverplace) that will spill over into the southwest corner of the St. Anthony district. It seems likely that as more and more people move into the area who have no roots there, changes must occur. Whether St. Anthony can retain its special characteristics in the face of intense economic pressures will be the primary question facing this district in the coming years.

Seward

In the western Seward area of Minneapolis is a small district that can be considered rebuilt. It includes a short two-block stretch of Milwaukee Avenue, and a portion of Franklin Avenue just north of it. The rebuilding process here took several forms: the rehabilitation of older houses on Milwaukee Avenue, the construction of new single-family homes nearby, and the construction of new apartment complexes along Franklin. The process here was much like that in other districts. The area around Milwaukee Avenue

Milwaukee Avenue in South Minneapolis.

This renovated streetcar strip provides a gathering place for the extremely diverse community.

was the oldest section of Seward, having been built up during the 1880s to house those who worked in nearby railroad yards. The largely Scandinavian population lived in closely spaced frame houses and duplexes. Descendants of this group lost interest in these units as more spacious sections of south Minneapolis opened for settlement. Over the years this part of Seward continued to house those who worked in nearby industries, but the population declined steadily.

This district was also pressured by institutional expansion in Cedar-Riverside. By the late 1960s old houses and apartments along Franklin were being replaced by large apartment complexes oriented toward the growing student population. The initial redevelopment plans for this area called for almost total clearance and new construction, but residents rallied to oppose such changes. Strong sentiment for historic preservation was beginning to emerge nationally. Those who objected to total clearance in western Seward hit upon the idea of having Milwaukee Avenue designated a historic district in order to preserve as much housing as possible and to delay clearance. As this proposal wended its way through local and federal channels, residents began

Older commercial buildings on Cedar Avenue shelter craft establishments as well as basic services for area residents.

This renovated house exemplifies Milwaukee Avenue's appeal to many more people than could possibly live on that small street.

working with the Housing Authority to plan the area's future. In the end, the city designated Milwaukee Avenue as a historic district, and HRA agreed to clear only structures that were beyond salvation.

As one strolls along Milwaukee Avenue today, one acquires a strong sense of appreciation for these rehabilitation efforts. The facade of the avenue is coherent both in age and in design. It is reminiscent of parts of Society Hill in Philadelphia, and other preserved nineteenth-century streetscapes. Most of the original brick houses were gutted and their interiors completely rebuilt. The exteriors have been uniformly surfaced with brick. The avenue itself has been turned into a pedestrian mall. The attraction and success of these renovated houses have had a clear influence on surrounding blocks. Almost every block contains one or more houses that are in the process of being rehabilitated. Experimentation is also evident in the area: one block from Milwaukee Avenue a "solar" home was constructed, and a few blocks away a group of earth-sheltered townhouses were built. The Housing Authority built some subsidized townhouses nearby for moderate-income families. These structures have shingled wood exteriors and interesting designs that blend into the historic character of the area. It is already clear that this small rebuilt area has generated more than its share of private investment in the blocks surrounding Milwaukee Avenue.

Rebuilt Areas of Saint Paul

In Saint Paul the Port Authority joined with the Housing and Redevelopment Authority in transforming neighborhoods. As a result, several old residential districts have been rebuilt as commercial and industrial areas. The two most extensive examples of this activity are (1) the upper levee project along the east bank of the Mississippi under the High Bridge, where an old Italian slum was replaced by a modern scrap yard and manufacturing activities; and (2) the enormous Riverview Industrial Park across the river from downtown. The latter project is interesting because here the Port Authority and the Housing Authority worked in concert to create a marketable industrial landscape and acceptable residential district out of the city's worst slum.

The rebuilt areas of Saint Paul might properly be called the rebuilding zone because the developers' plans have not yet been realized. For example, Capitol Village, just north of Interstate 94, is an attempt to build in the central city single-family detached housing selling at market rates. Although similar plans seem to have worked well in Minneapolis, development in this area has been plagued by financial problems.

Saint Paul River Flats

The so-called flats of the West Side had long been home to Saint Paul's newest and poorest immigrants. A little over a century ago this district was beyond the reach of the law, and harbored some of the area's most desperate characters. In 1874 it was annexed to Saint Paul, and law and order extended across the river. But living conditions did not improve when the city took charge. Because this area was liable to flood in the spring, landowners were not encouraged to invest much in their property. In fact, some immigrants remember moving into warped houses—they were cheap. The earliest occupants were French Canadians and Indians together with an undifferentiated mixture of impoverished individuals. The Indians and French Canadians left the area in the late nineteenth century, and they were replaced by Jewish immigrants from Eastern Europe and Russia. In the course of a decade the area became Saint Paul's first Jewish ghetto. These immigrants worked at whatever jobs they could find. Many walked across the old Robert Street Bridge to work in the garment factories on the eastern edge of the central business district. Others ran stores or worked in scrap yards. They were aided to some degree by the Jews from Germany who had immigrated earlier and who were by 1910 quite well established. The result was the founding of several synagogues and the Neighborhood House, a social outreach center.

The later immigrants to Saint Paul, the Blacks, Mexicans, and Indians, were also attracted to the cheap housing and tolerant population of the West Side. As the Jewish population gradually prospered and moved out of the area, their place was taken by Blacks and Mexican-Americans. Of all the immigrant groups to make their home in the Twin Cities, the Mexican-American population is the most diverse group. Among the residents of the rebuilt area on Saint Paul's West Side, where most of them live, are recent immigrants from Mexico eagerly awaiting citizenship, those

Torre de San Miguel, 1971 (above), and Sumner Field Housing Project, 1938 (below). These two projects span the more than thirty years during which attempts have been made to provide decent housing for low-income people in the Twin Cities.

recently naturalized, and some families with ancestors who have been citizens of the United States since the annexation of the Republic of Texas. All speak Spanish and are proud of their Mexican heritage. In the past few years they have been joined by families of Puerto Rican extraction who have relocated here from the larger cities in the East.

The Mexican population came to the state as migrant agricultural laborers. During the First World War a few responded to labor recruiters and settled down in Saint Paul to work in South Saint Paul's meat-packing plants. In 1920 there were approximately 70 Mexican families here; by 1930, about 400 permanent residents of Saint Paul were of Mexican origin. There is no way of knowing the size of the temporary Mexican population, but it must have been considerable. During these years the Mexican community lived quite apart from the rest of the urban population. Their large, extended families provided for most of their needs. Help was also available from the Mission of Our Lady of Guadalupe. Although the area was legally part of the city, it did not always look urban. Many families kept animals and fowl. Outdoor privys were common, and streets were not paved. On a warm summer evening when the sounds of guitars and singing spilled out of homes and cantinas into the warm damp air along the river, the flats seemed like a small Texas town to the occasional visitor from another part of the city.

In 1950 there were 4,000 Spanish-speaking residents in Saint Paul, most of them living on the low land along the river. Although the area was much better than the workers' camps many families had grown accustomed to, the 1950s brought renewal programs to Saint Paul. The flats housing was destroyed in the late 1950s and early 1960s. By 1970 several new housing developments had been constructed to rehouse the displaced residents. Torre de San Miguel has 142 units; the Phoenix, 48; Dunedin Terrace, 145; and Vista Village, 43. In addition to these, several single-family detached houses have been constructed along Concord Street on land cleared of dilapidated houses. But not everything here is new. The HRA made an effort to identify and preserve houses that had some historic and architectural character. Owners of such structures were eligible for low-interest rehabilitation loans.

Now protected from the river by a high flood wall, the old badlands of the West Side is a modern community that serves as the core for the greater Spanish community of the Twin Cities. The Spanish-speaking minority, now larger than the black population of Saint Paul, seems intent on making this area their home. Although there is some evidence that individuals at the edges of the community are dispersing into adjacent areas, there is no reason to believe that the group as a whole will abandon the area as did the earlier residents.

POPULATION

The environmental transformation of the rebuilt zone is only one part of the story. The other part is the residents. Who lives in these districts now? There have been changes as well as continuity. The overall characteristics of residents in some rebuilt areas have remained fairly constant. The population of other areas have changed dramatically. (See table 3, p. 146.) The one trait that is shared by all residents of the zone is a concern for the quality of life in the central city. People are willing to work at making their particular districts as attractive as possible, regardless of past problems.

St. Anthony remains slightly more ethnic than most of Minneapolis, both in popular perception and in fact. The sense of community here is still pervasive enough to make outsiders occasionally feel out of place. Many residents have strong ties to the area. In fact, many residents of the newer housing along the river grew up in the area, and made conscious decisions to raise their own children there. Of all the rebuilt districts, St. Anthony probably has some of the most content residents. They have downtown at their doorstep for major shopping expeditions. They have specialty markets and grocery stores right in the area. All their social and cultural institutions are intact. The major concern here is one shared in many parts of the city: the closing of local schools and the busing of children to meet the court-ordered desegregation plan.

The Near North, of which Sumner-Glenwood is a part, contains one of two major concentrations of blacks in Minneapolis—the other being on the south side. But numerous white residents can still be found in this area. People who live here, like most residents of the city, are basically concerned about the quality of their housing and the quality of their children's education.

The Gateway district's population today is drastically

different from what it once was. The old and poor residents were almost completely replaced by younger and more affluent downtown workers. At one time the district had a "swinging singles" aura, but since the conversion of the Towers to condominiums, this image has diminished. Most residents are single. If married, they are usually childless, or have already reared their children. Convenience is the key to life in this area. Gateway offers easy access to the cultural facilities of the central city; dependence on automobiles is minimized; and one need not be bothered with home repair and grass cutting. The one group that does not experience this life-style in the same way are the elderly of the Gateway. Since two or three subsidized highrises for the elderly have been built, Gateway is once again sheltering those in need of specific services.

Since Milwaukee Avenue's rehabilitation, the local population has changed somewhat, though the local citizens' group worked hard to ensure that some of the longtime working-class residents would be able to remain in the renovated houses. It is clear that to some degree these efforts were successful. But it also seems that relatively young and more affluent residents were attracted to the historic structures. In 1978, these new and renovated houses sold for more than $75,000, a price which virtually ensured a population shift. Living in this small district almost automatically implies an interest in, if not a commitment to, historic preservation.

COMMERCIAL DEVELOPMENT

In the nineteenth century each district in the rebuilt zone had enough local commerce to be relatively self-sufficient; all but major household purchases could be made here. As the districts deteriorated and lost population, the quality and sometimes the number of commercial facilities also declined. The rebuilding of residential sections of these districts gradually led to the transformation of the adjacent commercial sites as well.

The Sumner-Glenwood area presents a clear picture of the commercial decline that often precedes or accompanies renewal. The major commercial streets in this area were Glenwood Avenue, 6th Avenue North (Olson Highway), and Plymouth Avenue. In the early 1960s there were still many small supermarkets, barber shops, hardware stores, and cleaners on these streets. The commercial decline of Glenwood and Olson Highway was fully accomplished during the renewal process. Glenwood became predominantly industrial, and Olson Highway was upgraded to near freeway status. Merchants who were relocated from these streets in the early 1960s tended to stay on the North Side. Many of them, for example, moved to places that ultimately made a second relocation necessary (e.g., the I-94 corridor north of downtown Minneapolis). Ten years after relocation fully 60 percent of those businesses that had moved out of the project area were no longer operating. Although many normal retirements undoubtedly account for some of the closings, the difficulty of starting over at a new location is well documented. The one spectacular success story was the Lincoln Bakery on Olson—it moved to St. Louis Park, became the Lincoln Del, and now has two additional suburban outlets.

The commercial decline of Plymouth Avenue was aggravated by race riots in the mid-1960s. The number of shops had been stable prior to the riots. Soon after this, store owners indicated that business was down because customers were moving to the suburbs, and that vandalism was increasing. Most of the stores in this area were owned by older Jewish merchants. After the riots many of them simply retired. Those who remained in business moved their establishments closer to their suburban homes. By 1968 Plymouth Avenue was characterized by vacant and boarded-up buildings. Throughout the early 1970s the need for new commercial activity was acute in this area. The predominantly low-income population that could least afford travel to stores became almost completely dependent on outside areas, even for daily shopping. A strong effort has been made to induce businesses to invest in this area, and a small shopping center has opened on Plymouth, but the commercial needs of the area are far from being fully met.

St. Anthony's business district, lying along East Hennepin and Central Avenues, has had a major facelift in recent years. A small shopping center at Central and University continues to provide personal services, convenience goods, and grocery products. Many of the old business blocks had degenerated by 1970 to low-rent commercial uses; most of these have been removed or rehabilitated. A new bank was constructed and several restaurants, both old and new, serve the area.

Franklin Avenue commercial strip in the Seward district serves as an occasional playground for area children.

One of the local liquor stores, Surdyk's, has expanded so greatly and draws so much business that its parking lot is a local traffic hazard on Saturdays. One focal point of the area, though not specifically oriented toward the Northeast market, is the renovated Garden Court at Central and 4th Avenue. Another will surely be the new Riverplace development, with its condominiums and retail establishments, scheduled to open in 1983. New streets and curbs contribute to the area's refurbished character, as do the continuing improvements along nearby Main Street S.E.

The business district near Milwaukee Avenue has not fared as well. The old commercial center at 27th and Franklin Avenue got a boost when the Northwestern Bank relocated from Cedar-Riverside around 1972 and constructed a new building. The existing small retail shops and medium-sized supermarket continue to serve that section of Seward. Their clients are the residents of the nearby highrise for the elderly. There has been little new construction near Milwaukee Avenue. The only new businesses, other than fast-food outlets, are a cooperative grocery and cooperative cafe, a bar, and a new Mexican restaurant. Although the atmosphere here is not prosperous, it does seem to be stable, even in the face of extreme competition from the new Minnehaha Mall less than a mile away.

CONCLUSION

The rebuilt districts of both cities have clearly changed dramatically in recent years. Almost any evaluation would have to conclude that they are better places than they were. Twenty years ago most of the rebuilt districts were slums or near-slums. Now the housing in these districts is in good-to-excellent condition. Many poorer people still live here, but in much improved circumstances. Compared with most of the aging inner ring, the rebuilt districts are relatively problem-free areas.

It is hard to predict what the future of these districts will be. Some, like St. Anthony and Milwaukee Avenue, needed public investment to acquire properties and clear land. These places should now be able to generate enough private investment to guarantee their continued good health. Other districts, like the river flats in Saint Paul and Near North Minneapolis, may still need some measure of public involvement in the future. Whether it is public or private investment that maintains these districts, they shoud never again reach their former state of blight and deterioration. These districts were once considered unfit or undesirable parts of the cities. They have handily outgrown this stereotype, and not yet acquired another.

Panama Flats. Middle-income condominiums adjacent to downtown Saint Paul house the area's newest residents.

CHAPTER
V

The Turnaround Zone

During the last fifteen years American cities have presented a strong paradox to the casual observer. On the one hand, population decline and physical deterioration have continued unabated, particularly in northeastern and midwestern cities. On the other hand, portions of the same cities have demonstrated a remarkable resilience. Whole neighborhoods have been rescued from the bulldozers and restored to their former Victorian splendor, while commerical establishments have found new and profitable homes in such unlikely locations as former wharf buildings. The following examples provide two powerful and contradictory images of urban America today: the devastated buildings of Charlotte Street in the South Bronx which every serious national politician visits and promises to clean up, and the renovated, always crowded, shops of Quincy Market in Boston which millions of customers visit every year.

Why do some areas decline and decay, while others manage to reverse a long-term downward trend? What sorts of changes are involved when an area "turns itself around" and what is the impact of such changes on the area? These questions will be explored in this chapter on the turnaround zone of Minneapolis and Saint Paul.

In order for an area to be classified as a turnaround district, dramatic changes in the status of its residents and its housing must have occurred both historically and in the recent past. Most of the turnaround districts in Minneapolis and Saint Paul changed from high-status, high-income areas in the late nineteenth century to run-down areas with a poor population in the twentieth century. Recently, the zone gained substantial numbers of professional households, and housing values rose dramatically. Rental units were increasingly converted or returned to owner occupancy; older homes were painstakingly rehabilitated; and new construction was clearly aimed at an upper- and middle-income market.

Activities such as these had become so common in the last decade that many people came to believe in something called the "return to the city" movement. National magazines like *Time* and *Newsweek* have featured cover stories trumpeting the successes of rehabilitated "neighborhoods" and the commercial renaissance of the central city. The "turnaround" districts of some cities have become so well known that many are willing to believe that the urban crisis of the late 1960s has ended. In fact, the urban crisis goes on, but some parts of our cities are being salvaged anyway. There is no return to the city. During the 1970s suburbs continued to grow and central cities continued to lose population. The fact that certain parts of still-declining cities have been spontaneously renewed does not mean that the economic future of American cities is secure. It does show that not every part of every city is irrevocably doomed to decline.

Fifteen years ago common wisdom held that cities were dying. Their neighborhoods were losing population, especially the tax-paying middle class so dear to city administrators. Inner-city schools were being emptied. Only the most rose-colored view of the world could detect any benefit to cities in the explosion of suburban shopping mall and office construction. Cities, for the first time in our history, were being left to the poor and the underprivileged. But times change, and so have concerns about the city. Even limited evidence of middle-class resettlement now stirs the resentment of the poor and of minorities, who have been stewards of the houses and communities that others deserted. A true cynic might perceive the "middle class" to be the source of all urban woes. They fled in the fifties and sixties, leaving the city's problems behind them, and their reappearance in the seventies and eighties may spawn another set of difficulties.

LOCATION AND PHYSICAL CHARACTER

The most telling indicator of present-day turnaround districts is the location of the high-income, fashionable areas during the last part of the nineteenth century. Not all historic residential areas have survived, but those that have are potential turnaround districts. In Minneapolis, most such districts are located just south and southwest of downtown, indicating the original high-status settlements in that city. Saint Paul's pattern is similar, with most turnaround districts located on the bluff west of downtown. But there are also turnaround districts with less affluent histories, among them the Holmes and Willard-Homewood areas in Minneapolis and the West Seventh area of Saint Paul. (See map 5.)

Traffic patterns within the city have also played a major role in causing some areas to decay and others to regenerate. In areas greatly influenced by freeway construction, many older homes were razed in clearance programs. The population that could afford to move away from the noise and dirt of the major traffic corridors did so. In contrast, the less accessible portions of the older areas, in both the protected

genteel and the turnaround districts, attracted households seeking secluded homes, so that an area's lack of accessibility became a major resource. Although secluded, the turnaround districts were stigmatized by their proximity to downtown; today, however, the convenience of inner-city locations is drawing some members of the middle class back to these very areas. This is particularly true in Saint Paul where large numbers of government employees have been attracted to the housing near the Capitol and downtown.

Perhaps the most important locational feature of the turnaround districts is their nearness to the protected genteel districts. People in the protected genteel districts demonstrated to the metropolitan population the merits of living in older areas with high-quality housing. Because these districts could not satisfy the growing demand for older houses during the 1970s, people moved into nearby areas (or turnaround districts) and have been creating a new form of residential district.

The housing of the turnaround zones presents some interesting contrasts. One tends to think of decrepit Victorian mansions being brought back to life as the norm here. This is indeed happening, but it is only part of the story. For example, in Minneapolis rehabilitation has rescued large Victorian houses in Whittier and the Wedge, but the fever has also touched those buying bungalows in Willard-Homewood dating from the 1920s and thirties, and buyers of large apartment buildings in Stevens Square and Loring Park. Owners remove old carpeting, refinish floors, strip painted woodwork, and make every effort to salvage or replace distinctive architectural details. It is no accident that craftspeople who specialize in stained glass repair and replacement tend to choose the turnaround districts for their places of business.

Unlike housing in the other zones we have described, the housing in the turnaround zone is not particularly uniform. There is great diversity in its age, type, and quality. In the Wedge, for example, dwellings from the late nineteenth century stand next to brick apartment buildings from the 1920s. In Willard-Homewood, stucco bungalows constructed in the 1920s can be found near suburban-style houses built in the 1960s. In Loring Park, former mansions abut both older apartment buildings and recently constructed highrises. The mix of style and quality of housing in this zone accurately reflects the diversity of people living here.

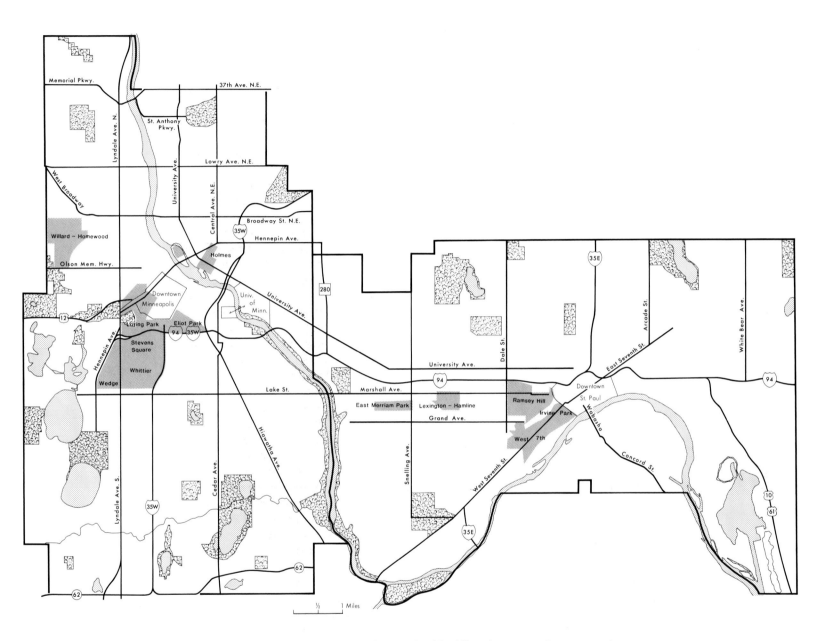

Map 5: The Turnaround Zone. The turnaround is characterized by Victorian restorations, expensive townhouse and condominium construction, and substantial housing rehabilitation.

Another interesting aspect of housing in the turnaround zone is the large amount of relatively new construction. This ranges from suburban-style single-family homes and townhouses to apartment buildings and highrise condominiums. Newer housing in these districts tends to be far more luxurious and more expensive than what it is replacing. In most of the districts the newer housing is spread throughout the area, not concentrated, so the predominant images of these districts do not reflect the newer housing. In some places, though, new construction is both dominant and inescapable. In Loring Park, for example, with the rising towers of condominiums and the "historic" facade of Greenway Gables, one's impressions are almost solely of cleanliness and newness.

THE TURNAROUND PROCESS

No district in Minneapolis and Saint Paul has yet completed the turnaround process, although smaller sections of some districts clearly have. These are the areas that, for a variety of reasons, are most responsive to sudden changes in the urban environment. They all exhibit a tendency to respond quickly to social or cultural shifts. These responses are then imprinted on the landscape through alterations of the housing or of business and commercial facilities. Yet many of the indicators of change are difficult to interpret, and the process, once begun, may be greatly altered by changes in the national economy or other outside forces.

One indicator of change that is relatively easy to measure is population movement. Dramatic shifts in the population of turnaround districts have occurred in recent years. Households that leave an area tend to be replaced by those with both higher incomes and higher social status. The population change has been mislabeled the "return to the city" movement (see p. 64). This term is incorrect because most of the households that move into such areas do not come from suburban locations, but are either new households or are experienced city dwellers. The term has caused some skeptics to discredit the change because population estimates and school censuses show that there has not been a real increase in the size of inner-city populations. Some have used the English term "gentrification" for this process because the so-called gentry are moving into deteriorated areas and taking them over for their own use. This term and its alter-native, "regentrification," can be applied to those areas into which young professionals have moved that were home to middle- and upper-income households before they cascaded to the lower-income groups, but they do not describe those places that are being revitalized by blue-collar households.

Although much attention has been devoted to what is happening in the turnaround districts today, few recognize that most of these areas have surmounted serious challenges at least once before. They are all, in a sense, survivors of earlier urban crises. For example, the Wedge and Whittier districts just south of downtown Minneapolis were middle- and upper middle-class residential havens during the 1890s. Thirty years later some of the large Victorian homes and many of the remaining empty lots were sold off to accommodate the first apartment boom. Three-story brown brick buildings soon dotted the landscape. During the late 1960s and early 1970s the same areas were subjected once again to a flurry of new construction. More of the older Victorian homes gave way before a deluge of two-and-a-half-story apartment construction. These ubiquitous buildings, flanked by blacktopped parking lots, were inhabited by young single renters.

Each turnaround district survived earlier challenges to the existing order, though, to be sure, each change diminished the district's social standing. This has been the unifying experience of the turnaround zone—to undergo changes without slipping into an irreversible downward spiral. Unlike the rebuilt zone and the aging inner ring, the turnaround zone has gone through more moderate physical changes. Another difference is that the turnaround zone began the process of change from a perceptibly higher socioeconomic position than did the other two zones.

Much of the change currently taking place in the turnaround zone is being sponsored in some way by the respective city governments. We can think back to the rebuilt districts of both cities and remember that city-sponsored renewal and rebuilding was one of the hallmarks of those districts. The tactics that each city currently deploys in its anti-blight efforts are far more subtle than they used to be. For one thing, neither city summarily designates areas for assistance or improvement as they used to do. That has an alienating effect upon residents. Now each city waits until area residents decide for themselves that they want some kind of assistance. Then the city can step in with a variety of helpful measures. The city and its agencies are not the main characters in this drama, but without their intercession very little would be happening.

Not only has the level of city involvement in any given district shifted in recent years, so have the approaches that are used. When the rebuilt areas were being transformed, implementation usually included total clearance and land write-downs to developers, or large-scale subsidized rehabilitation. Current methods encompass a wider range: low-interest rehab loans, urban homestead programs, historic-district designation, technical support for residents' planning efforts, and tax-increment financing. The old methods of clearance and new construction have not entirely disappeared—Loring Park's redevelopment was in part handled this way—but they are currently the least-used methods at the city's disposal.

During the 1970s billions of dollars, both public and private, were poured into new construction and rehabilitation in central cities. Not since the 1920s have so many substantial investments occurred wholly within corporate city limits. Even more interesting, perhaps, is the divisive reaction these investments have inspired. Certain groups applaud any evidence of reinvestment in the city; others automatically condemn it. Some eloquently extol the benefits of middle-class reverse migration. Others label these activities "insensitive" and "oppressive," claiming that speculators and investors are knowingly forcing poor people from their homes. The tension between these two positions is obvious, and to some degree each position is valid. As with many other topics of public concern, there is little room for compromise on these issues.

The ultimate outcome of the turnaround process is still in doubt. It is clear that the central-city districts of Minneapolis and Saint Paul are not yet the exclusive preserve of the middle and upper classes. The influence of these groups can be observed in areas that lacked any traces of them just a decade ago, but this is not enough to redirect an entire city's development pattern. If the commitment of the "new urban gentry" is genuine, inner-city areas may not decay as city watchers have predicted for the past twenty years. If the turnaround process merely describes a fad or trend, some areas of the city will be temporarily improved, and that will be the extent of its impact.

POPULATION

Viewed in terms of their residents, the turnaround districts have few common traits. The Northside portion of this zone in Minneapolis, for instance, is quite distinct from the Southside portion. Income levels vary significantly, as do population density, the proportion of households with children, and the proportion of resident homeowners. These distinctions are important to acknowledge because they underscore the variety of changes currently taking place within Minneapolis and Saint Paul. But they should not overshadow the fundamentally similar experiences of these districts during the last two decades.

The residents of the turnaround zone tend to be younger and more mobile than average. (See table 4, p. 146.) Except for the immediate University area, these districts have been more profoundly affected by the movement of the baby boom generation than any other part of either city. Much of the housing in these areas has been altered, or newly constructed, to cater to the housing needs of this age group. All the turnaround districts have lost population during the 1970s. Perhaps more important, all have lost over one-quarter of the families who lived there in 1970. There is nothing to indicate that new families are replacing them.

The number of households fluctuates widely among different parts of the turnaround zone. In 1978, some census tracts in Loring Park had as few as 300 households, while some in Whittier and the Wedge had over 2,000. These figures accurately reflect the relative amount of land devoted to residential use and the varying levels of population density. Almost all of the districts have recently experienced a net gain of households while continuing to decline in population. Throughout this zone the number of persons in each household is well below the city average, indicating larger concentrations of single people. Over half of the households in most of these districts consist of only one person. The major exception to this trend is in the Willard-Homewood area. This portion of the turnaround zone has continued to house substantial numbers of families. The far southern part of Willard-Homewood has Minneapolis' highest ratio of persons in each household, and it also has the highest percentage of households with children (53 percent).

The turnaround zone does not house as many elderly persons as we might expect. Only in Loring Park and Stevens

Pracna On Main was the first significant attempt at restoration in Old St. Anthony. Its success has spawned major commercial developments nearby.

Square are retired householders represented in higher than average numbers; these are the areas where city policies and local landlords have struggled to ensure that elderly residents will not be displaced.

Two areas of the turnaround zone have a racially mixed group of residents: the eastern portion of Whittier, and Willard-Homewood, one of the most well-integrated areas of Minneapolis.

A higher than average percentage of turnaround zone residents are unemployed, perhaps reflecting their youth and dissatisfaction with the job market. Hence it is not surprising that the level of public assistance is relatively high. A composite picture emerges of the turnaround zone's residents: they are relatively young, not yet settled into a chosen occupation, and not living in "traditional" family settings.

Distinctions between the north and south portions of the Minneapolis turnaround zone are depicted in the housing patterns. Willard-Homewood is an area of single-family homes, most of which are owner-occupied. In all other parts of the zone, renters overwhelmingly predominate. In all the turnaround districts south of downtown Minneapolis, over 85 percent of the housing is found in multiple-unit buildings. Recently there has been some evidence of more homeowners and a loss of multiple units in some of the turnaround districts. In 1978 the Wedge experienced Minneapolis' second-highest gain in homeowners and Loring Park lost more rental units (185) than anywhere else. The turnaround zone is becoming a place where owners are replacing renters, and where the rental stock of housing is increasingly becoming owner-occupied. Condominium conversions have been particularly strong in these districts, encompassing even the ubiquitous two-and-a-half story walk-up apartment buildings.

As in any area undergoing change, the level of petty crime in the turnaround zone tends to be high. For people moving into the zone the lessened degree of personal security is a trade-off that is willingly made for affordable housing with an aura of style.

COMMERCIAL PATTERN

The commercial facilities within the turnaround zone resemble those in other older parts of both cities. Corner stores can still be found, though shopping strips are the norm. Small shopping centers are of more recent vintage. Because all these districts are quite close to downtown, this zone provides better access to downtown commercial facilities than do most other zones.

Like the aging inner ring and settled mid-city zone, the turnaround zone has also suffered from commercial blight and deterioration in the last thirty years. Small merchants on most major streets have seen the purchasing power of surrounding areas erode with each successive population shift. As older stores have gone out of business, land-use patterns have shifted, and more stores now serve customers who drive to them. Fast-food outlets and other "drive-in" facilities have become common on most former streetcar strips. Parking—the bane of central city stores for the last thirty years—has been provided at the expense of residents along and just behind commercial streets. These shopping areas have so fully acquiesced to drive-in enterprises that a recent effort by Wedge residents to prohibit yet another fast-food restaurant was extensively covered by the press. Opposition of this kind is a relatively new undertaking in these districts.

Garden Court. This former fraternal lodge has been transformed into offices and shops.

This block in the Wedge area of South Minneapolis demonstrates the increase in privately funded restoration efforts.

The problems of the turnaround zone's commercial facilities are not always of their own making. For example, West Broadway's attraction to shoppers diminished greatly in the late 1960s, after riots occurred in another part of the Near Northside. West Broadway was untouched by the riots, but was profoundly affected by shoppers' memories of them. People who used to shop there began to be afraid, and some of the natural trade area simply disappeared when white residents fled the Near Northside.

All the commercial streets in the turnaround zone have suffered, too, from the development of suburban shopping centers. Competition from outlying centers has contributed directly to the decline of business activity on these streets. Business associations have worked to combat these problems, but their efforts have often been too feeble and belated. A cynic might characterize the value of the former streetcar strips to the city by alluding to the example of Nicollet and Lake. Anyone who knows anything about strip shopping realizes that merchants depend on passing traffic—especially cars—to generate business. The decision to close off Nicollet Avenue, and isolate the merchants there from passing traffic, eloquently illustrates the lack of "clout" that remains in the old streetcar commercial areas.

The commercial outlook for the turnaround zone is not entirely dismal, though. For all the symptoms of decline and disuse, there are still some bright spots. Efforts to improve the image of Hennepin Avenue near Lake Street are detailed in the chapter on the settled mid-city zone. For several years, there have been discussions about building a small shopping center on West Broadway near the Lyndale intersection. It is now under construction. Perhaps the most interesting commercial area anywhere in the turnaround zone is the one at 26th and Nicollet. Here the Black Forest Restaurant has been successful for years amid what looks to a casual observer like genuine commercial blight. Its success has been clearly demonstrated through expansion and interior renovations, as well as by lines at the door. In the last few years even more restaurants, bars, and entertainment enterprises have come to this area.

The impetus for such activity has been the somewhat recent arrival of the College of Art and Design in this area. When the Minneapolis Institute of Arts expanded its facilities and provided space for the College, the commercial facilities of the area began to display an "artistic" bent.

Once it became clear that there was money to be made in this area, new businesses appeared in order to tap the market.

Another portion of the turnaround zone that can anticipate some kind of commercial renaissance is Loring Park. Whatever appears here is likely to reflect the high-income character of the surrounding development. Some expensive restaurants have already opened. It would not be at all surprising if Loring Park also sprouted more art galleries and private clubs to complement the ones already operating at the new Hyatt Hotel.

DISTRICTS OF THE TURNAROUND ZONE

Superficially the districts in the turnaround zone have little in common. The housing differs from district to district, as do the changes currently taking place. An in-depth look at some of these places will provide a better understanding of the variations on the turnaround process.

Whittier

Parts of Whittier—for example, the Washburn-Fair Oaks area, where the large Washburn and Morrison mansions once stood—were settled as early as the 1850s. Because some of the wealthiest men in Minneapolis chose to live here, portions of Whittier have always had a rather grand and elegant aura. The mansions remaining near the Institute of Arts and along Pillsbury Avenue continue to demonstrate this. But the larger picture is more complex. While rich men built their stately homes north of 26th Street, the rest of Whittier filled up with large and small single-family homes, duplexes, and apartment buildings. Most of this building occurred between 1890 and 1920, when Whittier was established as a preferred residential location for the middle class. The area was well served by streetcar service to downtown. It proved attractive to white-collar workers who found the old elite image of Whittier to their liking. Surprisingly, many of the wealthy families remained here until well into the second decade of the twentieth century, and some even stayed until the early 1930s.

Although Whittier qualifies as a turnaround district on the basis of current rehabilitation activities, the truth is that this area has been changing at greater and lesser rates ever since the Depression. In the 1930s, many of the wealthy families still maintaining residences in Whittier also had summer homes at Lake Minnetonka. As fortunes were lost, choices had to be made. One longtime resident remembers the near wholesale desertion of the large mansions during this period. Families moved to their smaller-scale and less-costly country homes, where they could get by with fewer servants and a more casual style of entertaining. These hardships were clearly insignificant compared with what others suffered. Middle-class residents of Whittier began to double up in units that had formerly housed only one family. The poorer people of the area were unemployed and often hungry.

The changing status of Whittier residents was reflected in their use of space. As large houses were subdivided, the overall density of the area increased. Whittier had already become more crowded during the 1920s when many multi-family buildings were constructed. By the 1930s it was rapidly becoming one of the most densely settled areas of Minneapolis. This fact was further underscored by the city zoning ordinance of 1924. It established all of Whittier but the mansion areas at the maximum housing density permitted. The changing composition of the housing stock contributed to further population shifts. From the 1920s on, a younger and more transient group of residents seemed to be the new norm. Although these general patterns continued, Whittier never seemed to decline quite as much as some other older parts of the city. This was in part due to the original high quality of most buildings in the area. It was also due to the fact that upwardly mobile young workers continued to be attracted to the area. By 1950 Whittier was one of the few inner-city areas of Minneapolis that was not losing population. Many new housing units appeared during the fifties, primarily through conversions of older single-family structures. But this was just a ripple compared with what came later.

In the decade 1960-70 Whittier's landscape changed dramatically. Older homes were replaced by multifamily structures at an unprecedented rate. Approximately 1,500 new units were created—mostly in the form of two-and-a-half-story walkup buildings. Because additional amounts of older housing were removed during this period to make way for the construction of Interstate 35W, the visual impact of the newer buildings was quite striking. While other central-city neighborhoods were emptying out in the 1960s, Whittier

was holding its own, though possibly at the expense of its architectural heritage. The crowded character of Whittier was underscored once again when the newest zoning ordinance allowed the highest density possible for a residential area. The new apartment buildings going up all over easily met the new standard and expectations. This kind of intensive land use was permitted only in a few residential sections of the city, and Whittier was among this select group.

In the mid-1960s the City Planning Department proclaimed that Whittier was an "unusually diverse" area, with both good and bad characteristics. According to the department, the condition of most of the housing was good to excellent, though the surrounding environments were generally fair to poor. The prevalence of small residential parcels, mixed land uses, and the high level of hazardous traffic accounted for the negative environmental assessment. The population of Whittier was judged to have a high incidence of "social problems": young families had limited education and job skills; many elderly persons lived alone; and there were generally high rates of dependence and unemployment. The southern and eastern portions of Whittier were singled out as particularly in need of attention.

These harsh judgments were tempered somewhat by the department's assessment that, despite its problems, Whittier had some strong attractions and was thought capable of "spontaneous redevelopment." The department recognized the attractive qualities of the institutional complex next to Fair Oaks Park (the Institute of Arts, Hennepin County Historical Society, Northwestern Theological Seminary) but added a note of caution: the cultural complex was not being used to its full potential. It lacked a sharp identity, and city-wide access to this area was limited. Other institutions were reportedly seeking locations in Whittier, and a nucleus already existed to form a cultural center in the area. However, none of this would occur without hard work and significant changes in the environment.

By the late 1960s Whittier had not yet entered the turnaround category, though many indicators pointed in that direction. Plans were under way to expand the Minneapolis Institute of Arts (MIA) and to include facilities for the Children's Theater and the College of Art and Design. Within a few years these were all a reality. So was the commercial development district at Nicollet and Lake. Plans existed to designate the Washburn-Fair Oaks area a historic district, and there was growing appreciation for the architectural treasures of Whittier. More and more people were moving into large old Victorian homes that had been subdivided many times. They were restoring them to single-family use and salvaging whatever historic dimensions of the buildings they could. This was often a painfully slow and laborious process, especially since commercial lenders did not favor such projects. But steadily throughout the early 1970s "sweat equity" paid off. Many forlorn houses were saved, and some were even painstakingly restored to their original late nineteenth-century condition (although with modern conveniences in kitchens and baths). The recession of the early seventies effectively halted the construction of two-and-a-half-story walkups, so the growing interest in renovation received much attention in the press. All of this combined with a burgeoning preference in some quarters for older houses with natural wood-trimmed interiors and leaded or stained glass windows. It worked to ensure that Whittier's fortunes (defined in terms of population and tax base) were on the upswing.

In 1975 the Dayton-Hudson Foundation stepped into the picture. A concerted "adopt-a-neighborhood" strategy was just beginning to emerge in corporate circles around the United States—partly as a goodwill gesture toward corporate headquarters' locations, and partly as a shrewd investment in a new urban life-style. Dayton-Hudson already had a substantial investment in Whittier through its efforts to promote and fund the expansion of the MIA. In mid-1976, the Dayton-Hudson Foundation hired a local architectural firm, Team 70, to prepare a design plan for Whittier, and donated $250,000 to begin implementing the plan. The *Whittier Urban Design Framework* closely analyzed land-use and traffic patterns, crime, and commercial and open-space deficiencies. It made initial suggestions for improving traffic (both pedestrian and vehicular), for redeveloping the commercial areas, and for increasing recreational space.

Soon after the report appeared, a nonprofit corporation, the Whittier Alliance, was formed by delegates from institutional, business, and resident groups throughout the area. The avowed purpose of the Alliance was to get grants and help implement community goals. The Whittier Alliance received $1 million from Dayton-Hudson for a five-year improvement program, and was soon making low-interest loans and giving grants to residents for exterior rehabilitation

work. In 1979 a portion of the eastern section of Whittier was designated a "Neighborhood Strategy Area" by the city, making federal funds available to the area.

It is now clear that the scales have tipped in favor of Whittier. It is no longer perceived as an area in decline, either by residents or by knowledgeable outsiders. Problems remain, of course. Not all of the housing has yet been brought up to code, particularly in eastern Whittier. There is still some hostility about the closing of Nicollet Avenue. The saunas and adult bookstores along Lake Street still trouble many residents. But the commercial strip along Nicollet has retained its vitality. On some streets the two-and-a-half-story walkups from the 1960s are now selling as condominiums. Rents and housing prices are increasing, causing some concern about displacement of the poor and the elderly. Whittier now has momentum and a clear identity. Its turnaround is not complete, but it is certainly under way.

Willard-Homewood

The turnaround process in Willard-Homewood in north Minneapolis differs markedly from that in Whittier. There are comparable differences in the timing and style of development in the two areas. Willard-Homewood is younger—it was platted around the turn of the century. Most construction took place during the second and third decades of the twentieth century, and most of the housing is single-family dwellings. It was a very stable area until the mid-1960s when property values plunged rapidly along with public estimation of the area. This precipitous decline has been reversed in recent years as some people recognized the obvious: that good houses could be gotten in Willard-Homewood for much less than what they would cost elsewhere in the city. Unlike some of the turnaround districts, this is in no sense a "trendy" area. "Fern" bars, boutiques, and vegetarian restaurants are not in evidence. Willard Homewood looks for all the world like a family-oriented residential area. This is precisely what it has been and is. The "turnaround" here is not associated with either land use or life-style, but with the area's image and land values.

Willard-Homewood had some pretensions of grandeur in its early years. Like other Northside efforts to attract "elite" settlement, this goal was not achieved. When the

Homewood addition was platted in 1909, for example, it was a restricted area. Covenants attached to each piece of property specifically prevented parcels from being sold to Jews. Common prejudices of the period combined with popular notions about the "Jewish takeover" of Oak Lake and eastern Glenwood to produce these restrictions, but they were not very effective. Middle-class WASPs and Scandinavians did not move to Willard-Homewood in sufficient numbers. By the mid- to late 1920s many prosperous Jewish families were drawn to the Homewood area. It became one of the preferred locations of this group. The "foreign" character of Willard-Homewood persisted for many years. As late as 1950 the area had a high proportion of foreign-born persons (the highest in the entire city), and over half of these were Russian migrants.

As this group expanded into Willard-Homewood from the east, it left a cultural imprint on the area. Large synagogues were built. The western section of Plymouth Avenue sprouted kosher bakeries and butcher shops. Major purchases were made on West Broadway or downtown. From the mid-1920s to the mid-1960s Willard-Homewood was a prosperous and contented middle-class area. Abutting Wirth Park, possessing educated residents and well-maintained housing, it seemed to have everything going for it.

What deflected Willard-Homewood momentarily from continued stability was the same thing that tumbled many urban areas in the mid-1960s: racial tension and fears of change. Rioting along Plymouth Avenue in 1967 shook the contented world of Willard-Homewood and sent many residents fleeing to nearby suburbs. Even before the riots broke out, there were some signs of trouble. A 1965 City Planning report labeled most of the area's housing as sound and well maintained but noted the growing east-west disparities in the area. East of Penn Avenue residential overcrowding and deterioration increased markedly. Moreover, family incomes were lower than the city average in this section, and the unemployment rate was higher than average. The report also noted the large number of "for sale" signs in Willard-Homewood. Two possible explanations were given for this. One was the maturing of the local population, with many "empty nesters" living in larger houses than they needed. The other was fear and uncertainty about the future of the area, owing to an inmigration of blacks from the Grant and Glenwood areas to the east. (Ironically, this was precisely the path of mobility that Jewish families had taken forty years before.)

Between 1960 and 1970 Willard-Homewood did experience a substantial population shift. The Jewish community virtually abandoned the area. For the most part, it was replaced by upwardly mobile blacks. This transition was rapid and rather concentrated. The area south of Golden Valley Road, which had few or no black residents in 1960, ranged from 38 to 52 percent black in 1970. Just north of Golden Valley Road, the comparable figure was under 7 percent. The "white flight" from Willard-Homewood in this period exactly replicates migration patterns found in many other cities, where established Jewish communities suburbanized and were replaced by minorities (e.g., Lawndale in Chicago, Boyle Heights in Los Angeles). Whites left Willard-Homewood partly in response to violence that had occurred; but they were also drawn to the attractive newer housing in Saint Louis Park and Golden Valley.

Contrary to many other cities' experiences, the housing left behind in Willard-Homewood was in good condition. Most were single-family houses that represented a desirable life-style to those moving in, though there was a certain amount of price depreciation and some housing abandonment. The changes occurring were clearly reflected in the tenure of the new residents. Most of the Willard-Homewood's housing had been owner-occupied in 1960, but by 1970 sections of the area had lost 30 to 50 percent of the homeowners. Simultaneously the proportion of renters increased from 25 percent to 44 percent in parts of the area. At a time when the average value of homes in Minneapolis increased 30 percent, housing values in Willard-Homewood increased only 9 to 18 percent.

Declining housing values and the diminishing number of owner-occupants troubled both the city and area residents. The city's response was to target the area for urban homesteading, hoping to increase the proportion of homeowners and stabilize housing values. Through this program abandoned or run-down houses were acquired by the city and sold for one dollar. Purchasers were required to carry out sufficient rehabilitation to bring their houses up to code within one year. They were also required to live in their homes for at least three years. The program was so successful that Willard-Homewood soon had more urban homesteads than any other part of the city.

Whether the commitment of these new residents outlives their contractual obligation remains to be seen. Some say they are there to stay. But a *Minneapolis Tribune* interview indicated the complex nature of such a decision. This person had nothing but good things to say about the program and about the house he had purchased. However, he did have some clear reservations about the area's public schools. He said without hesitation that his family would move to the suburbs by the time his child was ready to start school.

By 1978 the area that had lost almost half of its owner-occupants between 1960 and 1970 had rebounded to an ownership rate of 74 percent. Willard-Homewood residents were actively promoting the area. The Willard-Homewood Organization (WHO) was formed in 1970 by residents concerned about housing deterioration. WHO focused on physical improvements, working on proposals for loans and grants to conduct rehabilitation. Many of these efforts were successful, particularly since the organization worked closely with the city's Housing and Redevelopment Authority to carry out projects. Willard-Homewood also became one of two city areas to receive federal community development funds for rehabilitation projects.

The turnaround in Willard-Homewood was well under way by the late 1970s. This was apparent not only in the increased levels of home ownership and maintenance, but also in the expressed concerns of residents. Sometime during the late seventies, young white professionals discovered Willard-Homewood and began to buy homes there. As more of this group moved into the area, current residents, many of whom were black and most of whom were renters, feared that they would be displaced. Neighborhood organizations are committed to integration, as are most residents, but such commitments can quickly evaporate. Willard-Homewood is also committed to home ownership, and if most of the new owners are white, that is what the area will progressively become.

There are clear indications that a measure of stability has returned to this area. In 1972 only 33 percent of the residents had lived in their homes five years earlier. By 1977 this figure had increased to 45 percent. People are no longer running away. Boarded-up houses can still be found in Willard-Homewood, but everyone who knows the area fully expects this to be a temporary situation. The turnaround here should be complete fairly soon. Willard-Homewood should once again be a stable middle-class residential area with few adverse images for either residents or outsiders.

Loring Park

The turnaround process in most districts takes the form of rehabilitation and is fueled primarily by private investment. However, the process under way in Loring Park superficially bears more resemblance to traditional urban renewal. What is happening in Loring Park is obviously so massive that more than private investment is needed to carry it through. But this is not urban renewal in its traditional guise, even though "blighted" buildings have been removed to provide middle- and upper-income housing. Rather, Loring Park demonstrates the increasingly sophisticated maneuvers cities use to shore up declining tax bases without federal assistance. One of the stated, most sacred goals of Minneapolis is to create more housing opportunities in the city for those with above-average incomes. Simultaneously, officials recognize that such people spend their leisure time and dollars pursuing "cultural" activities. So it makes sense to locate new housing for this group close to downtown, where most "culture" is to be found.

The tool available to accomplish this goal is called "tax increment financing." This procedure works as follows: the city designates an area as a tax increment district; it sells bonds as an expression of good faith in the reconstruction project; and it provides various means of assistance to private developers committed to the project. What the city expects to gain for its efforts is, of course, a greatly increased tax base and residents who neither want nor need expensive social services.

Loring Park was an obvious choice to become a tax increment district. It was within easy walking distance of downtown Minneapolis, close to the Guthrie Theater and Walker Art Center, and near the high-income district of Lowry Hill. More important, it was located near the slated improvements that would result from the construction of Orchestra Hall. It had a quantity of deteriorated housing that greatly needed improvement, but it also had retained some of its image as an elite residential area. Perhaps the most important reason for Loring Park's designation was the fact that it presented better opportunities for private investment than any other area near downtown, a fact

The south end of Loring Park, depicting the several generations of construction present in this and other turnaround areas.

which had been officially and unofficially recognized for ten to fifteen years before redevelopment started.

The history of Loring Park parallels that of Whittier. All of Loring Park fell within the original town limits of Minneapolis, but none of it was really developed until the 1880s. Some wealthy families built mansions in the Hawthorne area north of Loring Park in the 1870s, but Bassett's Creek and the uneven topography stopped settlement to the south of Hawthorne. Not until Central (Loring) Park was developed in 1883 did residential construction really begin in this area. In a very short time the area between the Park and Nicollet Avenue, north of 15th Street, was almost completely built up. Interestingly, the housing density in most of Loring Park was much higher than in contemporary parts of Whittier or Lowry Hill. Row houses, rather than single-family dwell-

ings, were the standard buildings here. Many small apartment buildings began to appear around the turn of the century as well. The only exception to this high-density pattern was on the ridge south of the park, where many extravagant mansions were constructed. Most of the people initially attracted to Loring Park were professionals (doctors, lawyers, businessmen), though some of the city's elite came too.

The trend toward high-density development in Loring Park was sustained and extended. By 1900 several large apartment buildings went up east of the Park. Some major nonresidential facilities appeared (Eitel Hospital), and some commercial enterprises began spreading into the northern edge of Loring Park from downtown. Very little new residential development occurred in ensuing years since the land in Loring Park was already built up. During the 1920s extensive redevelopment took place along streets like LaSalle and Oak Grove, as very large and sometimes ornate multifamily structures replaced the older row houses. This new housing was primarily intended for young couples and single persons since most of the units were small.

Loring Park was becoming a transient area as more and more families moved away. Commercial and institutional facilities continued to increase their hold on the northern fringe of the Park during the 1920s. In the next ten to twenty years Loring Park added many dwelling units, responding to pressures created by the Depression and World War II. The once-exclusive mansions were increasingly converted to multifamily use. Throughout these changing times Loring Park's population base was not substantially altered. While other areas were occupied by ethnic or racial groups unlike the original settlers, Loring Park continued to house an Americanized population. The presence of so many inexpensive rental units close to downtown and the lakes kept the area desirable for upwardly mobile young people.

During the 1950s Loring Park began to decline perceptibly. One-fourth of the total population left between 1950 and 1960, though the number of dwelling units increased. Some new luxury apartment buildings were built during the early sixties, but increased blight and social problems were more commonly encountered. The Loring Park area absorbed some people displaced by the Gateway renewal project at the opposite end of downtown. The commercial strip along lower Nicollet began to acquire a decrepit look as needy, often transient persons moved into the area. When Interstate 94 was laid out through this area in the mid-1960s, the still healthy section south of Loring Park was split in half. City planners expected the resulting "islands" to be used in the future for highrise apartment buildings. This expectation came true with the construction of the Summit Towers, though until very recently land use of this type was quite limited.

A city planning report of the mid-1960s identified the area's most serious potential problem: the large number of old, severly deteriorated rooming houses and apartments. These structures were labeled a "blighting influence," since they were potentially detrimental to increased investment and maintenance in Loring Park. The city seemed to have no clear agenda, except to address the social problems of the area, and possibly to get rid of the worst buildings. In

the early sixties a Nicollet-Loring businessman's association had planned a complete facelift for Nicollet Avenue, but could get no assistance without having the street declared a renewal area. Police complained about the presence of drunks along Nicollet, though others thought the area was improving. In 1963 Northwestern College announced its decision to develop a liberal arts campus in Loring Park. Several years later Metropolitan Junior College also decided to build its campus in the area. A thriving neighborhood association was already active in the area, working on flower and shrub planting and tree trimming.

By the early 1970s major changes were under way in Loring Park. More and more young people were drawn into the area by the expanding institutions, and ever-increasing numbers of speculators were making investments. The future direction of the area was becoming clear enough to worry current residents. A community survey in 1973 found that most residents fell into one or more of the following categories: elderly, retired, welfare recipients, disabled, and unemployed. Most residents earned $2,000 a year or less, and 75 percent of all residents lived alone. The survey also found that most current residents wanted to remain in the Loring Park area. By the following year, as plans for future development moved closer to reality, bad feelings were rampant in the area. A local group organized to oppose the construction of 2,700 middle- and upper-income apartments. The group asked for an environmental impact study, claiming that approximately 1,400 residents would be displaced by the project without any relocation benefits or replacement housing. The study was deemed unnecessary, but the City Council did support the group's appeal for replacement housing.

The projected scale of redevelopment in Loring Park emerged in the early plans. A 1973 design plan envisioned a ten-year development in the area east of Loring Park. Parking lots, aging commercial buildings, and four-story apartment buildings would be replaced by new highrise and townhouse construction. Ultimately, 7,000-10,000 new units were to be built. The developer claimed that most of the people being displaced would be eligible for public housing. The first phase of the project had several components: the extension of Nicollet Mall to Grant Street; major improvements for Loring Park (e.g., the Berger Fountain); the expansion of Metro Junior College; and the construction of

Greenway Gables (front) and Loring Green (under construction). These expensive condominiums demonstrate one form the turnaround process takes. This site had been occupied by apartment buildings dating from the 1920s.

2,600 new dwelling units. Residents continued objecting to development plans for the area, correctly fearing that there was no place for them in most of the plans, but the process had too much momentum by then to be ended easily. The decision makers of Minneapolis and the financial community were set on improvements for the Loring area. They would ensure that the projects would go forward.

Today, even a brief drive through the Loring Park area leaves no doubt that major changes have occurred. The landscape is filled with the equipment of the construction industry. Office buildings are now under construction, and a

new Hyatt Regency hotel has been built. Metropolitan Junior College has grown to over twice its former size. Across the street is the new Minneapolis Technical Institute. New highrises dot the eastern edge of the Park, dispersed among the new townhouses. These residences—1200 on the Mall, Loring Green, Loring Way, and Greenway Gables—are all condominiums, and they were eagerly snapped up by buyers when they first went on the market. Rental units in the older apartment buildings have been converted to condominiums at a rapid pace. There have also been some provisions for low- and moderate-income people in the redevel-

Ramsey Hill near downtown Saint Paul at the start of its turnaround phase.

opment process. A new subsidized building for the elderly is now occupied, and the Volunteers of America have a residential facility in the area.

People have now lived in the redeveloped part of Loring Park for several years. Most seemed well pleased with their choice. Loring Park is no longer considered a dangerous or undesirable area. People no longer worry about drunks in the Park or prostitutes on the streets. The image of Loring Park is becoming that of an attractive urban environment. Barring unforeseen disasters, that is what this area will be for a long time to come.

Ramsey Hill

Ramsey Hill lies to the north of the Saint Paul protected genteel district of Crocus Hill. For purposes of this account, Ramsey Hill is considered to consist of Census Tract 358. Although the tract includes some areas that are not expe-

riencing turnaround these areas do not comprise a significant portion of the district.

This area became the focus of the "neighborhood conservation" movement in the late 1960s. In 1967 the residents of Crocus Hill organized the Summit Hill Association, and a reinvestment cycle was begun that would soon spill over into Ramsey Hill. A group of white "urban pioneers," composed of nontraditional households and young professionals, moved into large houses on the fringe of the black community in Saint Paul. At first they bought buildings on or as close to Summit Avenue as possible. These buildings were magnificent relics from the grand days of the community, and the newcomers took comfort in their proximity to beautiful Crocus Hill. The young professionals, because of their greater buying power, occupied the more secure areas, whereas nontraditional households—voluntary poor— moved into high-risk areas and sought to form alliances with the resident population. These newcomers were able

78

to forge new organizations, and in 1969 the Summit-University Model Cities Program was begun. Although liberal organizations like the Saint Paul Tenants' Union voiced their strong disapproval of the newly arrived members of the middle-class buying houses in the area, most of the established property owners were happy to see land values rise. Large numbers of speculators were active by the early 1970s. Between 1971 and 1976 the number of homeowners in the area increased dramatically, and by 1976 Ramsey Hill was no longer considered the place for low-income families to find cheap rental units. Some units were combined to make more valuable larger rental units, and finally, as the supply of detached housing began to run out, the older apartment buildings were converted into condominiums.

Between 1976 and 1978 the district lost thirteen housing units, or 3 percent of the loss experienced by Saint Paul. Vacancy rates are quite high in this district (4.56 percent in 1978) compared with the city's average of 2.93 percent. It is interesting to note that the vacancy rate in the protected genteel area to the southwest was 1.77 percent and the rate in the aging inner ring district to the north was 14.95 percent.

Slightly over 3,000 people lived in this district in 1,568 households in 1978. Average household size was nearly the lowest in Saint Paul (1.9). Obviously the number of smaller rental units in the district attract young singles. The presence of several homes for the elderly in the district also lowers the average household size.

The best indication of the district's attractiveness is that it experienced a 2.28 percent increase in households between 1976 and 1978. This increase means that the vacancy rate has declined rapidly in recent years. Finally, we note that in Saint Paul only the newest of the suburban-in-city districts and one area of the aging inner ring have a lower percentage of retired persons as heads of household than does Ramsey Hill. In this district only 15.69 percent of the head of households are retired, whereas the city figure is 26.14 percent and the middle-class zones generally have rates in the low 30s.

Not only is the population of the district undergoing a marked change in family status, it is also experiencing a change in social and economic status. Between 1976 and 1978 only one district gained more professional and mana-

gerial households than Ramsey Hill. Although the percentage of high-status households in the district (26.9 percent) is well above the city's rate of 16.9 percent, it is comparable to most of the other middle-class districts. All these changes in demographic and social structure within the district have combined to produce an average yearly income per household of some $15,000 (in 1978 dollars). However, because the household size is smaller in the district, the money available for consumption is somewhat higher than the average income might indicate. In addition, the aggregate money income for all households in Ramsey Hill has increased 1.8 percent, whereas that in Saint Paul has increased 1.29 percent.

Home ownership rates in this district are low. Only 25.8 percent of the households own their homes, as compared with 58.8 percent for Saint Paul. Few districts in the city have a larger fraction of their population living in rented quarters. At the same time, the turnover rate in this district is one of the highest in the city. At 71 percent it is nearly twice the city-wide rate.

The demographic changes this district is undergoing have caused concern among certain segments of the community. Because this area contained a large number of lower-cost rental units, the reinvestment has reduced the housing options open to low-income households. Housing activists argue that many lower-income families have difficulty finding suitable rental quarters because landlords prefer to rent units to households without children, a practice which reduces their maintenance costs. Consumer advocates have argued that some of the landlords within the district are discriminating against families with children, depriving these people of their civil rights.

This emotional issue is typical of the sorts of problems that are involved in turnaround areas. Most problems seem to be reducible to the question of who controls or is going to control the area. The name we have applied to the district implies that the middle-class home buyers moving into the area will eventually become the dominant force in the local community.

Irvine Park and the West Seventh Community

A political alliance of several different types of residential districts exists in Saint Paul's West Seventh Community

Saint Paul's Irvine Park has been transformed through the combined efforts of the Saint Paul Housing and Redevelopment Authority and enthusiastic new house-owners.

which gives the area a special identity. Among the small districts within the area are several that might be examined as examples of turnaround districts. By taking a somewhat arbitrary slice of the area, Census Tract 360, we can glimpse a few of the changes under way. This tract also contains rebuilt districts because there have been several large and successful city-sponsored redevelopment projects in the zone. Sherman Forbes, a large project containing subsidized housing for families, is located on the corner of West Seventh and Grand Avenue. The city has also established two programs here, known as Identified Treatment Areas, that are intended to encourage home maintenance and rebuilding. In addition, the United Hospitals complex has had a great impact on the area, both through the direct removal of housing and through proposals for new housing. But the most notable renewal project has been the Irvine Park project begun in the early 1970s. It is this project that serves as the core of the turnaround district. In 1973 Irvine Park became the first area in Saint Paul to be placed on the National Register of Historic Places. The Leach-McBoal area, which lies to the southwest of Irvine Park, has also attracted some reinvestment, and now that the Cliff Street area has been designated an Identified Treatment Area, it carries the promise of continued reinvestment in this district.

Although we will use the term "Irvine Park" in our discussion of this area, it must be clearly understood that it is an umbrella term covering several smaller residential districts. The area contains relatively few households—only 600. Previous clearance projects and the large number of commercial areas within this part of Saint Paul have combined to give these districts a small population. The population has increased by about 200 people in the past five years. Almost all the growth has resulted from migration into the area by people interested in the new housing units. Between 1976 and 1978 the area lost eleven housing units, or about 2 percent of the available housing in 1976. (Although there have been complaints about the loss of housing in Ramsey Hill, that district's housing stock decreased only .7 percent during the same two-year period.) The high vacancy rate in Irvine Park (6.69 percent in 1978) reflects some uncertainty about the future of the housing market and the presence of new developments.

In 1978 about 34 percent of the households in this area

included children. This rate is essentially the same as the city-wide average. The number of households with children remained constant between 1978 and 1981, which indicates that population turnover in the area is not the sort feared by people opposed to gentrification and the displacement of low-income families by middle-class couples. Although a few retired households moved out of the area in the past few years, the number of retired houshold in the districts is the same as the city average. This again supports the contention that displacement is not yet a problem in the district. Of course, the best measure of displacement is the number of professional- and managerial-level households that have moved into a district. This part of West Seventh has a lower percentage of high-status households than other parts of the community. The large subsidized housing projects in the area undoubtedly deflate the rates. The average household income in the area is also lower than it is in other parts of the West Seventh Community. Clearly, the turnaround process in the area will be different from that experienced by Ramsey Hill.

Only 41 percent of the households in the area own their own homes, one of the lowest rates of home ownership in Saint Paul. The large number of rental units undoubtedly is the reason for the area's rather high turnover rate. Over 50 percent of the housing units experienced a change in occupancy between 1976 and 1978.

Although the turnaround zone in Saint Paul has two historic areas, Ramsey Hill and Irvine Park, the districts within the zone are quite distinctive. Ramsey Hill appears to be going through the gentrification process, while the lower Seventh area is experiencing a change in occupants without a comparable change in status.

CONCLUSION

What impacts have the turnaround districts had on Minneapolis and Saint Paul? Certain trends are visible in both cities. Decayed older, though once-elegant, homes are being rescued and refurbished. The cities are becoming the preferred residential option for certain people, primarily professional and childless. There is little sign of a "back to the city" movement. But some young people, who might once have been presumed destined for suburbia, are instead making their homes inside the cities. Some commercial strips

are benefiting from the rehabilitation activites in nearby areas—restaurants and bars crop up regularly and appear to be doing a booming business. Does any of this mean that the gloom-and-doom prophesies of city watchers in the 1960s are obsolete?

The answer to this question is not yet clear. Much of what people believed about the future of cities in the late 1960s was somewhat exaggerated to begin with; not every city was doomed to economic misfortune as business and industry moved to the suburbs, nor was every city equally affected by residential migration to the suburbs. The health that many cities demonstrated in the 1970s clearly contradicts many firmly held beliefs and fears of longtime city watchers. And yet, problems do remain for many parts of many cities. If the gloom-and-doom prophesies of the 1960s have not come true, it is only because these ideas were so generalized that they could barely distinguish between healthy and declining parts of the same city. As we have seen so far in this study, there are many fine-grain differences that distinguish sections of every city. These differences must be taken into account in order to think about the future of any particular place.

Changes occurring in the turnaround districts may signal a new future for American cities, but there is little reason to believe that these places alone can salvage any city. The turnaround districts of Minneapolis and Saint Paul are becoming desirable residential areas, and the commercial success stories are a positive sign. But the turnaround districts are geographically limited, and the benefits generated there have not extended to other parts of either city. The relationships of turnaround districts to abutting portions of the aging inner ring are often quite tenuous. Residents of the areas that are not improving have little in common with residents of improving areas. The interests and goals of these groups can be directly at odds. Some people in the aging inner ring feel threatened by the possibility of displaced refugees from the turnaround zone inundating them. This would put even more pressure on any affordable housing that was still available. So while many applaud the changes occurring in parts of the city that are upgrading, others view these quite negatively. The actions occurring in the turnaround zone are favorable for people moving there, and possibly for the city, but this may not be the final assessment.

Bargain-hunting on weekend mornings is a popular pastime in the settled mid-city zone.

CHAPTER
VI

The Settled Mid-City Zone

In the half-century after the introduction of streetcars into the Twin Cities, several economic panics and booms caused the construction industry alternately to wax and wane, thereby creating a set of ringlike residential zones. Although most of the housing built during the streetcar era has changed dramatically, buildings in a few scattered areas have been modified to a lesser degree and retain their original design. Never home to the elite, such areas have sheltered middle-class families for years and are the proverbial "nice older neighborhoods." We have combined these residential districts into the category of "settled mid-city" zone.

The districts in this zone were built up as the last phase of the pure streetcar city. Because they were all constructed within a twenty-five-year period, between 1900 and 1925, these areas occupy similar positions in the transportation network of the Twin Cities. Their location is simlar to that of many aging inner ring and protected genteel districts, except that the settled mid-city districts were originally on or beyond the outer edge of the built-up city. The streetcar lines that spawned these districts were concentrated in a few portions of each city. In Minneapolis most lines were south of downtown, especially in the southwestern sector toward the lakes. In Saint Paul most lines ran to the west

and north. As a result, the settled mid-city districts are concentrated in these parts of the Twin Cities. They are separated from the central city by a band of neighborhoods of comparable age but with different characteristics. The only exceptions to this pattern are the Mounds Park and the Cherokee Heights districts in Saint Paul. These areas are separated from downtown by major topographic boundaries which have protected them from encroachment by commercial and industrial activities. However, these and other districts have experienced encroachment of the residential blight that produces the aging inner ring type of districts.

Macalester Park and Hamline Village in Saint Paul, and Linden Hills in Minneapolis, were all built beyond the urban fringe. They are therefore surrounded by newer houses.

The settled mid-city districts are particularly vulnerable to change because they lack the spectacular houses of the protected genteel districts. This means that they have not attracted the attention of the preservationists. At the same time, they do contain large houses that can be subdivided for tenants, and which are relatively expensive to maintain. These pressures were the causes for the turnover of all the other old middle-class areas. Yet the settled mid-city districts are survivors. They have retained their essential character because each has some special feature that continues to attract middle-class families and thereby maintain the value of the housing. These special features consist of excellent designs, proximity to public transportation or to amenities such as parks, lakes, or recreational facilities. (See map 6.) Although these special features vary from district to district, there is one locational aspect that all the districts share: None is on a major traffic artery. Many are bounded by a busy street, but all are buffered from the dramatic changes associated with the upgrading of streets to carry higher volumes of automobile traffic. This may seem odd, since the old streetcar routes that served these districts when they were new later attracted buses and car traffic. These streets have tended to become edges for the districts, separating them from areas in poorer condition and occupied by less wealthy households.

Because the residential structures were added one at a time for about two and one-half decades in the beginning of the century, there is a mixture of house styles and sizes in most districts. The subdivisions created during the streetcar era in the Twin Cities, however, all share several design characteristics. Lot sizes are generally modest but not as small as in areas developed prior to the introduction of the mass transit system. Most blocks have alleys, although many houses did not have garages when they were built. The lots are aligned along a regular grid pattern of streets which is related to a set of arterial streets on which the streetcars ran. Commercial establishments are located at intersections along the old streetcar routes. (Shop owners wanted to take advantage of the business generated by streetcar riders.) In many districts multiple family units are also found along the major arterials.

The zone is characterized by generally level terrain. This is due to the fact that in the early twentieth century developers were discouraged from building on hilly ground because the streetcars had difficulties climbing steep slopes. In hilly western Saint Paul, which was laid out during this period, development lagged until the Selby Avenue streetcar tunnel was constructed to replace the complex system of counterweights that helped the cars climb the steep bluff. This advance in transportation technology dramatically reduced the travel time from the city fringe to downtown, and caused a spurt in growth.

The landscape today is quite different from what it was originally. Developers had to contend with several small streams and bogs in many of their subdivisions. In almost all cases they filled in the water courses with material excavated locally, and eventually placed houses on every piece of vacant land. Although most of these districts were originally prairies or mixed oak groves and grasslands, the real estate promoters and residents convinced each city government that boulevard plantings were needed to beautify the areas. Like the rest of the city built before 1940, the settled mid-city districts were planted with elms. By the late 1960s great elms with branches like cathedral beams overarched the streets and screened the aging houses from the casual glances of visitors to the districts. Heavy shade in the districts made gardening difficult. Vegetables were confined to the backyards and the front yards were devoted to grass and shrubs. The result is an attractive but not showy landscape.

THE DEVELOPMENT PROCESS

It is hard to overstate the importance of the streetcar in the expansion of the Twin Cities. As we have seen, when this area was first settled, people tried to live as close to their jobs as possible because nearly everyone walked to work. Under these circumstances only those who could afford to maintain horses could live on the edge of the built-up areas where the conditions of life were quite pleasant. Early innovations in mass transit in the Twin Cities included the horse car, the cable car, and a steam train in Minneapolis. These innovations had no impact on the settled mid-city zone, however. It was the installation of the electric street-car systems in the early 1890s that signaled the true beginning of development in this zone.

City leaders and investors across the country realized that a transportation system that could carry large numbers of people at low cost would cause an extraordinary boom in land values on the edge of urban areas. Others believed that a decrease in the population density in the older areas would enhance public health conditions and make cities more governable. The combination of sentiments prompted the municipal governments to issue franchises to streetcar companies, who then built private right-of-ways for their railroads. In many districts the beds for the tracks were in

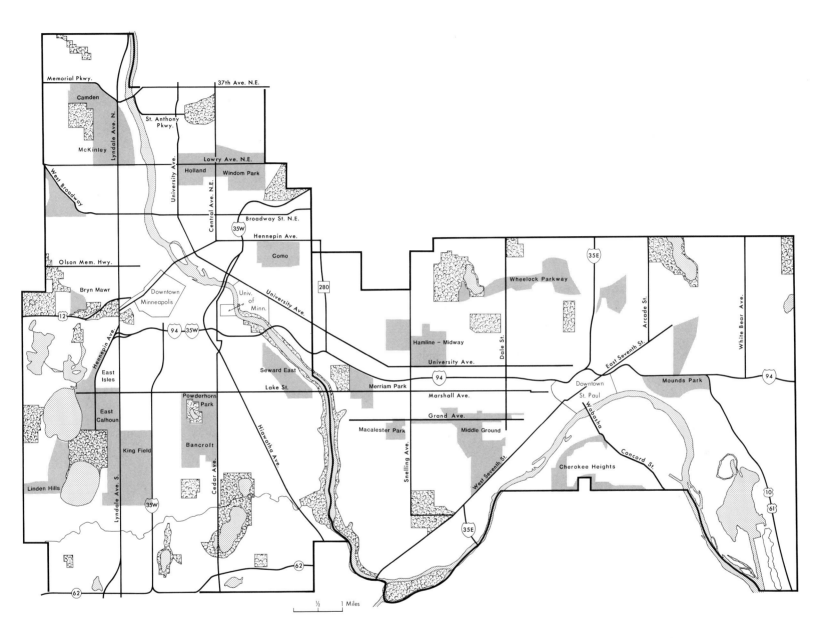

Map 6: The Settled Mid-City Zone. This zone has housed middle-class residents since it was constructed between 1900 and 1920. For many people it is the ideal older urban "neighborhood."

before the streets were paved, and commuters frequently waded through mud to get onto the cars.

Because the right to operate streetcars was conferred by local governments, two separate companies were chartered in the Twin Cities, one for Saint Paul and another for Minneapolis. The investors in both companies were men involved in real estate. Wright and Wann in Saint Paul and Thomas Lowry in Minneapolis were the early promoters of the systems. It is interesting to note that the Grand Avenue line, Saint Paul's first electric route, ran as far as the Grand and Victoria intersection, one short block from Wann's home on Summit Avenue. The major part of the line ran through Wann and Wright's Summit Park addition to the City of Saint Paul. Thomas Lowry was the organizational genius behind the streetcar network of the Twin Cities. The Minneapolis system was more extensive than Saint Paul's. Although neither company was profitable, the Minneapolis organization was better capitalized and was the stronger of the two. Thomas Lowry and his fellow investors eventually acquired the Saint Paul company, and the Twin City Lines were formed. Under Lowry's leadership the system was extended to Lake Minnetonka on the west, White Bear Lake and Stillwater on the east, and South Saint Paul on the southeast. In the early twentieth century the company actively promoted suburban development to increase ridership. In the 1920s the company also built and managed amusement parks on Lake Minnetonka and White Bear Lake. In addition to being profitable in their own right, the amusement parks promoted travel on weekends. Holiday and Sunday specials ran to the ends of the lines all through the summers, carrying people from the crowded older districts to the open countryside around the recreation areas.

Although the streetcar company did not pay dividends, Lowry and others actively promoted the expansion of the tracks. Real estate developers were constantly badgering the company to open lines to their property so they could sell more lots. In a sense the streetcars were a "loss leader" in the development of the fringe real estate. The owners of the streetcar company were all involved in real estate development and reaped their profits from the sale of land, not from the fares earned by the company.

The subdivisions developed by promoters during the streetcar era were intended to house populations that were much more homogeneous than those living in the older districts. Because land costs were high in the older sections of the city and travel expensive, upper-income families lived relatively close to lower-income households. The real estate developers understood that the wealthy wished to live apart from lower-income families. As a result, they developed housing areas for the various income levels within each city. Although historians argue that some entrepreneurs had a master plan for the separation of economic classes, there is no reason to believe that a master plan to segregate the city was developed by the builders. The latter group did, however, determine the range of housing costs for districts and thereby ensured the concentration of households by income level. As a result, housing styles and income levels in the settled mid-city zone tend to vary from district to district. Yet the range of income is all within the bounds of the middle class.

Builders took clues from the landscape when laying out subdivisions for particular income levels. Where possible, they developed land near natural amenities such as lakes or hills because these places were preferred by wealthier households and could be sold for a high price. Thus the lake district of southwestern Minneapolis was soon occupied by higher-income families. In Saint Paul, the rather uniform landscape in the western section of the city was built up for the middle class, as were the shores of Lake Como. In general the east side of the city was occupied by lower-income households. With few exceptions, fringe development that resulted from the expansion of streetcar lines resembled the older housing in the vicinity.

In Minneapolis both Linden Hills and a portion of Northeast were developed before the rest of the zone. Linden Hills was spawned by the streetcar to Lake Harriet which ended its journey there. For a time in the 1890s this was an exclusive residential area for those who wanted some distance between themselves and the city. The graceful homes and spacious character of Linden Hills Boulevard are a clear reminder of this period. Parts of the Northeast district also made an attempt to be somewhat more exclusive. An area east of Central Avenue near 24th Avenue N.E. was laid out in the 1880s by a developer named Henry Beard. He got the street railway extended to this area, platted a group of wide streets, and built about a hundred houses. Soon this development was engulfed by growth outward from the city. The Central Avenue streetcar line, for example, was extended beyond the present city limits by 1905.

The rate of construction within the areas served by the streetcar lines depended upon the strength of the economy and the rate of immigration. In boom periods such as the 1880s and the first fifteen years of the twentieth century, hundreds of new houses were built in a score of subdivisions. The boom was cut off by the First World War when the number of housing starts dropped almost to zero and the development process that produced these districts essentially ended. In the modern period there has been a considerable amount of rebuilding in some districts, as well as numerous conversions of large single-family houses into duplexes.

HOUSING

At the turn of the century houses were built according to a few basic plans. Where possible, contractors used precut lumber so dimensions were becoming standardized. Decorative trim of all sorts, stained glass windows, windows of special shapes, fancy cut wooden trim, or gingerbread, could all be ordered from catalogs. Large mail-order houses would sell customers entire houses precut, but most people in the Twin Cities used local carpenters and contractors to build their homes. Many higher-income households had individually designed homes, and some of these structures still stand within the settled mid-city zones. For the most part, however, middle-class families selected a house from one of the half dozen or so general styles popular at the time. Frequently, changes in superficial decorations were made, and there appears to have been some effort to avoid the sort of regularity that typifies modern subdivisions.

Because the variations within the housing stock give character to the individual districts, detailed descriptions of houses will be provided for each area discussed. Nonetheless, a few generalizations can be made about the zone. The houses built before World War I were overwhelmingly single-family detached frame structures. Few were over two stories high. Most would be considered story and one-half houses because the slope of the roof extends down to the level of the first-floor ceiling. As a result, the second-story walls have a steep pitch. During the 1920s duplexes and apartment buildings were constructed in many parts of these districts. These structures occupy corner locations and are found along the major streets. Most of the builders in the twenties and the thirties preferred stucco to the older wooden siding. Larger apartment blocks were generally constructed of brick.

Today these houses are in good repair. For example, a recent survey of housing conditions in Saint Paul determined that in the settled mid-city zone the percentage of structures requiring major repairs ranged from less than 4 percent to 20 percent, depending on the district surveyed. In several districts a great deal of new construction has occurred, both as infill on vacant property and as replacement housing. By and large, the new construction has consisted of multiple family units. In the area east of Lake Calhoun large numbers of massive apartment blocks have been constructed along Douglas Avenue, the old streetcar route serving the area. In other areas new houses have been built on vacant lots.

COMMERCIAL SERVICES

During the first half of the twentieth century the residential communities of the Twin Cities were served by convenience stores and professional offices located on intersections along the streetcar routes. In a few districts small grocery stores located on corners within the residential areas, but they were not common in the settled mid-city districts. Most residents depended upon the large department and furniture stores in downtown Minneapolis and Saint Paul for major purchases. Local stores provided groceries, drugs and sundries, hardware and clothing. Doctors, dentists, and lawyers maintained their offices on the second floors of commercial blocks, which typically housed a corner drug store as well.

This pattern of commercial land use dominated all the residential districts, and occupants of the settled mid-city shared the commercial districts with other newer developments as well as with the older, more elite areas in the vicinity. Although the social characteristic of the settled mid-city districts has remained relatively unchanged, the commercial areas serving these sections have been profoundly altered by dynamics within the aging inner ring and prewar areas. The declining population density of the older communities greatly decreased the viability of shops located on streetcar routes, and in the 1950s the number of convenience stores plummeted on all the shopping strips. In several places sites were cleared of old structures to make room for new supermarkets. As the number of convenience stores declined, their places were taken by new operations that served a wider segment of the urban population. These shops depended upon customers who came by cars, and so parking problems developed along the streets. One solution to the situation was for the successful establishments to demolish neighborhood buildings to make room for parking lots. In so doing, the owners changed the character of the old streetcar strip. In some areas the facade of shops and apartment buildings has a rather "gapped tooth" appearance. Needless to say, the several small parking lots created in this fashion have not solved the parking problem. Traffic congestion and the shortage of parking spaces during the rush hours continue to plague the settled mid-city districts.

Several streetcar strips in the settled mid-city zone developed into substantial shopping districts. Hennepin and Lake was the largest, and is still the most successful of these. It has many specialty stores and offices, a large grocery store, a bank, and two movie theaters. It is the shopping area most accessible to the protected genteel districts of Kenwood and Lowry Hill, and this accessibility accounts for its sustained business fortune over many years. Currently, plans for a new shopping center (Calhoun Square) with parking facilities are nearly complete. This center is to be built on a former school site near the main intersection. The income profiles of residents in surrounding districts are not sufficient to warrant this investment, so spillover from the more well-off areas is clearly taking place. The other factor that determines the planning of new commercial facilities is how residents' income is spent. Income levels in the East Isles and East Calhoun areas hover around the city average, but much of it is disposable. That is, the area has an extremely high proportion of singles and couples without children. These people rent apartments and have few fixed expenses. They may not have a large amount of money to spend, but they can often spend a greater fraction of what they do earn on nonessential items than can people raising children.

Other commercial strips in Minneapolis districts that remain viable include 43rd and Upton South, 42nd and Lyndale North, and Central Avenue Northeast from 18th to 28th Streets. None of these are quite as prosperous as Hennepin and Lake, but all have managed to retain physi-cians' offices, small grocery stores, and other convenience facilities in the face of intense competition.

POPULATION

Because this zone houses a variety of middle-class households, it is essentially as difficult to describe as is the social category of middle class. Accordingly, the districts range from areas that are occupied by professionals and higher paid skilled workers to places where the majority of the population would be classified as blue collar even though their incomes are high. These groups are united in this zone because they share similar values. They all prize home ownership and are careful to maintain their property to the best of their ability. Unlike the occupants of the protected genteel area, they are not enthusiastic supporters of historic preservation. Few homes in this zone have been restored, although many have been modernized and redecorated. Others have been maintained in a state that resembles the original design. In Saint Paul occupants of this zone seem to share an unwillingness to become active in neighborhood associations or similar organizations. The low level of community participation may seem surprising in light of the considerable investment of time and money that the residents have made in their property, and considering the presence of local organizations in similar districts in Minneapolis.

It would appear that two factors lay behind this situation. First, the residents perceive no immediate threat to the continuation of the living conditions in their areas. In several different surveys administered in Saint Paul districts during the 1970s, we asked residents to list problems facing their community and to comment on the level of city services they were provided. Local schools were an issue in some districts, and a fear of criminal activity existed in others. But the overwhelming majority of respondents could list only one or two minor concerns and they were satisfied with the treatment they were receiving from the city. The lack of major issues in the districts makes the task of establishing an organization through standard community-organizing techniques nearly impossible. This is not to say that people living in the zone have no pride in their community. On the contrary, they seem to be almost smug in their complacency. The second factor contributing to the lack of organization in the areas is the fundamental conservatism of the population. These are districts in which people tend to mind their own business. As long as no serious changes are made in the status quo, the people will remain, living a fairly independent life.

The people who live in the settled mid-city zone today are very much like their neighbors occupying interwar districts adjacent to them. As we have indicated, the population is middle-class and earns a range of incomes that span the median income for the Twin Cities. (See table 5, p. 146). The households are predominantly white, two-parent families who own their own homes. Renters are common, however, and in some districts the percentage of tenant households is as high as 70 percent. During the 1970s, total income in the settled mid-city district increased slightly, while total income in the rest of both cities remained essentially unchanged. Like the rest of Minneapolis and Saint Paul, these districts gradually lost population during the last two decades. As is the case in other middle-class districts, a population decline results from changing family structures, not from abandonment of the city or destruction of housing units. Although there is some variation among the districts, the population tends to be aging as young adults mature and leave their parents' homes. In addition, elderly individuals who wish to remain in familiar parts of the city but can no longer maintain a house move into the apartment buildings scattered along the major streets. In a few districts it is possible to see the beginning of a counter-trend. There young adults are competing with the older people for apartments and smaller houses in the districts. If current trends continue, these young people cannot be expected to have many children. Therefore, the population of the districts will undoubtedly remain fairly constant in the foreseeable future.

DISTRICTS OF THE SETTLED MID-CITY ZONE

Macalester Park

Macalester Park, one of the several "Tangle Towns" that exist in the Twin Cities, is a nineteenth-century garden suburb that failed. Its failure is the very foundation of its charm and the reason it has been selected to illustrate the settled mid-city category. Instead of booming and filling up with wealthy families as the developers expected, the area was built up gradually during the first decades of the twentieth century. A few wealthy households were attracted to this area, but most residents of the Park were middle-class professionals and businessmen, with a few skilled tradesmen and academics mixed in. Despite the pressures of the changing economy and the expansion of Macalester College, the district has remained essentially as it was— middle class. There are more academics living in the area now, and some of the houses are a little worn, but the atmosphere of comfort and stability remains intact.

It all began in 1881 when the Trustees of Macalester College decided to relocate the institution to the suburbs. They purchased the Thomas Holyoke farm, the 160 acres bounded by Snelling, Grand, Fairview, and Saint Clair Avenues. After deeding forty acres to the college to be used as a campus, in 1883 they created the community of Macalester Park from the remainder. The winding streets, odd lot sizes, and mixture of housing styles distinguish this area from the newer developments around it.

Its romantic design was popular among landscape designers, architects, and the elite of the Victorian era. The idea of garden suburbs such as this grew out of the garden city movement sparked by the British reformer Ebenezer Howard, who sought to establish an alternative to the dark and unhealthy industrial cities. He believed that if factories could be located in the country, and if workers lived nearby in residences along curved lanes shaded by trees and surrounded by gardens, a humane style of life would prevail. His ideas reached influential leaders of the United States about the time the streetcar was invented. Real estate developers quickly seized the superficial aspects of the garden city concept—its landscape design—and pleasing suburbs were laid out along streetcar lines in nearly every city of the country. Patterned after Shaker Heights near Cleveland, Macalester Park became one of the first streetcar suburbs in the Northwest. Earlier suburbs in the Midway district, Merriam Park, and Saint Anthony Park were based upon rail commuting.

The area surrounding Macalester Park had long been considered an attractive place for outings. It was described in 1890 by an enthusiast writing in the Northwest Magazine as follows:

Reserve Township with its groves of oaks and elms, its hills commanding extensive views over both cities which form the dual metropolis of the northwest, its winding roads, its bold wooded cliffs along the river, deeply creased with picturesque ravines, where little streams leap over the brown rocks and hide in the thickets of ferns and flowering shrubs, is, indeed, one vast natural park.

The establishment of the streetcar lines in the early 1890s opened this area for recreation as well as settlement. At first people were attracted to the area for recreation. Again from the Northwest Magazine:

On holidays and Sundays and the long summer evenings, the cars are crowded with lovers of nature, eager to escape for a little while from the brick walls and paved streets, to breath the pure air of the country and to wander under green boughs along wood paths. It is a very orderly crowd, for there are no amusements—no games and no saloons—at the end of the route to attract the rough elements of the city's population.

The writer went on to say that

Once up the hill the train turns on Grand Avenue, here a pleasant shady street with more vacant lots than dwellings and a general air of village quiet. The dwellings are rarer and newer as you advance. A little stretch of open prairie is crossed, then a bridge over the shortline tracks which run to Minneapolis, and just beyond, the broad avenue cuts through a noble grove of oaks. Macalester is soon reached with its group of handsome red college buildings, its green campus, its rows of pretty villas where live the professors and other people who are fond of living in the shadow of institutional learning and who appreciate the beauty of landscapes.

Although the streets were named after famous schools—Cambridge, Princeton, Dartmouth, Amherst—the area did not attract the population the college hoped for. The original plan of selling lots to provide an endowment for the college was soon abandoned, and the promoters resigned themselves to watching the district develop slowly as single houses and occasional duplexes were added each year.

Because Macalester Park was not developed by a single contractor or architect, a walk through the area will reveal several different house styles. The oldest housing is the eclectic cube. This balloon frame structure with two full stories plus an attic, porches front and back, and usually with a bay window on the side, was popular until the First World War. The foundations of such structures are generally made of blocks of gray limestone about a foot and a half thick. There were enough rooms to house the large families of the day, who lived without servants. Most houses have a living room, dining room, a large kitchen and pantry on the first floor; four bedrooms on the second; and an unfinished attic. The backstairs and maid's room so common in the protected genteel districts are extremely uncommon here. Over the years the interiors of most houses have been altered, but aside from the presence of aluminum combination windows and occasional aluminum siding the exteriors look much as they did during the summer when the Archduke was assassinated in Sarajevo.

The second most common style of house in the area is the bungalow of the 1920s. Modeled after California houses, these are one-story structures with a small attic above and a basement underneath. On the first floor are two bedrooms, a bathroom, kitchen, dining room, and living room. These houses usually have a screen porch as well. They, too, have remained essentially as they were when first built, although some have new kitchens. Some have had only two or three owners.

During the 1920s a third type of house was built, also influenced to some extent by California styles: the large three-bedroom, two-floor duplex with red tile roof. These structures were an accommodation to the increased building costs of the twenties and usually occupy corner lots. The units were luxurious for the day and are now in great demand because they provide comfortable and efficient housing.

There are of course other styles in the area, colonial revivals, Queen Annes, and variations of the three major types. Two stables still stand in the district, but because the area was built up during the streetcar era most families did not keep horses. A few small "Model T" garages still can be found, but these are gradually being replaced. The college villas described by the promoter in the 1890s have long since been replaced by dormitories.

As the population of Macalester Park and the surrounding area grew, a set of commercial establishments sprang up along

The garden suburb planned for Macalester Park is clearly evident in the comfortable houses on large lots.

The Grand Village commercial area west of Snelling is a thriving local shopping district.

The Grandview Theater provides first-run movies for the entire western section of Saint Paul. Its art deco facade has been remarkably well preserved.

Snelling, Grand, and Saint Clair Avenues. These places provided convenience goods such as drugs, groceries, and services like dry cleaning. During the twenties, movie theaters were added and even a few saloons. These, together with medical practitioners located above the drug stores, prospered until the 1950s. During that decade the local decline in population and competition from new shopping centers forced many stores out of business. They have been replaced by more specialized establishments with larger trade areas, which profit from the reputation of Grand Avenue and the increased purchasing power of local residents.

The recent history of the district reflects the historic or older communities' experience everywhere. The middle- and upper middle-class families that formed the backbone of the community for decades moved away in response to changes in the household structure. Older couples whose children had grown relocated in smaller quarters nearby or in distant retirement communities. The children of the first families often relocated in other cities or moved to high-status suburbs like Mendota Heights, Arden Hills, or North Oaks. They were attracted to these locations for essentially the same reasons that brought people into Macalester Park. The families who moved into the district during the 1960s did not stay long. Most were upwardly mobile and viewed Macalester Park as a stepping-stone to more prestigious communities.

In the early 1960s Macalester College began to expand its campus. In addition, the college purchased several dozen houses with the intention of holding the land for future expansion. In the meantime these houses were rented to faculty and students. This changed the basic nature of the area by mixing in some three dozen tenant households in the place of homeowners. An expansionist plan for the campus was made public in 1968, and the local residents were aghast. The 1968 plan is representative of the relationship between large institutions and surrounding communities that existed during that decade. Museums, hospitals, schools, churches, and art galleries were expected to grow indefinitely in response to the exciting increases in wealth and population that characterized those years. Residents in the vicinity of the college did not have long-term commitments to their space, so that few that protested the college's program received little support from their neighbors.

In the early 1970s Macalester was preoccupied with internal problems, and expansion plans were shelved. At the same time the value of older housing was widely promoted by preservation enthusiasts. The elite districts of the nineteenth century were attracting a new population, and a similar, although smaller, trend occurred in Macalester Park. By 1973 houses in the area began to turn over at an increased rate as mortgage money became increasingly available. Higher-income households replaced the out-migrants. By 1977 property values were increasing so fast that realtors struggled to predict housing values.

This portion of the census tract has approximately 800 housing units, less than 1 percent of the total supply in Saint Paul. This number has been essentially constant for decades. Vacancy rates are low here, but the turnover in units rented by students produces a vacancy rate somewhat higher than in other middle-class areas. The population of the district is estimated to be about 2,200 and is shrinking slightly.

The perecentage of owner-occupied units in the districts, 54 percent, is below the Saint Paul rate of about 58.8 percent. This low rate is due to presence of large apartment blocks along Grand Avenue, and the duplexes and housing owned by Macalester College. Many of the properties owned by the college are being sold to families, so the ratio between renters and owners will be closer to the city-wide rate in the near future.

The presence of the rental property has attracted large numbers of single-person and childless households to the district. Therefore, the average household size here is lower than in other middle-class districts. The percentage of single-person households is the highest of any area in the western section of Saint Paul and twice the rate in the suburban-in-city district. Although there are large numbers of single-person households in Macalester Park, there are also many large families. This is understandable, given the great variety of housing. The large eclectic cubes and story and one-half houses make ideal homes for large families. Over 30 percent of the households here have children, which again distinguishes this district from other areas in the southwest section of Saint Paul. The number of retired persons who are the heads of households here is slightly lower than the city-wide figure and considerably less than it is in adjacent districts which are made up of newer and smaller housing. The reason for this is evident. Older couples have tended to leave the large units when maintenance becomes a burden.

This pattern of households and housing stock has combined to give Macalester Park a high turnover rate. Forty-four percent of the housing units changed hands between 1976 and 1978. This is much higher than the city-wide rate and nearly twice the rate in the prewar grid districts immediately to the south. On some blocks 95 percent of the housing units have changed hands in the last decade.

A turnover rate as high as this usually indicates a residential district with severe problems or one declining in status. This does not seem to be the situation here. The percentage of heads of households in professional and managerial occupations is among the highest in the city, and the Polk Data indicates that more professional households have moved into the district between 1978 and 1980. Several districts in the west-central zone of Saint Paul are experiencing a net inmigration of high-status households, which may be associated with a reevaluation of the qualities of life in these older areas.

Despite the professional population, the large numbers of students and recent graduates living in the district give it an income level only slightly above the average for Saint Paul. Not only is the average income of Macalester Park lower than that of the surrounding districts, it is declining slightly.

The presence of the college has a two-edged effect on the district. On the one hand, it has attracted many professional people to the district, and its program of neighborhood investment and beautification is helping to maintain the character of the area. On the other hand, its students tend to rent quarters off campus and remain after they graduate to take advantage of the area's convenience. They are certainly middle-class, but their incomes are quite low and skew the standard statistics used to describe populations.

The new professional and managerial households have little to do with Macalester, but they enjoy the amenities that attracted residents for half a century—variation in housing styles, comfortable homes, spacious lots, and pleasant landscaping. The convenience of the district is also a factor drawing people who work in the central city or at the University of Minnesota.

Most residents are busy adapting the streetcar-era landscape to modern life styles by adding garages and renovating houses. But here, unlike the protected genteel areas, there is no need for extensive renovation. Macalester college sold most of its houses with the provision that they be purchased by owner-occupants, and so the area is even more middle-class now than it was ten years ago.

Neighborhood organizers frequently throw their hands up in despair at this district because the usual problems that can be used to organize people do not attract much concern here. The presence of the college stabilized the housing market when it was most threatened. Today the area's major problems are the condition of some rental properties owned by small-scale landlords who rent to college students, and the absence of a large public playground.

The Middle Ground

Along West Seventh Street in Saint Paul, at a point where the high terrace above the Mississippi reaches its broadest extent, is a settled mid-city district that is quite different from Macalester Park. Known locally by the intriguing name "the Middle Ground," it stands between the lower-income districts of the West Seventh Community and the new, wealthier areas of Highland Park. Its boundaries are the cliff top on the west, Saint Clair Avenue on the north, West Seventh on the east, and the I-35E right-of-way on the west and south.

Like the older areas toward the city center, the Middle Ground was built to house workers employed in the manufacturing plants located near the railroad tracks. The railroads themselves employed large numbers of men who also lived in the districts.

There was no elaborate plan for the Middle Ground. It was developed along the grid pattern of streets platted to take advantage of the early streetcar line out West Seventh and Randolph Avenue. The houses here are predominately single-family detached, built in the story and one-half style. Although there are a few brick buildings, the houses are essentially frame, with a few having stucco siding. There are a handful of apartment buildings in the district, and some of the larger houses have been converted into duplexes.

The high cliffs and West Seventh corridor surrounding the district are barriers that have to a large extent insulated the residents from the rest of the city and promoted a special sense of place. Nonetheless, as an extension of the streetcar landscape, the Middle Ground shares many of the problems found in the other sections of West Seventh, but most of them are not as severe. Housing remains in good repair. Lawns and gardens are immaculate, and public facilities such as streets, sidewalks, and sewers are in good shape. One of the many landscape differences between the Middle Ground and other settled mid-city districts is the number of vegetable gardens. Here, unlike other districts, most lots have at least a tomato plant or two, and many a garden seems to be productive enough to make a household self-sufficient.

As in the Macalester Park area, residents here tend to avoid organizations. Although many of the residential districts nearby are very active in the West Seventh Federation, people in the Middle Ground are not. To the outside observer it would seem as if these people are content with the status quo and do not feel any strong ties to other districts in their part of the city.

There are slightly more people here than in other settled mid-city districts, about 2,300, living in about a thousand housing units. The population is essentially stable. As in the other districts in this zone, the population declined somewhat recently because of a lower birthrate. Most of the households own their own homes.

In spite of the nationwide decline in birthrates, the households in the Middle Ground are still somewhat larger than what one might expect. In fact only in the suburban-in-city districts, and areas influenced by large minority populations with birthrates significantly higher than the national average, are the average household sizes greater than in the Middle Ground. Many households have five or more members. They account for about 16 percent of the households in the district. This is a greater fraction than occurs in Saint Paul as a whole but is considerably lower than that found in the other areas with a high average household size. Thirty percent of the families in this district have children, only slightly more than the city average and considerably lower than the suburban-in-city zones and the other districts with larger households. Thus, because of the great number of households composed of adults, we infer that in the Middle Ground, children stay with their parents after they are eighteen for a slightly longer time than they

do in other districts. This indicates the strength of family ties in this area as well as the problems children from lower middle-class families have getting jobs that will enable them to live independently.

Another striking difference between the Middle Ground and the rest of the zone is the low number of single-person households. The rate is almost 10 percent lower than Macalester Park's.

The West Seventh area as a whole has a large number of retired households. Many live in highrises for the elderly, but the majority occupy houses or apartments scattered through the area. The vast majority of these people have lived most of their lives in this community. It is not uncommon to encounter individuals who have spent the last fifty years here. Needless to say, they are quite proud of the area. Over a third of the household heads are retired, which is more than in most parts of the city, and 8 percent higher than Saint Paul's average.

There are only a few places in the Twin Cities more stable than the Middle Ground of West Seventh Street. According to the Polk Directory data, 33 percent of the housing units experienced a change in occupancy between 1976 and 1978. This is well below Saint Paul's average of 39 percent for that period.

The average income in the area approximates that of Saint Paul and shows no sign of increasing. There are few high-status households living here and their number has been essentially unchanged in recent years.

Unlike Hamline Village, Macalester Park, and other settled mid-city districts, the Middle Ground is an inward-looking area. People resent leaving the area to shop; they like to do their socializing nearby; and they think of their neighbors as friends. Some observers have described this community as provincial because of the pervading sense of isolation that one gets in the district. Change is coming to the Middle Ground, however. The right-of-way for Interstate 35E coils around the area, and when a road is actually built here the serenity of the district will be greatly changed. The decline of population has brought about a reduction in the number of stores serving local needs, and local schools have been closed because of a lack of students. Teenagers are no longer able to perform their entire round of activities a few miles from home. They are now sent to larger high schools across the city from their parents' homes where they encounter

The middle ground community near Saint Paul's west 7th Street has housed working-class households for generations.

new attitudes and values. The traditional family life of the Middle Ground may be significantly changed.

Despite this, young blue-collar families are attracted to the area in ever increasing numbers. They are eager to buy the smaller, older houses from retired couples because these are some of the few good buys in single-family housing still available. This is the place for "do-it-yourselfers." As they fix, paint, and rebuild the houses, they ensure the stability of the district. In fact, during the late 1970s and early 1980s housing prices in the area increased at one of the highest rates in the city.

Camden

Camden, on the far north side of Minneapolis, has a longer history than most of the settled mid-city districts. In the early 1850s the Dows and the Bohanons, two families, settled in the area far beyond the town limits of St. Anthony. They farmed this region for many years and eventually formed the nucleus of a small community. Even in the 1870s they were still outside the city limits of Minneapolis, but the district was already growing at a rapid pace.

The small stream that emptied into the Mississippi at 42nd Street North had been christened Shingle Creek after the shingle mill built there; the adjoining community was referrred to by this name as well. As the area grew, new residents felt this name was unsuitable, so the district was renamed after Philadelphia's sister city—Camden, New Jersey. Both people and industry were drawn to the area. By the 1880s Camden had a brickyard, a stockyard, a water pumping station near 42nd Street, and the sawmills had expanded upriver to this point. The district was also incorporated into the city during this period. But the real development of Camden, like that of other settled mid-city areas, hinged on transit expansion. Streetcar lines reached this area in 1892. Within two years a thriving business district, complete with a hotel, developed at 42nd and Lyndale.

Although Camden's early growth was related to industrial opportunity, the real impetus for development derived from its residential potential. Closer-in parts of the Northside were already declining after 1900. Camden offered exactly what the middle class wanted: an opportunity to live far away from undesirable people or influences, and to com-

mute easily to downtown. Between 1890 and 1912, all of the area east of Crystal Lake Cemetery was filled with houses. The pattern of settlement spread west rather than north from the center of the community because the Soo Line Railroad was a formidable barrier. As the district grew, its industrial character began to change. The lumber mills disappeared by 1920. They were increasingly replaced by grain elevators, brickyards, and storage facilities.

The housing built in this period represented the range found throughout the settled mid-city zone. Some duplexes and apartment buildings appeared along streetcar lines, and a few large and expensive houses were built along Webber Parkway. Most of the housing consisted of frame or stucco single-family houses, inhabited by the people who owned them. A mid-1920s analysis of the community claimed that most residents of Camden were of American or Scandinavian backgrounds. It portrayed the housing as "comfortable" and well maintained, reporting that lots were large enough to provide space for playgrounds, gardens, and pets.

Over the years Camden has not experienced any dramatic changes. While many parts of the city lost population in the 1950s and 1960s, this area remained quite stable. The slight population decline of the 1970s probably resulted from changing household characteristics rather than movement of the population. A recent sampling of blocks in Camden indicates a home ownership rate of 75-82 percent. Over half the people who lived there in the late seventies had been there for five to ten years. Residents are predominately blue-collar workers, with large numbers of skilled and service workers, and many retired persons. In the past, upward mobility was not characteristic of residents. Long-time residents whose parents were laborers tended to have careers as clerical or skilled workers. Few children were sent to college, and even fewer finished. Camden may have changed slightly in this respect in recent years, but it still exemplifies the tradition of training children for well-paying jobs without worrying about their status levels.

Today Camden is a pleasant, unpretentious residential environment for families. Most houses are in good condition. Community groups actively monitor potential problems. Many park areas are close by, and the area has a well-used community center. A full complement of churches sponsor many activities that are fully subscribed to by residents. The only major problem in Camden is the status of the old business district, which has declined in recent years. Plans for renovation and some rebuilding exist, but community leaders worry that residents are too attached to nearby suburban malls to be drawn back. Now that I-94 is completed along the district's eastern edge, it is even easier for residents to take their business elsewhere.

Como

The eastern portion of the Como district demonstrates how the settled mid-city zone contrasts with the aging inner ring. Located south of East Hennepin and extending from 18th Avenue S.E. to the city limits, this district developed gradually as settlement expanded out from St. Anthony during the last years of the nineteenth century. The portion of the Como district west of 18th Avenue S.E. has deteriorated somewhat and now falls into the aging inner ring category. The eastern portion has remained more stable and retains its middle-class character. The environmental distinctions in the two areas emerged during the last two decades. The western portion of Como is closer to the University of Minnesota, and thus more attractive to students. Consequently, it was also more attractive to apartment developers. It lost much of its original housing, and single-family houses were frequently subdivided into smaller units. The housing of the eastern Como district dates primarily from the late 1890s and early twentieth century, though some infill construction did occur after 1940. Most of the houses are substantial frame dwellings with three to four bedrooms. Many of them contain lovely carved woodwork and interesting construction details. These are often hidden beneath the now-stucco or asphalt-covered exteriors.

Eastern Como, much like similar parts of Bryn Mawr, Seward, and Powderhorn Park, has always housed both skilled workers and professionals. Both University professors and employees of the railroads and grain elevators found this area to their liking. It offered enough housing options for both types of people. In the early twentieth century, status was achieved through personal merit and not income, so that a continuum of middle-class society could happily coexist in a residential district. This is what happened in eastern Como. It was never a fashionable area, but it was a comfortable one.

Longtime residents of eastern Como, many with Scan-

dinavian backgrounds, are generally pleased with the area, though they are willing to admit its deficiencies. The most obvious, residents contend, are the commercial decline of Como Avenue and the influx of students into the area. Many homeowners worry about plans the University may have to expand its supply of student housing. Longtime

This portion of the settled mid-city in South Minneapolis has the range of housing types and styles typical of this zone.

*Hennepin and Lake intersection (above);
interior of Lunds supermarket (below).*

residents also feel that the area is somewhat less "neighborly" than it was in the past. One resident pointed out the adverse effect of "the fences," maintaining that the sense of friendliness declined some years ago when many residents built fences around their back and side yards. In the late sixties the Como area, like other portions of this zone, took part in a code enforcement program. Residents were offered low-interest loans to make home improvements, streets were upgraded, and paving was replaced. This concerted effort to prevent blight from spreading into the area was quite successful.

Nonresidents perceive eastern Como as more run-down and transient than it actually is. It is a quite pleasant and well-maintained area, one that retains residents who could easily afford to live elsewhere. Downtown Minneapolis and the cultural facilities of the University are easily accessible. Although local shopping facilities have declined in recent years, most items can easily be gotten in nearby Dinkytown. A sampling of blocks in the area indicates that eastern Como is as stable as some portions of the suburban-in-city zone and far more stable than parts of the protected genteel districts. Interestingly, this area has been more successful at retaining residents than Prospect Park, which also 'serves the University's housing needs. Eastern Como continues to house clerks, skilled workers, and professionals. In fact, the number of residents affiliated with the University has increased in recent years.

East Calhoun

Perhaps the most satisfied residents of the settled mid-city zone are those who live in the lake district of South Minneapolis. The areas east of Lake of the Isles and Lake Calhoun developed around the turn of the century into solidly middle- and upper middle-class residential districts. As in other parts of the settled mid-city zone, development here was aligned with streetcar extensions. The areas closest to the Hennepin Avenue streetcar line developed first; those closer to the lakes were built up later. In the years between the late 1890s and the early 1920s these districts were filled in with architecturally interesting houses: late Victorian, classical revival, prairie style, and numerous independently crafted residences that blended several styles. Large single-family dwellings predominate, and some are of near-palatial proportions. Although most of the very wealthy lived on or near Lowry Hill, these nearby areas attracted many doctors, lawyers, and businessmen with high incomes. The evidence of their spending power remains on the landscape, though some houses have been removed to make way for commercial facilities. During the 1920s numerous apartment buildings were built to serve the many small households wanting to live close to the lakes. This initial challenge to the low density of these districts was formalized in the 1924 zoning ordinance. This in turn ensured that the next boom in multiunit construction would also be felt here. During the 1960s, portions of these districts were indeed subjected to major new apartment construction.

The only real change in East Calhoun over the years has been this increase in its population density. The district remains an extremely attractive residential environment, especially for unmarried young people. Opportunities for inexpensive recreation are abundant here, with Lake Calhoun's beaches and bike paths. And yet there is also room here for middle-class homeowners whose primary concern is property maintenance. Tolerance is one of the hallmarks of this area—a "live and let live" attitude prevails. In the last few years many homosexuals have moved into East Calhoun and begun extensive remodeling of older houses. Longtime residents do not view this trend with alarm; rather, they welcome the physical improvement that has occurred. This is in many ways an activist area. The East Calhoun Community Organization (ECCO), after which one district is now named, is one of the city's oldest neighborhood groups. ECCO works on development and housing issues, sponsors many social events, and publishes a neighborhood newspaper. East Calhoun is a settled mid-city district that exudes pride and satisfaction. But it is also ready to defend itself against threats of any kind.

CONCLUSION

Each of the settled mid-city districts owe their existence to streetcar expansion. Consequently, their early history is much the same. Developers hoping to attract middle-class families developed the areas a few blocks at a time between the turn of the century and the First World War. Most areas are close to some sort of physical amenity, but some are more directly associated with centers of employment. The appearance of the city-scapes varies somewhat throughout the zone because some districts have a higher percentage of large houses whereas others have greater concentrations of multiple family units. Today there is a range of incomes in the zone, but most residents have an income that approximates the Twin City average.

Despite their similarities, these districts are faced with different sets of problems. In some areas the major problem is the number of absentee landlords who do not maintain their property to the satisfaction of the nearby homeowners. In the district near Hamline University in Saint Paul, there is concern over the growing crime rate. Because all of this zone is either adjacent to or very close to the aging inner ring, most residents tend to worry about the spread of urban blight onto their blocks. Most often this is not articulated, but the concern over crime and absentee landlords is a clear expression of the uneasiness in the districts.

Although the settled mid-city zone is not large, it may be one of the pivotal areas within the Twin Cities. Its districts have remained a haven for middle-class families for over a half-century. If this zone is buttressed by continued investment and if the residents' confidence in the future is maintained, it should serve to stabilize the adjacent aging inner ring districts and prevent the deterioration of the prewar grid zone.

This scene in North Minneapolis is typical of the prewar grid zone in both Cities.

CHAPTER

VII

The Prewar Grid Zone

The prewar grid zone was the first area of the Twin Cities to be developed with the automobile in mind. Houses here were built with garages, and some particularly farsighted builders included garages in apartment buildings. The zone was built up between 1920 and 1933 to house the growing middle class, particularly tradesmen and middle managers. Although there are few prominent landscape features here, and open space is at a premium, the middle class has continued to be attracted to this zone because of its comfortable, family-oriented housing.

The zone stretches like a broken ring around the streetcar era districts. The pattern is not continuous because certain areas either were avoided by developers during the twenties or were already occupied by older industrial suburbs. There are also a few small and scattered districts located on the eastern and northern sides of Saint Paul and in south Minneapolis near the river. (See map 7.) In the southwestern section of Saint Paul, the zone is quite extensive. Here and in south Minneapolis the qualities of the zone are best preserved. The zone is laid out in a grid pattern—hence the name.

Because the prewar grid zone was constructed under generally the same economic conditions as those influencing the older communities in the Twin Cities, the differences between the present prewar grid zone and those portions of the older zones still in their original condition are difficult to see. (The development pattern of the prewar amenity zone, to be discussed in the next chapter, was similar to that of the prewar grid zone, but the physical landscape of the former is so distinctive that it is difficult to confuse the zone with the prewar grid zone and the older middle-class areas.) The essential difference between the prewar grid zone and the older communities is, of course, that the automobile was taken into account in the design and layout of prewar grid developments. Therefore, when you walk along the alleys of this zone you cannot find the small barns or carriage houses of the earlier developments. If you are lucky, you will find the small, or "model T," garages that were constructed to house the early cars. Although most of these garages were built of wood, a number of metal garages were also erected. Many of these buildings have been pulled down to make way for roomier structures needed by the larger cars of the fifties and sixties.

Residents of the prewar grid districts at first used the streetcar system to commute to work, but as an increasing number of people came to own automobiles, it became ever more popular to use the car not only for commuting but also on pleasure and shopping trips. Thus began a decline in the drawing power of entertainment and shopping facilities located in downtown areas. More and more stores and theaters relocated to areas that would attract customers arriving by car. This movement was most pronounced in the zone we call the suburban-in-city.

From the above, it can be seen that the prewar grid zone represents a transition zone both in location and in function. It lies between the older zones and the post-World War II developments, and it has to a large extent built around the existing pattern of streetcar lines, while also serving the needs of the automobile owner. Moreover, it embodies significant aspects of both the older and the newer building styles.

THE DEVELOPMENT PROCESS

The prewar grid zone is characterized by single-family bungalows, story-and-one-half structures, individualistic styles, and duplexes. Houses here are smaller than those in the older districts, owing to a decline in family size that began in the 1920s and which reached a historic low in the mid-1920s. During this period the three-bedroom home became the standard and kitchens became smaller. Gas and electricity made possible the development of household appliances. Apartments and duplexes became popular for the first time during this era. The duplex, or double house, excited large numbers of young couples who intended to buy a building and use the income from the second unit to offset the loan payments. The size and quality of the duplexes varied considerably. In some locations three-bedroom units with fireplaces and fine interior finishes were constructed. In others the duplexes were smaller and had fewer design features.

The fashion that we continue to refer to as modern was popularized during the twenties and thirties, although these principles of high design seem to have had a rather limited influence on the prewar grid districts of Minneapolis and Saint Paul. The architect-designed homes built during this period were constructed in the prewar amenity zone rather than in these districts. A few poor man's versions of the prairie school styles exist in the prewar grid districts, but for most people the modern style was not the uncluttered open interior spaces of the Chicago school but a Spanish neo-colonial patterned after California suburban housing.

Saint Paul's 1922 zoning law designated fringe grid districts as either A or B residential. The difference between the two classifications is that the A zone has large lots and no apartments. Duplexes, schools, and churches could be built in both zones. This land-use compromise was necessary because people did not take to using the car as extensively as they would twenty years later. Most workers continued to commute by streetcar, and walking was still an accepted human activity. As a result, services were built within the districts. Large churches were built on residential blocks, some by new congregations; other buildings housed congregations relocated from the older sections of the city. Even though most households in the zone had a car, habits were slow to die and the churches were built without thought of providing parking lots. Small stores located on corners of the nearby commercial street were common and popular.

The burgeoning population also needed schools, which were built with large playgrounds. The location of these buildings gives us an indication of the sense of place that pervaded these communities as well as the philosophy of urban life that dominated intellectual writing of the time. These were "neighborhood" schools. Pupils were expected to walk to and from homes within a mile radius of the buildings. In addition, the population living in the vicinity of the school was expected to and did view the school as the center of their community.

The homogeneous population of the prewar grid zone had many racist feelings. They did not want immigrants from Southern and Eastern Europe living in their communities. Anti-Semitism was very strong here and elsewhere in the Twin Cities. During the First World War a trickle of blacks began moving into Minneapolis, and received a hostile reception. In fact, the Ku Klux Klan was active in the Twin Cities during these years. Residents of this zone were caught up in the prevailing fears of the day and attempted to protect themselves and their community from invasions of newer immigrants. A large percentage of the people who moved into the new houses came from older neighborhoods that were being abandoned to the Jews and Italians.

Real estate developers and salesmen were the image builders who worked hard to promote the image of an ideal community in the prewar grid districts. The general literacy

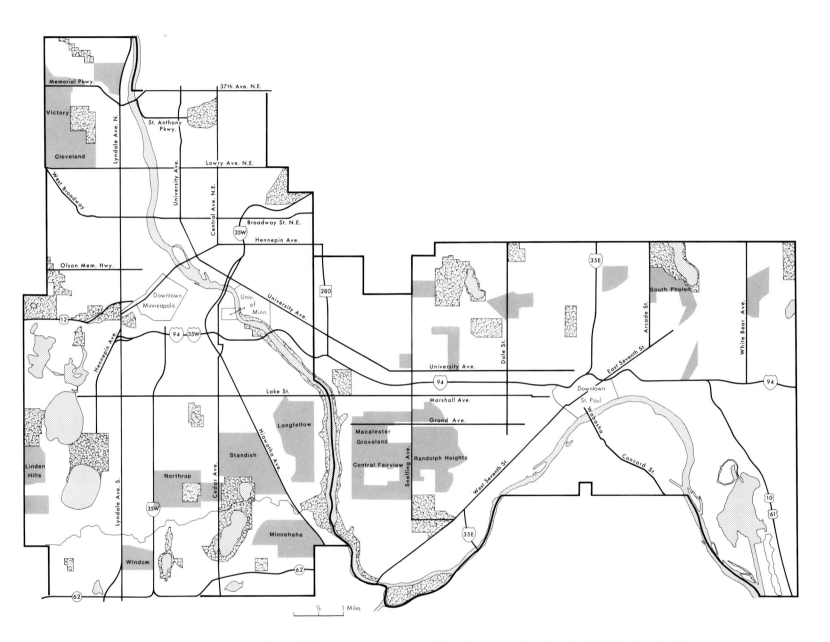

Map 7: The Prewar Grid Zone. This zone includes some of the first parts of both cities built for households with automobiles. Its residents have been and continue to be workers with stable jobs.

of the population and popularity of newspapers made advertising a potent tool in the cause of urban development. Many individuals believed the newspaper ads and participated in the subdivision of land themselves. Hundreds speculated on individual town lots. It was quite common for a household to buy two adjacent lots, build their home on one, and keep the other as a garden or part of their lawn for a few years, waiting for its value to increase before selling it.

Little is known about the individuals who had the greatest influence on the development of the zone. Although people who promoted real estate in the last years of the nineteenth century have gone into history books as the founders of both cities, the second generation of developers has largely been forgotten. Den E. Lane (1881-1952) was one of these people. An Irish immigrant and graduate of Saint Thomas College, Lane began speculating in real estate in Saint Paul while still a student. He was known as the "own your home man," because he was such a strong advocate of private, single-family housing. He apparently was the leading developer in Saint Paul in the 1920s and 1930s. He created the Highland Park area of the city and developed residential districts along the Mississippi River boulevard and on the city's eastern and northern boundaries. He is reputed to have handled more than ten thousand property transactions by 1925. By his own reckoning he laid out and named 50 percent of the new streets added to the city between the mid-teens and mid-twenties. His career spans the era in which this zone was developed, for he laid out the last streets in his Highland Park development in 1945.

The prewar grid zone was developed by men like Lane whose ideas about urban landscapes were formed during the streetcar era. Their genius was their ability to foresee the impact of the private car on development. At first they believed that the car would be a supplemental form of transportation, and they sold land within a quarter mile of streetcar lines. As the sales of cars increased during the twenties, promoters soon realized that it would be possible to live beyond an easy walk from the streetcar lines, and a new land boom was on. The Stock Market Crash ended the boom and the careers of many speculators. During the 1930s paved streets ran through open fields in Lane's Highland Park development. He continued the pattern of the 1920s, building houses for middle-class families at low

cost and selling land to individuals wishing to build a more substantial structure with a private contractor.

Today, with many houses enlarged and tall trees surrounding them, the prewar grid zone is a uniformly pleasant urban environment.

HOW THE DEVELOPMENT OF THE PREWAR GRID DISTRICTS AFFECTED THE CONCEPT OF THE NEIGHBORHOOD

At the close of the nineteenth century, working-class households were confined to inner-city ethnic communities near their place of employment, while the wealthy were moving to more pleasant settings at the edge of the city. The development of the streetcar system allowed the middle class to move away from the center, but the coming of the First World War interrupted the process. During the economic boom of the twenties, large numbers of households accumulated enough money to move into new housing at the edge of the city. The combined income of young couples allowed them to enter the housing market sooner than their parents had. This was particularly true of second-generation immigrants who were able to leave the ethnic communities of their parents and become integrated into the new districts. The grid areas being developed were attractive to lower middle-class households. Housing was affordable, the streetcar lines provided adequate transportation in some sections of the zone, and cars were available for commuting from houses more than a quarter-mile from a streetcar line. Builders cited the convenient location, the affordable housing, and the lower population density to attract home buyers to this zone.

The concept of neighborhoods was also a part of the sales pitch. This notion was picked up from sociological theories that argued that residential areas of cities consisted of small pieces, called "natural areas." Particular areas were said to attract a certain kind of household, and once in an area individauls were further differentiated from people living elsewhere. These urban residential areas were thought by some to be partway between the idyllic rural villages and the harsh, impersonal industrial city. Home ownership was good, local control of government was good, and segregation into natural areas was the way things should be.

Today we look back nostalgically on the way of life that characterized these districts when they were new and consider it the ideal urban life-style. In fact, such communities served as the model for postwar urban developments. Young families, headed by individuals raised in such areas, sought to find a similar situation in the postwar suburbs. Central-city politicians still seek to develop programs that will reestablish neighborhoods of this variety in the modern city. It is therefore necessary to look at the features of this zone that produced the sense of place so envied by succeeding generations.

The new districts were less densely settled than the other parts of the city, making them attractive to households wishing to raise children. The pleasant backyards and school playgrounds of this zone gave children ample recreational space. In addition, these districts were close to the actual edge of the built-up area. Consequently, the more adventurous children roamed the fields beyond the city.

POPULATION

Residents of the zone in the 1970s have nearly the same demographic and social characteristics as did the zone's original occupants. (See table 6, p. 148.) After the Second World War a great cultural shift occurred in Saint Paul. It was then that the Jewish population moved through the district. Today in Saint Paul the Jewish population is concentrated in the Highland Park area, where families live in houses built over a thirty-year period. Except for this major change, little about the contemporary population or landscape of the zone would surprise its builders.

Homeowners are still in control of these districts. In some sections over 80 percent of the households own their housing unit, which is usually a modest single-family home. (Multifamily units in most of these districts average less than 10 percent of the total dwelling units—a figure comparable to that in most of the suburban-in-city districts.) The people are older now, and there are a considerable number of single-person households. In most districts income levels match or are a little higher than the city-wide median. There is approximately a $2,000 variation in average income over the zone. The inflation-adjusted incomes of households in this zone have not increased in recent years, although in a few districts an immigration of higher-status

Groveland School (above) and the now-razed Mattocks School (below). These two Saint Paul schools, built in the 1920s, served as focal points for local residents. The recent decline in school-age children caused the closing of Mattocks and other schools in this zone.

households has occurred. The income levels in the districts are greatly affected by the high percentage of households living on fixed incomes. In this zone about 30 percent of the households are retired, as compared with a figure of about 25 percent for Minneapolis and Saint Paul. Only those districts with high- and mid-rise apartment buildings designed for the elderly have a greater fraction of the population over age sixty-five.

The total population of the zone has declined in recent years owing to the shrinking size of families. The total number of households has remained essentially unchanged, however. This pattern has been the norm for most cities in recent years. Its chief impact seems to be the decline in school enrollments.

Because the houses in this zone are by and large less than a half-century old, maintenance is not a problem. When asked about problems in their districts, residents reported only two anxieties: the lack of open space and the concern about continued property maintenance. The shortage of recreational space stems from the fact that these areas were planned by realtors before small parks became fashionable. As a result, most of the districts are an uncomfortable walking distance from the large parks that were laid out at the edge of the cities or are across busy streets from the few major playgrounds in the zone. There is little to be done about this problem because all the available land is covered with structures. Park and recreation departments in both cities cannot afford the cost of clearing houses to get open space. In a few districts school sites may be available for community recreation when they are declared to be surplus or obsolete by the school board.

The concern over maintenance levels is the result of people believing in theories about the process of neighborhood turnover and the filtering of houses from one income group to another. We have been told for decades that neighborhoods, like water, run downhill. This self-fulfilling prophecy makes everyone nervous. Will today's unmowed grass lead to tomorrow's peeling paint? This fear will be present in all districts as long as individuals lack confidence in each other.

Stability is a prominent characteristic of the zone. Sample areas of the south Minneapolis portion of the zone indicate that from 60 to 75 percent of the residents have lived in the same house for ten years or more. From its inception this zone has sheltered skilled workers and service workers. Although the housing was sound and income levels reflected a middle-class population, professionals and managers did not choose to live in these districts. But our recent experience with inflated housing prices has brought in some professionals, who could obtain good housing at affordable prices here. As pressure on the cities' housing supply increases, some of the prewar grid districts will be considered better and better places to live by middle-class professionals.

COMMERCIAL FACILITIES

The zoning laws of the 1920s concentrated commercial land use along the streetcar routes, and so residents of the prewar grid districts shopped with their neighbors from other districts. The growth of the zone's population prompted new establishments to open, and the shopping strips were gradually filled in. Neighborhood movie theaters, with facades of pseudo-Moorish or modern design, became common during these years and attracted considerable numbers of area children and young adults. Drug stores with soda fountains, confectioneries, and other shops provided both conveniences and a friendly meeting place for residents of the district.

The quality of the construction in the new districts, the national prosperity, and international peace of the twenties combined to give residents of the zone a profound sense of well-being. Politicians were also pleased with the development of this area because new land was entered on the tax roles and the population of the city was increasing. Downtown merchandising was profitable because the zone's population still looked to the city center for specialty products and entertainment.

The commercial configuration established during the twenties holds residual problems for current residents. Over time neighborhood stores lost trade, as did commercial facilities on the streetcar lines, primarily as a result of suburban competition. There were few genuine strips and no centers in this zone to begin with, so there is not much that can be revived. The commercial centers that did evolve appeared in the nearby prewar amenity districts. Consequently, residents of the prewar grid zone must drive elsewhere to do their shopping. In Minneapolis, residents of the northside districts shop at Brookdale, and residents of the southwest districts shop in Edina, especially at South-dale. Residents of the districts south of Lake Street and east of Hiawatha find it most convenient to shop in Highland Park across the river in Saint Paul.

The low-rent character of commercial facilities in this zone has enabled some rather old-fashioned services to flourish here. Two of the best butcher shops in the Twin Cities, each located within a modest-sized grocery store, draw customers from far outside the local area. Handmade chocolate is available in both the Minneapolis and Saint Paul portions of the zone. The south Minneapolis districts are dotted with tiny cafes, able to seat no more than eight to ten people. These places serve hearty meals and cater to the social aspects of coffee drinking for their Scandinavian customers.

DISTRICTS OF THE PREWAR GRID ZONE

Attempting to describe the prewar grid districts in detail presents some challenges. There is little about these districts that stands out, except to the most intimate observer. The landscape meets almost everyone's preconceived idea of what middle-class urban housing looks like. There are few anomalies here; large houses from an earlier period and apartment buildings are both in short supply. But though these districts may all look more alike than those in other zones, there are perceptible differences among them.

South Phalen Park

This prewar grid residential district is bounded on the northeast by the shore of Lake Phalen, on the west by Arcade Street, and on the south by Maryland Avenue. The area does not have a name in the folk geography of Saint Paul. We will refer to it as South Phalen Park. Although this district is close to Phalen Park, the course of its development was not greatly influenced by the park. The presence of a state hospital on the edge of the park provided an institutional atmosphere for the locale.

There are 1,445 housing units in the district. The number of housing units declined slightly in the 1970s, there are very few vacancies and the housing market is very tight.

The current population of this district is about 3,800,

living in 1,429 households. The average household size in this area is somewhat larger than it is in the city as a whole, but it is about the same as that found in other districts made up of large numbers of single-family houses. There has been a reduction of the total population in the district in recent years owing to the removal of a dozen or so housing units and the lower birthrate in the city. The decline has been so small, however, that when compared with other districts the population here seems to be essentially unchanged.

Families with children are not as common in the district as they once were. In 1978 some 34 percent of the households had children, which is essentially the same as the city-wide rate. This figure is considerably smaller than that in the adjacent suburban-in-city zone, where up to 45 or 50 percent of the households have children. The lower rate is due to the fact that many mature couples whose children have left home still live in the houses they used to rear their families. In addition, when people leave the district they are frequently replaced by couples without children. The prewar grid zone is still attractive to young families, but a net outmigration of families with children may indicate that the conditions for rearing children here are deteriorating. This is a cause for concern.

Single-person households are becoming more common in the districts as individuals move into apartments formerly occupied by couples and small families. Retired individuals make up a sizable portion of the district's population. In fact over a third of the households are headed by retired individuals. This is much the same throughout the zone. It would seem that the population is neatly divided into thirds: retired households, families with children, and adults without children. Most of the latter are middle aged.

Although the number of professionals in the district is declining, South Phalen Park is still a middle-class area. Most of the population are skilled trade persons and middle-level white-collar workers. Professionals and managers make up about 14 percent of the households, a figure which is lower than the fraction of such households within Saint Paul. It is also lower than the percentage of such house-holders in most other parts of the zone. In this respect the South Phalen Park district resembles the population of the greater East Side which is more blue collar than other sections of Saint Paul.

This combination of high-paid skilled tradesmen and

middle-level managers gives the area an average income somewhat higher than the average for Saint Paul. The total income in the area remained steady during the 1970s, and there is no indication that the income situation will change in the near future.

Central Fairview District

The large section of the prewar grid zone that lies in the southwestern quadrant of Saint Paul contains many subtle differences and is occupied by a population without a well-developed sense of place. The area is best understood in terms of a small but representative district which we are calling Central Fairview for lack of an official name. This district is bounded on the north by Saint Clair, on the west by Cleveland, on the south by Highland Parkway, and on the east by Snelling Avenue. (Note that it is slightly larger than the Central Fairview area for which data are presented in table 6, p. 148.) Fairview Avenue forms a seam between the eastern and western portions of the area. Although there are few commercial facilities on the avenue to provide residents with space for social activities, most people drive along it several times during the week. Therefore it is a well-known part of the landscape and serves as a landmark for the local population.

There has been little change in the make-up of the landscape in this district in recent years. Along the fringes, commercial development and apartment construction have combined to make the boundaries of the district more sharply defined. Of late, a few more large apartments have been constructed, and some commercial structures have been put to new uses, the most obvious of these being the conversion of corner gas stations into office buildings and professional offices.

The area has been attractive to homebuyers throughout its history. Today the vacancy rate is extremely low. Only the suburban-in-city zone in the northeast corner of the city had a lower percentage of vacant units in 1978. Houses along the heavily trafficked streets are frequently on the market, but they sell very quickly.

Central Fairview has a population of about 7,600, up slightly from the early 1970s. This growth results from the formation of new families. Here, as in the new areas of single-family housing, young couples settle in, expecting to have children and to rear them in pleasant surroundings. As a result, the average household size in the area is somewhat larger than that in most areas of the city. The birthrate in Central Fairview is undoubtedly also affected by the large population of Roman Catholics in the district. One of Saint Paul's largest parishes, Nativity, is located here and continues to attract those families interested in being part of an active congregation. About one-third of households have children residing at home, which is about the same figure as that for the city as a whole and considerably less than that for the suburban-in-city zone.

There are about 2,100 housing units in Central Fairview. About 80 percent of the households own their homes. Only a handful of residential districts have a higher proportion of owner-occupied housing units. On many streets in the area, every house on the block is owner-occupied. Renters are concentrated in apartments and a few single-family houses that have been converted to duplexes. Although the houses here are quite comfortable, they are not large. A four-bedroom house is quite uncommon, and only buildings with postwar additions have more than four sleeping rooms.

Only a quarter of the households in the district consist of a single person, as compared with 37 percent in the Macalester Park area. Other districts adjacent to the Central Fairview district also have more single-person households. Most people in Central Fairview live in residual families—married couples with grown children. The eastern portion of the district, which is heavily influenced by multiple-family units, has had an ever so slight increase in single-person households during the late 1970s.

There appears to be an interesting trend in this part of the district. The number of retired households is slightly higher than the average for the city, but it is declining because there has been a net outmigration of retired persons from the area. Many of these people are leaving the state, whereas others are moving into group or institutional quarters. Their places are being taken by couples without children. Many of these young couples may eventually have children, but they have decided to postpone indefinitely the starting of their families. Therefore, the district has some potential for rapid demographic change.

While the entire district is certainly dominated by middle-class households, the number of high-status individuals is not especially great. In 1978 approximately 26 percent of the household heads were employed in professional or managerial careers. This is higher than the city rate but much lower than the rate in adjacent districts. The elite population in Central Fairview has been stable, whereas that in some older districts has increased.

In terms of income, this district is a transition zone between the lower-income families occupying the settled mid-city zone and the aging inner ring to the north and east, and the suburban-in-city and prewar amenity districts to the south and west. It is possible to see the effects of this income differential in the landscape as one moves through the district. Housing is better maintained, landscaping more elaborate, and alleys are cleaner in this area than in the areas to the north. Nonetheless, the Highland Park district to the south receives a greater annual investment in lawn care and housing maintenance. The most visible evidence of this difference can be seen on a summer weekday. As one travels south from Saint Clair to Highland Parkway, the number of lawn service crews cutting grass, trimming hedges, sweeping sidewalks, and raking leaves steadily increases.

The configuration of income and status in Central Fairview is accounted for by two factors. First, the housing in the Central Fairview district is rather plain. It was well built and has been very well maintained, but it was never intended to house people interested in decorative architecture. In addition, the topography of the district is not particularly interesting. The major landmarks are playgrounds which are not known to attract higher-income people. Unless there is a dramatic and unprecedented increase in the demand for in-city houses among the higher-income groups, Central Fairview should continue to shelter the middle-income families and childless couples, of the sort who were attracted to it in the 1950s and 1960s, well into the future.

Like other parts of the inner city, Central Fairview has attracted young couples interested in owning their own homes but unable to purchase housing in the suburbs and unwilling to undertake extensive remodeling projects that typify the turnaround districts. Many of these households have two incomes, and this enables them to move into homes at a younger age than their parents' generation could. The life-style of this group is slightly different from their more established neighbors. They patronize the food co-ops located just outside the district. They choose to ride the bus rather than drive, and they can frequently be seen riding

Cleveland commercial strip, Saint Paul.

bikes or jogging on the quiet streets. In short, the culture of the Central Fairview district seems to be undergoing subtle and gradual changes. This is not a trendy area, and it is unlikely to become an "in" place to live. Nonetheless, white-collar households, civil servants, accountants, and teachers are slowly taking over the area.

The new residents may have some long-term impact on the conservatism of the area. This district is one of the many areas where "single issue" politics are dominant. Here the right-to-life issue figures in nearly every election. Politicians must be absolutely sure of their positions on the issues if thy intend to serve this population. It would appear that the newcomers are politically inactive and apathetic at present. Yet they are well educated and therefore have the potential to be an important local political force should a cause compel their attention.

Until that happens, Central Fairview and the other districts in the zone will remain parts of the city that people drive through quickly. The especially observant visitor may notice a neat house and quiet street and thereby may be moved to make a comment about the "nice neighborhood." But it will remain a vague unknown area in most people's mental maps of the Twin Cities.

109

Northrup-Standish

Like Central Fairview and South Phalen, the Northrup-Standish area of South Minneapolis is not well known to most city residents. There is little reason for those who do not live in the area to go there. If people recognize this area at all, it is probably from speeding along its eastern border (Hiawatha Avenue) from downtown to the airport—not a vantage point that would yield an intimate knowledge of any area. The boundaries of Northrup are Chicago Avenue to Cedar Avenue and 42nd Street to 48th Street. Standish extends from Cedar to Hiawatha, and from 36th Street to 43rd Street. Like most of the prewar grid zone, these districts developed slowly during the 1920s and 1930s. Many lots were left empty until the late forties. This pace of development left an impression of homogeneous facades, though few houses were exactly alike.

The local topography was part of the reason for the leisurely pace of building in these districts. Northrup-Standish encompassed some low-lying parcels of land with severe drainage problems. During the twenties and thirties builders avoided these parcels, leaving the pattern of development somewhat spotty. Some of the most swampy blocks were eventually pumped out and turned into parks or playgrounds (e.g., Sibley Field). Even today the prewar grid districts of South Minneapolis contain some of the areas most prone to flooding in the entire city. The blocks where residents routinely canoe down their streets after a heavy summer storm are primarily in these districts.

The Northrup-Standish area is unlike other prewar grid districts in certain respects. The residents of this part of Minneapolis are overwhelmingly Scandinavian, including many former immigrants who are now senior citizens. "Ole," "Sven," and "Bergit" are common first names here. This was one of the preferred settlement regions for Swedes and Norwegians who had "made it" by the 1920s. Many residents moved here from Seven Corners and from Seward once they had good jobs and could afford a house. The Scandinavian background of area residents led to the establishment of complementary institutions. Northrup and Standish are full of Protestant churches, particularly Lutheran ones. Not only are the churches visible, but so is their ethnic diversity. Swedes, Norwegians, Danes, and their descendants each have their own religious institutions, often within a block or two of one another. Bakeries are a common element of local commerce—quite in keeping with the legendary Scandinavian devotion to cakes and tortes.

Perhaps the best way to convey a sense of the Northrup-Standish area is to describe part of it in some detail. A small portion of the Standish area will serve as an example of the larger district. This segment extends from 38th Street to 42nd Street and from Cedar Avenue to 21st Avenue South. The fourteen blocks of residences surround Sibley Field, the major recreational site for a much larger area. The housing in this small area is overwhelmingly composed of single-family houses, though a few duplexes and small apartment buildings appear near Cedar. Most of the houses are small, rather closely spaced, in good repair. There are few definable styles of architecture to be found here. Stucco bungalows and aluminum-sided boxes predominate, though an occasional cabinlike structure can also be found.

The life-style of this area, like much of the prewar grid zone, is family-oriented. Children are constantly underfoot, often using the streets as playgrounds. Sibley Field is used by everyone. Children congregate on the playground at the south end, and from April until early October adults monopolize the ballfields on the north end. Few residents hold white-collar jobs with working hours from nine to five. Car engines start roaring around 7:00 A.M. as residents set off for work; many men are home by 4:30 P.M; and lights are out by 10:30 P.M. Traditional mores are highly valued here. People worry about their children and about outside influences on them. They also worry about the value of their homes and the future of the immediate area. Evidence of deterioration is close enough at hand to make residents wary of even small changes.

The Northrup area, just south and west of Standish, developed a bit more slowly. It was only about half filled-in by 1940. Most of the retail establishments and churches in the area were not built until the 1950s when residential construction resumed after the war. Interviews with long-time residents revealed some interesting aspects of the area. Most residents had lived in the area twenty years or more, and most had grown up in nearby areas. When people moved into the Northrup area, whether in the 1930s or the 1950s, the only other residential option seemed to be in similar parts of the north side. Because most of these people had

One of the many small cafes found in the heavily Scandinavian section of South Minneapolis.

some attachment to south Minneapolis, this location seemed a more natural choice.

For most people the Northrup area had several distinct advantages: a new elementary school (in the 1950s), good public transit, and excellent fire protection. Most people also thought the area was a good one in which to raise children, and this was one reason they moved here. Many people could identify the area's advantages: its centrality, safety, and the high level of home maintenance. They were also aware of potentially harmful changes; the closing of the grammar school and a slight increase in petty crimes were frequently mentioned in this regard. Everyone felt strong ties to the area, but also said they would move away if it began to "deteriorate." As in other parts of the prewar grid zone, residents here are very practical people, seeking to protect their investments in their homes at all costs.

CONCLUSION

The various districts of the prewar grid zone were developed in response to the growth of commuting that resulted from the dramatic improvement in transportation facilities during the 1920s. In those years the streetcars still provided

excellent service, and the improved and affordable automobiles made it possible to drive to work from areas without streetcar service. The developers of this zone laid out communities for tradesmen and middle managers. The result has been a solidly middle-class population. In the 1970s these people enjoyed good incomes. Like other middle-class households, they have continued to invest in their property.

The occupants of the prewar grid zone, like all other middle-class residents of the Twin Cities, are worried about the increasing costs for home heating and about maintaining their aging houses. In addition, they must deal with a relative shortage of recreation facilities. This problem will become worse as schools are closed and as housing is constructed on the abandoned school sites. Each of these problems is essentially beyond the control of the individual households, but is subject to the influence of collective action. For example, group purchasing and shared labor will greatly diminish the cost of home repair. Nonetheless, the population of the prewar grid area seems to be composed of very private individuals who have shown little inclination to join neighborhood associations. Such reluctance may disappear if conditions in the zone worsen and households feel an actual threat.

111

The shore of Lake Harriet typifies the open space found in this zone.

CHAPTER

VIII

The Prewar Amenity Zone

Certain residential areas in Minneapolis and Saint Paul are highly prized, and well used, by both outsiders and local residents. Houses here are much sought after and tend to sell quickly because they are all located on, or within easy walking distance of, a major amenity. Sites near the lakes in both cities come most quickly to mind, but the amenity zone is not limited to lakeside areas. It also includes stretches of land along the Mississippi River and along Minnehaha Creek, some areas near large parks, and one section of Northeast Minneapolis located atop a hill of near-San Francisco proportions.

The landscape of the prewar amenity zone is among the most inviting in either city. The terrain is broken up by occasional hills and rolling areas. All of this zone offers relief from the standard urban grid pattern. Although grid streets are still the norm, they offer abundant vistas of trees or water. Grid street patterns are regularly interrupted by avenues that curve alongside the river, a lake, or the creek. The most common landscape feature throughout this district is open space—the extensive system of wooded parks and boulevards. Where they have not been decimated, tall elms form cathedral ceilings over most streets. The elm trees are joined by conifers, cedars, maples, and other vegetation, particularly along Minnehaha Creek.

Districts in the prewar amenity zone have more than physical amenities in common. Much of the zone was inaccessible during the streetcar era, so the majority of houses date from the 1920s and 1930s. The housing is more varied here than it is in most other zones. This variety is not due to a high incidence of architect-designed houses, as in the protected genteel zone, but rather to the fact that builders in the prewar amenity zone constructed houses individually, often for a particular client. Aesthetic variation came about naturally as a result of the differences in people's tastes.

A special quality of this district is its quiet nature. To be sure, on a weekend this zone has more than its fair share of runners, joggers, walkers, and children on bicycles. Parts of the zone must contend with either freeway or airport noise. But it is also possible, on a weekday afternoon, to encounter an unexpected stillness. The prewar amenity zone epitomizes the urban forest at its finest.

The prewar amenity zone in Minneapolis is much more extensive than that in Saint Paul, owing to the presence in Minneapolis of Minnehaha Creek and many lakes. (See map 8.) Ninety percent of the prewar amenity districts in Minneapolis are in the southern half of the city, forming a semicircular pattern. Beginning at Bryn Mawr and the western shores of Cedar Lake, the zone extends down the western shores of Calhoun and Harriet, eastward along Minnehaha Creek, and then northward along the Mississippi bluff. This zone also includes a section of Northeast Minneapolis near Deming Heights and eastward along St. Anthony Parkway. The prewar amenity zone in Minneapolis comprises about 15 percent of the city's residential area.

Only three small pieces of the prewar amenity zone are located in Saint Paul. All three are situated near parkland: the first is along the Mississippi gorge on either side of the Seminary of Saint Paul and west of Cretin Avenue; the second lies just northeast of Lake Como; and the third is a narrow strip of housing along Edgecumbe Road near Highland Park and Golf Course.

HISTORICAL DEVELOPMENT

The development of this zone was not linked to the expansion of public transit. Like most of the prewar grid zone, these areas were intended for people who owned automobiles or who could afford to spend extra time commuting to work. A few streetcars did extend into this zone as early as 1905: the Central Avenue line went to the city limits in Northeast Minneapolis, and both the Nicollet Avenue and Hiawatha lines went as far south as 50th Street. There were even a few houses constructed by that time. This was a clear example of streetcars being extended beyond the line of profitable service in anticipation of, and certainly encouraging, future growth. By 1940, when this zone was almost fully built up, it was well served by radial lines from downtown.

The entire zone filled in slowly during the twenties and thirties, and not all available land was used by 1940. Low-lying fields that were too swampy for inexpensive development or were unattractive to potential residents remained empty until the postwar housing demand made it economically feasible to build on them.

Perhaps the hallmark of the prewar amentiy zone's development was its relatively slow pace and individualistic character. Housing here, unlike that in some older parts of the Twin Cities, was not constructed hastily. Each house was built to reflect the taste of either its builder or the person for whom it was constructed. During the 1920s and 1930s there were still many craftsmen who took pride in their work. Great pains were taken even with the small bungalows in the prewar grid district. Given the more lavish budgets of people in the prewar amenity zone, even more diversity was possible. The great building boom of the 1920s is evident in the zone: most of the land near the lakes and north of Minnehaha Creek got built up then. During the late 1930s, after the WPA had bridged the Creek in several places and sculpted Minnehaha Park, the area south of Lake Harriet and the Creek began to fill in with houses.

It is important to remember what a barrier Minnehaha Creek and its ravine were to the normal pattern of development. They were large enough to thwart private developers from building their own bridges so that they could construct houses on both sides of the Creek. Unlike the Mississippi River, though, this barrier was not sufficiently large for the city to take action. Lowry's streetcar company bridged the Creek at Bryant Avenue at its own expense, to encourage further high-income settlement to the southwest. East and west of Lake Nokomis, unsettled areas bordered middle-class and worker's housing north of the Creek. It was not clear that any private investment would be made to increase this supply of housing, so the WPA efforts served this corner of Minneapolis as well.

People's motives for moving to these districts when they first opened were fully consistent with traditional American values. Houses here were better (i.e., newer), if not bigger, than they were elsewhere in the city. And homes came equipped with every "modern" convenience. This part of the city was "countrylike," but still had plenty of urban services: streetcars, nearby markets, and local schools. These districts contained every advantage of city living but none of the disadvantages. This is still a large part of their attraction today.

POPULATION AND HOUSING

The people who originally occupied this zone had higher incomes and better jobs than the population at large. They were the professionals and managers who emerged in great numbers during the 1920s, and they were the people who survived the Depression with either their assets or their careers intact. They were not the elite of the city—that group was already abandoning Minneapolis and Saint Paul for Minnetonka and White Bear—but they were just a step

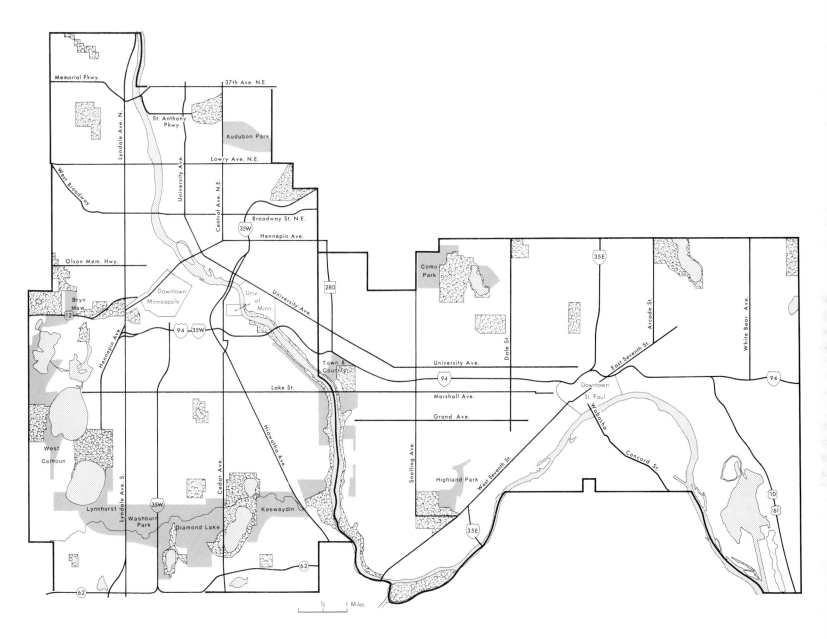

Map 8: The Prewar Amenity Zone. This zone contains amenities such as lakes, creeks, and extremely rolling terrain. Housing in most sections is large and expensive.

Spanish colonial house in South Minneapolis is one of many examples of Period Revival architecture found in this zone.

or two down the socioeconomic ladder. This is a fair description of current residents of this zone as well.

Today's residents of the prewar amenity zone are among the best housed and most financially secure in either city. Income levels here tend to be much higher than average. As might be expected, professional and managerial occupations predominate in this zone, but a larger percentage of these households still appear in the protected genteel districts. Certain occupational groups are attracted to particular districts: more blue-collar workers live in Bryn Mawr than elsewhere; and more business owners live on the parkways on both sides of the Mississippi. Bryn Mawr is also the most ethnically diverse of these districts, retaining clear traces of its Finnish background.

The population of these districts is predominantly two-parent families with children. (See table 7, p. 148). Household size in almost every part of the zone is well above average. The presence of children is taken for granted in this zone, but recently there have been indications that some families with children are moving away. A partial explanation for this may be the closing of public schools, which local residents strongly oppose. Retired people who live in this zone usually have spent most of their lives here—it is not an area to which older people move. Subsidized housing for the elderly was unheard of in the zone until very recently, when a few buildings of this type appeared.

The prewar amenity districts are among the most stable in either city. Close to 70 percent of the people who live here have been in their houses for ten years or more. Interestingly, residents' attachments to these areas seemed to increase in the 1970s. In some areas home ownership has been increasing slightly from already high levels.

Over 90 percent of the structures in the prewar amenity zone are owner-occupied, single-family houses. Houses here are not ostentatious, though they tend to be larger than average. Most are set on adequate-to-large-sized lots. Almost nowhere in this zone does the environment feel cramped.

The houses themselves represent a wide range of styles and architectural trends. The influences of contemporary European building fashions are apparent. So are both traditional and more modern American styles. Two-story brick Georgians or half-timbered Tudors are found next to clapboard or brick Colonial Revival-style houses. These shapes are all quite conspicuous, as are their clay-tiled or

116

colorfully patterned shingle roofs. Far less numerous are the low-lying, boxlike "prairie" style houses and some streamlined Art Deco dwellings. The zone also includes a few blocks of modified-ranch houses and bungalows dating from the 1950s.

Many houses fall into a category that might be called "arts and crafts" style. These can vary greatly, but they share vaguely English antecedents. Most often they are stucco boxes with low-pitched hipped roofs, and one or more porches. These houses are also found in great numbers throughout the settled mid-city zone. A contractor could easily modify this style of house to fit a client's wishes. It was the style most favored by the suburbanizing middle class—and this zone shares many traits with 1920s suburbs in other metropolitan areas.

In addition to the single-family dwellings in the zone, there are a few older, elegant apartment buildings gracing the western shore of Lake Calhoun. Some newer apartments and condominiums have been constructed there and along Minnehaha Creek. Because there is a great demand for housing in these locations, pressure for this kind of investment is strong, especially near Lake Calhoun.

Housing values fall into the highest category in almost every part of this zone. The composite picture that emerges is that of a well-tended residential area that is ideally suited for anyone who can afford to live here. These districts remain a bastion of upper middle-class families.

COMMERCIAL DEVELOPMENT

Commercial establishments in the prewar amenity zone developed along the various streetcar routes, as they did in other parts of both cities. The one exception to this was the commercial strip along Lyndale Avenue in Minneapolis, two blocks away from the Bryant Avenue streetcar. During the 1920s and 1930s small local centers appeared every six blocks or so on the streetcar lines. They usually had a grocery store, a drugstore, a hardware store, and occasionally a barber shop or a creamery. Most of these commercial centers remained relatively small. They were a counterpart to today's convenience stores; the area they served was limited to the distance people were willing to walk for small purchases.

Each of these small centers remains viable today. Most have a service station, a real estate or insurance office, and a convenience store like 7-11 or Tom Thumb. In Minneapolis, a few "neighborhood" movie theaters have managed to survive in this zone; the Hollywood, the Boulevard, and the Parkway all have discount showings of recent first-run films, and seem to attract sizable crowds. These small commercial centers continue to exist in the face of competition from nearby large supermarkets and regional shopping centers. Their ability to do this clearly testifies to the strength of the market in this zone.

Only one of the "neighborhood" centers in this zone served a larger market. This was the section of Lyndale Avenue between 53rd and 55th Streets. Even before World War II, this area had grown into a sizable shopping district. It had several drugstores (one with an old-time ice cream parlor), several hardware stores, gas stations, bakeries, and corner groceries, and perhaps the first Dairy Queen in Minneapolis. In addition to these common services, the area boasted a bowling alley, a car dealership, a large garage, a large lumberyard, a candy factory, and the Boulevard Twins theater with its wraparound restaurant. A good-sized business block contained a hairdresser, an insurance agency, a real estate office, a women's accessory shop, and a shoe store. One former resident fondly recalled a staple of every urban childhood: the decrepit storefront run by a mean old man who collected pop bottles and sold penny candy and ice cream. By the late thirties this area also featured one of the earliest "supermarkets" (Super Valu).

Until the Hub Shopping Center opened in the early fifites, this was the largest commercial area below Lake Street in all of south Minneapolis. The Lyndale strip served a captive market that was large and relatively well-off. Like most commercial areas inside the Twin Cities, this strip began to decline in the mid-fifties. Competition from the new suburban shopping malls was keenly felt—Southdale was less than three miles away. There was no room to expand parking facilities, and the large market the Lyndale strip had served was being drawn to newer and larger facilities with parking. The strip clearly had to shrink back to a small scale. During the 1960s, some businesses closed, and old buildings were torn down. The only expansion taking place was that of Bermel-Smaby realty, who transformed the Boulevard Twins restaurant into its corporate office. Now this area looks like an aging commercial center struggling to keep up appearances. There is little evidence of its former glory.

DISTRICTS OF THE
PREWAR AMENTIY ZONE

Bryn Mawr

Bryn Mawr is an islandlike area on the western edge of Minneapolis. It is surrounded on three sides by parkland: Wirth Park on the west, Bassett's Creek Valley on the north, and Bryn Mawr Meadows on the east. Highway 12 is the southern boundary. Because major roads go around rather than through Bryn Mawr, it is a corner of the city that is relatively unknown, despite heavy traffic flowing past it each day. People encountering this area for the first time are generally surprised to find its lovely, well-maintained homes. Residents of Bryn Mawr have long prized the fact that few people know about the district. They believe they have the best of both worlds: the good qualities of small-town living as well as the benefits of city living. They live very near downtown Minneapolis, but are cut off from surrounding areas. Indeed, this is one of the few areas in either city that genuinely fulfills people's ideal of what an urban village should be.

Not all of Bryn Mawr fits our "prewar" description—some houses were built in the 1890s and a portion was not developed until the 1950s. But all of it fits the notion of an amenity area. Not only is a bountiful amount of parkland nearby, so are three lakes: Cedar, Brownie, and Wirth. The eastern area near the Meadows contains an old bank of an ancient Mississippi River channel. This has caused occasional problems of water seepage and land settling. The notoriety of these problems underscores the fact that residents encounter few major difficulties here.

The area that became Bryn Mawr was farmed as early as the mid-1850s. During the next fifty years pieces of the original farm were sold off, and the area began to attract residents. Some of the earliest were employees of the nearby Milwaukee and St. Louis Railroad shops. The fact that laborers settled in Bryn Mawr quite early may account for the variety of small industries found there. A clock company, a beekeepers' supply company, two bottlers of spring water, a mill, and a macaroni factory all appeared between 1890 and 1920. Even Burma Shave Company got its start here. When the first streetcar appeared in 1900, professionals and proprietors began moving into the area. Most of the early residents had English or American backgrounds. Foreign-born residents were from Sweden or Finland.

Most of the houses in Bryn Mawr were built between 1915 and 1930. By that time the area had a thriving buisness section at Cedar Lake Road and Superior Boulevard (which became Wayzata Boulevard and then Highway 12). There were several grocery stores, a butcher shop, a drugstore, a hardware store, a small notion shop, and a dentist's office. During the twenties Bryn Mawr began to grow beyond the small outpost it had been. Many people came here to enjoy the "countrylike" surroundings. Organizations proliferated during this period: a community church was started, as were several benevolent associations and a masonic lodge. Bryn Mawr was home to hard-working people who were financially comfortable, well-mannered, and solid citizens. They lived in one of the best settings in Minneapolis and appreciated their advantages.

During the fifties and sixties Bryn Mawr remained the middle-class haven it had always been. Its population was aging, and its young people were moving to the suburbs—a common experience of communities throughout the Twin Cities. The old business center was obliterated when Wayzata Boulevard became a freeway, but the small-town atmosphere remained. The major challenge to the community came in the early 1970s, with the projected routing of I-394 through the area. A coalition of area residents and freeway opponents from surrounding suburbs have managed to delay this project indefinitely.

Today Bryn Mawr retains its placid residential character. On a typical block there are lawyers living next door to retired laborers, and engineers next door to truck drivers and bartenders. There are few other areas in Minneapolis and Saint Paul where white-collar and blue-collar residents are so well mixed. Newer residents tend to be more highly educated and have better jobs. Old-timers view this positively, claiming it is a way to ensure that Bryn Mawr will remain a good area in which to live. People who move here tend to remain for a long time—this is one of the most stable communities in Minneapolis. The area has a substantial number of senior citizens who have stayed in their homes, and these houses are among the best-kept on any block. Feelings of neighborliness are strong in Bryn Mawr. People know their neighbors, and block clubs are active. Residents maintain that the churches are the centers of activity in the community.

Most of the housing in Bryn Mawr consists of owner-occupied, single-family houses. Apartment buildings are almost nonexistent, though recently some large older homes have been converted to apartment units. Houses are well maintained. With styles ranging from Victorian gingerbread to newer ramblers, the visual diversity of the community remains strong. A 1965 study of Bryn Mawr labeled the district "sound" and "stable." The only potential problem it identified was an aging population that might not replace itself with younger families. Area residents claim that this has not happened. Young families are drawn to the area by its amenities and varied housing styles. It seems likely that Bryn Mawr will continue to attract a population that values the kinds of housing and the quiet atmosphere it has to offer.

Lynnhurst-Washburn Park

Lynnhurst and Washburn Park in southwest Minneapolis were built up during the twenties and thirties, but portions of each district predate this period. Lynnhurst lies at the southeast corner of Lake Harriet, and Washburn Park lies north of Minnehaha Creek from Stevens Avenue to Lyndale. Each place is considered an established residential area for the more successful citizens of Minneapolis. Indeed, Garrison Keillor's "Ode to the Street System" gently pokes fun at this pervasive image:

> For years, successful men have reckoned
> By this system, trained the self
> To follow Lyndale and hang a Ralph
> At Fiftieth, into a neighborhood
> Where homes are stable, children good,
> Earnings are high and soundly invested
> In products Consumer Reports has tested,
> Where life is not paranoid, moody or radical,
> But Republican, Lutheran and Alphabetical.

Lynnhurst got its start in 1893. An overly ambitious plan of Charles Loring's (of Loring Park fame) established a colony on Fremont Avenue between 46th and 47th Streets. Nine "outstanding" young married men in Loring's employ were given three lots each. The only condition was that they use the land to build homes that could not cost less than $3,000. This was not entirely a philanthropic gesture. Loring, who was also a partner in the Street Railway system, hoped to promote development in this outlying area. The developers lost the land around this colony in the 1893 panic, but the residents on Fremont remained. They named the area Lynnhurst after the many linden trees. This colony was extremely isolated for many years—the streetcar terminated over a mile away at 42nd and Bryant. Lynnhurst residents were forced to pool their resources. They evolved a kind of cooperative arrangement, sharing one telephone and three cows among the nine families. It was not until 1903 that the area north of the colony was finally platted. Even then settlement in the area was slow.

Washburn Park was platted in 1886 by Senator W. D. Washburn and a group of investors. Their aim, as stated in the first advertisement, was to provide a "fine suburb" where "men of business can get away from the noise of the city and the inconvenience of small lots and crowded neighborhoods." The 220 acres surrounding the "park" were laid out by the well-known landscape architect H. W. S. Cleveland, to follow the natural contours of the site. The park itself was the location of the Washburn Memorial Home, an orphanage built in the same year with the money bequested by Senator Washburn's brother. A portion of this district was subdivided into quarter-acre lots, on which houses costing at least $3,000 were to be built. To attract buyers, the investors sponsored a new streetcar line to run on Nicollet from the orphanage up to 31st Street, where it would connect with the existing system. Like many other speculative developments of the late nineteenth century, this one was not an immediate success. Even those who owned land did not rush to build on it. Architect Harry Jones was a good case in point. Although among the original group of investors, Jones did not design and construct his own home on Elmwood Place until after the turn of the century. The area was obviously attractive, but it was just too far away from the center of activity in Minneapolis.

Real development in Washburn Park did not occur until around 1910. The depression of the 1890s had caught some of the investors short, and the platted land remained largely empty for almost a quarter-century. Some houses were built

Large middle-class houses in Bryn Mawr just north of Highway 12. Blocks of this style and shape are spread throughout this zone.

Commercial strip at 54th and Lyndale in South Minneapolis demonstrates the streetcar landscape transformed by automobiles.

during the second decade of this century, but large-scale construction did not take place until after 1920 when the upper middle class poured into the area to build expensive homes. The park in Washburn Park was soon lost in this rush to develop the land. The city purchased the former orphanage site for school construction in the early twenties.

From the time of the first settlement in Lynnhurst and Washburn Park, an aura of comfort prevailed. Residents tended to be native-born Americans with good incomes and good breeding. The housing constructed in these areas exudes a tasteful quality often found in expensive older suburbs on the East Coast. Both areas experienced population booms during the twenties. From 1920 to 1930 the population of south Minneapolis along the Creek grew 300 percent or more. Settlement patterns were not dense, nor was all available land filled in. But this is clearly where most building was taking place. The fact that Washburn High School was constructed in 1925 serve an area virtually empty ten years earlier emphasizes the dramatic scope of this area's growth.

Today both Lynnhurst and Washburn Park are stable upper middle-class residential areas. Lynnhurst is bordered by Lake Harriet and Minnehaha Creek, and families seek out the local amenities. The area has some distinctive residences; a number of Purcell and Elmslie Prairie houses dating from the teens are scattered through the northern part of the community. Washburn Park is probably best known for its water tower—a tall Gothic monument decorated with enormous Teutonic Knights. With its hilly winding streets, this "tangletown" is one of the most phsyically attractive areas in the city.

In both areas people appreciate and enjoy their environment. There are some block clubs organized to monitor airplane noise and other environmental problems. These tend to be watchdog organizations. Their task is to ensure that the high quality of life here is maintained. Residents say the only change that occurs is the occasional turnover in housing. Older people remain in their homes as long as possible, but are replaced eventually by younger families. Many of these newcomers are people who grew up in these areas. Access to other parts of the metropolitan area is relatively easy from here. The commercial facilities of the suburbs are near enough to provide most goods and services. Residents are content, safe, and aesthetically wealthy.

The Saint Paul Amenity Zone

The 1920 plan for Saint Paul called for a system of boulevards that would connect all the major parks. These roads were laid out, but the city did not expand rapidly enough to create a demand for housing lots so far from the city center. Therefore, most of the Grand Round, as it was called, was not built up until after the war.

The housing in the prewar amenity zone of Saint Paul tends to be large and brick. The River Road housing is magnificent. Here tudor revivals and colonials are set in large lawns which seem to extend to the river's bluff. Most residents concentrate their outdoor activity in their spacious and private backyards to avoid the prying eyes of joggers and tourists who cruise the River Boulevard.

This area was built up by stockbrokers, lawyers, and physicians together with business executives before the great crash. At first all the residents of the district worked in Saint Paul and generally ignored their proximity to Minneapolis. In the last two decades, however, this area has become increasingly attractive to individuals working in or near downtown Minneapolis. In addition, some of the faculty of the University of Minnesota have located here. Needless to say, they are among the better paid members of the teaching corps. The population obviously enjoys a high status. In fact, this area has the greatest concentration of managerial and professional households in Saint Paul and is second only to Kenwood in the Twin Cities.

The rather large apartment buildings along Marshall Avenue depress the home ownership rate in the district somewhat. But at 66 percent the home ownership rate is still higher than that in all but the newer parts of both the prewar grid and the suburban-in-city zones. If the strip of rental units along Marshall is not taken into account, the ownership rate becomes more than 90 percent.

The large homes and lots are attractive to upper-income households with children. There are few single persons or retired households living in the single-family dwellings. Perhaps the families are attracted to the exciting wintertime activities of sliding and skiing in the marvelous hills of the Town and Country golf course. Turnover is slow here despite the population of renters. There appears to be a gradual inmigration of families with children who have to

some degree replaced the retired households who no longer cherish the responsibility of home maintenance. The area's chief problem seems to be teenaged revelers along the river bank.

Unlike the River Boulevard, the older portion of Edgecumbe Road is very private. It is also the smallest of the districts, comprising only twelve blocks. Homes on the bluff side of the road are set far back from the street, with thick hedges to screen them from the occasional traffic. Here the houses are of two types: the mansion and the mini-mansion. Both types are meticulously landscaped to capture the flavor of the greenway down the center of Edgecumbe. The result is a splendid district that appears to be nearly all open space, when in fact most of the houses are quite close to each other.

The third prewar amenity district in Saint Paul is the forty-block area north of Midway Parkway and west of Como Park. Snelling Avenue gives this area a sharp western border, and the city limits form its northern boundary. Unlike the other districts, this is not an especially high-status or exclusive area. Like much of south Minneapolis, it contains middle-level bureaucrats and managerial people who work for state government, the University of Minnesota, or suburban employers. The houses are small; three bedrooms predominate. Lots are neat and well maintained, but homeowners do their own yard work. While visitors to Como Park create small traffic jams in the summer and roaring lions and barking seals in Como Zoo are reputed to disturb the area's peace, nothing compares to that frantic last week of summer when the State Fair is on. Millions of people pour into the area looking for a free parking space or just to rubberneck around the neighborhood. A few people living on Snelling turn their yards into parking lots, but most residents either go on vacation or wish they had.

The area was embroiled in a bitter controversy in 1978 and 1979 over the proposed conversion of the former Bethel College campus into a Job Corps training facility. Bethel had moved to a more suburban location in the early 1970s and for several years had sought to dispose of its former physical plant and grounds. The property, though extensive, is located in an area zoned residential and therefore cannot be used for many of the development schemes discussed. The establishment of the Hubert Humphrey training center is by no means a compromise. Neighbors believe the values of adjacent property will decline and that the atmosphere of the district has already been significantly altered. Although this controversy is now resolved, it illustrates the dilemma posed by the presence of large institutions in residential areas.

CONCLUSION

The prewar amenity district is relatively free from the problems normally associated with urban life. Incomes are high, open space is abundant, crime is almost nonexistent. People who live here are stable and maintain their own homes. Perhaps the only difficulty in this zone, at least in Minneapolis, involves the public schools. Three areas, Audubon Park, Bryn Mawr, and Washburn Park, lost elementary schools before 1978. The area near Minnehaha Park lost both an elementary school and a junior high school in 1978. Several more grammar schools in this zone are being closed this year (1982), along with Ramsey Junior High School. Unlike most other parts of Minneapolis, districts here have not yet lost a high school. One of the major goals of Minneapolis' "Plan for the 1980s" is to make the city attractive for families. The prewar amenity zone is an area that families, especially upper-income families so beloved by city tax collectors, still choose to occupy. Thus the school-closing policy seems to be at odds with the ultimate achievement of the goal of the plan.

The suburban-in-city zone provides ample open space for athletic activities for all ages.

The Suburban-in-City Zone

Perhaps no two things in the literature about urban areas and city life are as confusing as the term "suburbs" and the often discussed distinction between city and suburb. Scholarly literature during the late 1950s was filled with reports of a "new" form of urban landscape and "new" life-styles. The "suburb" was said to be a homogeneous landscape filled with ticky-tacky houses occupied by middle-class refugees from the older areas who were climbing some economic or social pyramid. Social commentators described these places as female-dominated and child-oriented areas where people returned to religion and changed from Democrats to Republicans. Social life was said to revolve around the California-style backyard or patio barbecue and the local Little League. The best that could be said for the suburb was that it was somewhere between the liberalism and vitality of the city and the unsophisticated simplicity of the small town. These popular and academic images of the postwar communities seem to derive in large measure from a handful of scholarly and journalistic studies made of the fringes of New York and Philadelphia in the late 1950s.

Unfortunately, it is difficult to apply the conclusions of the East Coast studies to the sections of the Twin Cities built up after the second World War because the patterns of residential development in the two areas of the country were not analogous. On the East Coast, "true" suburbs were forming on vast tracts of land located outside the city limits. In the Twin Cities, on the other hand, new residential areas were being developed on less-extensive tracts *within* Minneapolis and Saint Paul as political subdivisions of the central city.

At the end of the war there were still large undeveloped areas within the Twin Cities. In some cases developers had platted streets and planned to build in these areas during the late 1930s, but nothing materialized. The areas were finally developed in response to the tremendous demand for housing that characterized the postwar period in the United States. The housing shortage resulted from the lack of housing starts during the Depression and World War II. Returning servicemen, seeking their piece of the American dream—a wife, children, and a single-family house in an attractive and peaceful neighborhood—heightened the demand for housing. A double boom was the result, one in babies, the other in home mortgages.

When the war ended, most places of employment were still in the central portions of the metropolitan area, and before the freeway system was constructed, commuting was time consuming and frustrating. Therefore, those undeveloped areas within the city were among the first areas to be built up after World War II. As can be seen on map 9, the suburban-in-city zone occupies the outer edge of both cities. Although the popular image of Saint Paul is that of the older "dowagerlike" twin, the majority of this zone actually lies in Saint Paul rather than Minneapolis. In addition, it is the second largest zone in Saint Paul. This is because Saint Paul grew much more slowly than Minneapolis after 1900. As a result, when the postwar housing boom occurred, a larger part of Saint Paul was still vacant, awaiting development.

The fact that the suburban-in-city zone is part of an established political and educational system is significant. Residents of the postwar districts of the central cities cannot avoid the issues of urban decay and declining central business districts to the degree that their neighbors beyond the city limits can. This lack of isolation deprives them of a separate identity, and, in some cases, their needs are overlooked by city administrators concerned with more dramatic issues of older areas.

Although they are politically part of Saint Paul and Minneapolis, these areas look like adjacent suburban communities. Because these districts range in age, there are greater differences within the suburban-in-city zone than there are between particular districts and their adjacent suburban neighbors. The intra-zone differences are essentially a function of age of the housing and income level of the occupants.

RESIDENTIAL DEVELOPMENT AND HOUSING

The growth of this zone was concentrated in a few distinct areas. Land adjacent to railroad tracks and industrial areas that had been left vacant (for example, the Midway district of Saint Paul) were developed as small pockets of middle-income housing. On the edge of the city, developments were concentrated in long-established growth corridors which were based on major transportation arteries. Prewar development had filled in most of these limbs of the city in Minneapolis, but in Saint Paul there was still room for postwar developments along the old route to White

Bear Lake and Stillwater as well as on the road to the southeast near Mounds Park. In other parts of the city, the suburban-in-city zone filled in the undeveloped areas between earlier developments. Those areas were not well served by mass transit but were ideal for people who commuted to work by car.

Topography had a great impact on the development of the zone. At first builders were attracted to level pieces of land, in such areas as the northern edges of Minneapolis, that could be prepared for building at low cost. Modest bungalows and Cape Cod houses soon sprang up in these places. Builders avoided the rolling land, cliff edges, and low places until the 1960s and 1970s, when they constructed rather expensive houses in the split level, rambler, and two-story colonial styles. Thus the suburban-in-city zone contains specific residential districts developed in two distinct eras.

Those districts developed in the 1940s and 1950s are essentially extensions of the prewar communities of the central cities. The landscape consists of small single-family homes. Most of the builders active during these two decades were capable of constructing only a handful of houses each year. At first they built houses of less than 1,000 square feet, and later, houses of 1,200 square feet of living space were most common. In several areas the home buyers did much of the finishing work on the houses themselves. Nearly everyone did some of the decorating and outside landscaping. Some built their own garages and driveways. Neighbors frequently banded together to help finish the construction process, and a spirit of cooperation prevailed.

Two basic styles of housing dominated the early phase of postwar construction, the "Cape Cod" and the "Ranch House." Neither house looks much like its namesake, but people liked them just the same. Sited on standard city lots, these houses are now surrounded by mature vegetation. In Minneapolis nearly all the alleys are paved and the sidewalks are in. Boulevards in these areas were not planted with elms, so the lots here have more evergreens and flower beds than those in older areas. Some locals refer to them as "grass neighborhoods," as opposed to "tree neighborhoods" which are dominated by mature urban forest.

For most people the layout of streets and the styles of houses are the most important characteristics of an urban landscape. Here in the Midwest the curved streets of the

126

Map 9: The Suburban-in-city Zone. This zone contains those parts of both cities developed after World War II. The population here is predominantly middle-class and white-collar.

Smaller Cape Cod house in Saint Paul's Highland Park.

modern subdivisions provide a sharp contrast to the traditional grid of the nineteenth-century development. Therefore, whenever we encounter an area of the city with curved streets and one-story, single-family houses, we immediately associate it with suburban developments. This is a problem only when we overlook the fact that most suburbs have many miles of straight streets and that extensive portions of the inner cities were built during the modern area and are "suburban" in nature.

Housing developments of the postwar era were of course designed for families with cars, and are said to be automotive landscapes. The curving streets and names that conjure up images of pastoral landscapes have been used by developers to highlight the differences between "city" and "suburb" —differences in the density of housing and population. Occupants of these low-density areas need their cars for mobility because services are spread over a large area and because the mass transit system cannot economically provide service to such extensive residential districts.

Many of the developments built during the late 1940s and early 1950s were laid out on the grid pattern—straight streets and alleys. Some even had sidewalks installed to serve the occasional pedestrian. This was a time when most families had only one car and wanted to keep it in their own garage; hence small, inexpensive garages were the order of the day.

In 1958 and 1959 the nature of residential development in the zone underwent a profound change. Builders of inexpensive homes now concentrated their efforts in the suburban communities where large tracts of suitable land were still available at low cost. This meant that the new construction within the city was increasingly confined to the remaining vacant lots and consisted mainly of larger, more expensive houses built by custom contractors.

The newer districts, developed in the 1960s and 1970s, occupy the more scenic landscapes in the zone and frequently are more similar to adjacent suburbs than to nearby older parts of the city. These areas also contain apartment complexes (see p. 130) and Saint Paul's oldest public housing projects, John J. McDonough Homes on the far north side and the Franklin D. Roosevelt Homes in the northeast sector.

In Saint Paul the zone can be thought of as having four distinctive components: the southwestern (Highland Park), the north side, the northeast quadrant, and the southeastern quadrant (greater Battle Creek). To some extent each of these areas is an extension of older communities, but there are several important differences. The southeast Saint Paul quadrant contains houses of both eras. Although the section of the city due east of downtown was developed early in the city's history, growth did not extend far from the major roads. During the 1950s the expansion of employment opportunities at Minnesota Mining and Manufacturing made these areas attractive, and modest single-family houses were built on extensions of the old grid pattern streets. The area south of Highway 12 (now I-94) was built up later. Apartment complexes were built near the highway in the early 1960s, and stretches of rolling fields and cliff tops were transformed into upper middle-class communities in the late sixties. This area is still developing. The northeastern quadrant is a continuation of the traditional East Side community. It follows the historic growth corridor toward White Bear Lake and blends almost imperceptibly into the new subdivisions in Maplewood. Largely an area of modest single-family homes, it has been changed slightly by the recent construction of multiple-family homes on sites where it was unprofitable to build single-family houses.

The northern city limits, or the "inter-park district" between Como and Phalen Parks, is more complex than either the northeastern or southeastern quadrants, although it is not as extensive. Here topography has combined with the influence of transportation routes to create a mixture of residential districts. The western area, with its hilly terrain,

Apartments in Saint Paul's North End were built in the mid-1960s to house members of the baby-boom generation as they left home.

attracted builders of single-family homes that were sold to people wishing to live close to Como Park. Builders avoided the ancient river valley that cuts a wide swath through this area because of the high water table and large boggy areas that need fill. In the 1950s the McDonough Housing project was built on the western slope of this valley only one block away from the city limits. Its residents live in the midst of an open and undeveloped landscape exactly the opposite of stereotyped public housing projects. The easternmost district in this band of postwar development is a continuation of the East Side communities and is essentially a neighborhood of single-family houses.

The southwestern section, or greater Highland Park, is also made up of several districts. Along the Mississippi River cliff top is a district of sumptuous housing, whereas the Saint Paul Avenue area, near the Ford Plant, was developed for middle-class families who could only afford rather modest houses. There are also a few large apartment complexes in this area. The area around the golf course is an extension of the Edgecumbe Parkway development and contains luxurious houses on large scenic lots. Below the high terrace of the Mississippi, along West Seventh, an extensive apartment complex was constructed during the early 1960s. A few multiple-family units are added to this district each year.

In Minneapolis, the suburban-in-city zone hugs the far edges of the city on the north and south. There are additional small patches of the zone along the eastern and western city limits, and another in south-central Minneapolis atop a former swamp. The zone can be segmented into the far north side (Shingle Creek), the northeastern edge (Waite Park), and the southern city limits. In contrast to the Saint Paul suburban-in-city zone, the Minneapolis zone is not extensive. Because Minneapolis' population surpassed Saint Paul's in 1880, it contains more housing built in the late nineteenth and early twentieth centuries than does Saint Paul. By the time the postwar housing boom was under way, there was little land left in Minneapolis to feed it. Consequently, most of the suburban-in-city zone there was filled with houses at the start of the postwar boom — during the late 1940s and the decade of the fifties.

Small, single-family houses dominate the landscape in Minneapolis. As in other places, they have been saved from total uniformity by extensions, additions, and decks. The more expensive suburban styles of the 1960s appear sporadically around Grass Lake and along East River Road. Unlike the Saint Paul portion of the zone, the Minneapolis section contains few shopping strips and centers. Almost every portion of this zone in Minneapolis is within two or three miles of a major suburban shopping center, so the need for local facilities is greatly diminished. Even though gasoline is expensive, most residents seem content to drive the short distance to the Dales and other shopping centers quite regularly.

One of the more interesting aspects of housing in the Minneapolis portion of this zone is the presence of dwellings dating from the teens and twenties. This is not, and never was, a completely homogeneous landscape. Some farmhouses remained from the time when these districts were primarily truck-gardening areas. Other houses in this zone were built in the teens by pioneers who needed some breathing room. But many were simply moved into this zone from farther out in the suburbs. During the forties and fifties, when land was being cleared for freeway rights-of-way, a good number of structures that might have been razed were moved to a new location. Usually this was in the city, where streets and utilities were already in place. So the modern housing of the suburban-in-city zone occasionally abuts a remnant of an earlier era.

Because the districts on the edge of the city are close to major parks or stretches of open land, recreation facilities do not seem to be a great concern in these areas. The local schools were among the best equipped in the Twin Cities until they were consolidated recently.

129

In the early to mid-1960s a mini-boom in apartment construction began in the Twin Cities. Although most of the great complexes were built in the suburbs, an extensive development occurred along the northern limits of Saint Paul near Rice Street. These are nearly all three-story walk-up buildings that were built upon low land that was thought to be unsuitable for single-family houses. The structures at first housed Saint Paulites who could not find satisfactory housing in the older areas yet who wished to be close to their former residence. The area has continued to attract apartment builders. Between 1970 and 1975 some 2,000 apartment units were built in the vicinity of Rice Street. Because the area still contains a considerable amount of vacant land that has been designated for multiple-family housing, this trend will undoubtedly continue for the next few years.

The apartment boom of the late sixties never really took hold in Minneapolis because districts here were almost completely built up by the late 1950s. As mentioned earlier, the Minneapolis zone's housing is predominantly single-family dwellings. There is a smattering of small multiunit buildings along major arterial streets, but the only concentrations of these structures are along the Crosstown Highway near 35W and near the airport. In these areas as much as one-third or more of the housing is in multiple units. Elsewhere in this zone multiple units comprise less than 10 percent of the total. The residential character of the zone is undisturbed by commerce.

COMMERCIAL FACILITIES

The commercial establishments in this zone are either found along major streets (in a variation of the commercial strip development typical of the streetcar landscape) or in small shopping centers. The auto-oriented commercial strips have several basic features in common. First, the commercial buildings are set back from the street in order to provide a modest parking lot in front of the stores or offices. On most streets these mini-parking lots have direct access to the street, so traffic flow is somewhat impeded by turning cars. Second, the buildings are almost always single-story structures made from concrete blocks. Signs are quite variable, but clearly intended to attract the eye of passing motorists.

Because this part of the city was built during the early years of the franchise explosion in the United States, most streets have at least one major franchised establishment which tends to set the tone for the street.

The focal point of the small shopping center is its centrally located parking lot, not an enclosed shopping mall. These centers are more like the old commercial blocks of the early twentieth century than the luxurious malls of the suburbs. A few are rather large, with upwards of a dozen establishments, but most contain between six and ten stores or offices. They are almost devoid of ornamentation. Their chief competition comes from suburban malls.

Like all commercial enterprises, the strips and shopping centers reflect the wealth of the residential districts that they serve. However, because the wealthy residents of the zone are very mobile and shop for luxury goods in all parts of the city, the establishments within the zone tend to specialize in convenience goods. Exclusive shops are extremely rare.

The range of goods and services located in these commercial areas is impressive and can be divided into two general categories; those that serve the local area and those that serve a section of the city and surrounding suburbs. The establishments serving the local area provide convenience goods like groceries, drugs, and personal services. The regional-oriented establishments provide a range of professional services and consumer durables such as furniture, recreational equipment, household goods, and the like. The establishments serving the wider community are located in this zone for essentially two reasons: ease of access to heavily trafficked streets, and the availability of rather large sites and/or buildings at lower costs than those in suburban shopping centers.

There are two major problems within the suburban-in-city residential districts. Residents are concerned about heavy traffic in the commercial areas, and the successful regional-oriented establishments want more commercial space, which could lead to the encroachment of commercial facilities into areas of single-family housing. To some degree, these problems are similar to those generally experienced on older streetcar shopping strips, but the problems appear to be greater in the newer developments. The problems can be best seen by using a case study.

The northeast sector of Saint Paul is served by three commercial areas: a large and busy shopping strip along

White Bear Avenue; the Hillcrest Center (located on White Bear Avenue) begun in the late 1940s and finished in 1961; and the Phalen Center built between 1959 and 1961 at the intersection of Prosperity and Maryland Avenues. The Phalen Center serves both the suburban-in-city districts and the older areas closer to downtown. In this part of the city residents are quick to point out four basic problems. First, the design of the Phalen Center's parking facility does not adequately allow a smooth flow of cars and pedestrians in and out of the area. Second, many residents and shoppers consider the outdoor advertising along White Bear Avenue to be "visual noise." These people would like to see a greater investment in signs, street furniture, and lighting. Third, the centers were built for cars, and as a consequence pedestrians from the area encounter difficulties in trying to use them. Finally, local residents are apprehensive about the impact of continued expansion and intensification of the shopping areas on White Bear Avenue. Although they realize that some expansion may be necessary, they are seeking ways to separate the commercial from single-family residential districts by constructing apartment buildings as buffers.

These problems, of course, are not unique to the East Side. They result from the lack of a definite plan for the areas built up during the postwar era. Each contractor built to suit his purpose, but the combination of several individual projects did not always produce a harmonious landscape. The signs are designed to attract the attention of passing motorists and not to provide an attractive facade that would blend well with the surrounding houses. The traffic problems are in part the result of trying to take a suburban phenomenon designed for areas where space was not a constraint and transfer it to the city, where space was restricted. Cramped traffic patterns were the unavoidable outcome.

It should be noted that the case study is drawn from the portion of the zone developed in the 1960s. Newer areas are less constrained and have fewer shopping centers providing convenience goods. These newer districts do not usually contain commercial establishments serving large sections of the city because that function is provided by outlying shopping centers.

The prosperity of commercial establishments throughout the suburban-in-city districts in both Minneapolis and Saint Paul depends upon the strength of the local market and the nature of competition from the regional shopping centers in adjacent suburbs. In general, we find that the commercial districts located on the inner edges of the zone are less prosperous because a part of their trade area is made up of the poor older districts toward the city center. These centers do not have large numbers of vacancies, but merchants frequently describe their businesses as fair, and several express the desire to relocate in a "more suburban location." Part of their problem is the increasing obsolescence of the centers built in the 1960s. These were designed to provide a mix of convenience goods and services for the surrounding residents who would be attracted to the center because they could do most of their shopping in one location. However, three developments have decreased the attraction of these locations. First, the local market in the older areas has become weakened owing to the aging of the population and the decreasing population density. Second, a change in the mix of the stores in these centers has occurred; as some of the initial establishments went out of business, they were replaced by dissimilar operations. Third, the growing traffic on the arterial streets made the centers' parking lots more difficult to get into. As a result, shoppers drive past them to regional shopping centers located just a few minutes farther down the road. The commercial strips within the suburban-in-city zone seem to be thriving because the establishments along them depend upon single-purpose shoppers. These shoppers find the strips more convenient than the regional centers beyond the outer edge of the zone because they need not contend with lines in parking lots.

Both the centers and the strips must deal with growing competition from shopping centers and discount stores farther out in the suburbs. The latter are newer and larger than the centers in the suburban-in-city zone and are, therefore, able to compete in accessibility and in merchandising techniques. Over the past decade the successful establishments in the suburban-in-city zone have exhibited a tendency to relocate farther out rather than undergo the costly and time-consuming process of expansion in the established centers and strips. In another decade the centers will undoubtedly be characterized by a larger number of offices and neighborhood services, whereas the strips will be dominated by establishments that serve the wider community.

POPULATION

As might be expected, the population of the suburban-in-city zone bears a closer resemblance to residents of neighboring fringe communities than to the residents of the older inner-city communities. In general we find that people living in the postwar housing are white, middle-class home-owners, living in two-parent families. (See table 8, p. 148.) Home ownership averages over 90 percent throughout the Minneapolis districts. At the same time, the amount of residential mobility is relatively low. In some districts the median income equals the Twin City median. In the newer areas or those that are still developing, incomes are considerably higher, as much as 70 percent higher than the Twin City median in some places. During the 1970s the total income of residents in the suburban-in-city districts in Saint Paul increased significantly, whereas the total income for the rest of the city, with few exceptions, remained unchanged. The great increase experienced in these districts resulted from more families moving in rather than from an increase in the income of families living in the area. These high dollar districts together with a few protected genteel areas comprise most of the market for retailers in the center cities.

Although the population of Minneapolis and Saint Paul has continued to decline over the past two decades, the Battle Creek area of southeastern Saint Paul has undergone a population explosion, growing 240 percent between 1960 and 1970 and an estimated 53 percent between 1970 and 1975. Those districts built up during the 1950s, however, have experienced a population decline. As the children of the households living in these areas matured and left home, their parents remained in the houses or were replaced by households with fewer children. Thus the decline in the birthrate as well as migration patterns have had an impact on the suburban-in-city zone.

The population of Minneapolis' suburban-in-city districts differs slightly from that of Saint Paul. Most of these areas in Minneapolis are slightly older, and their residents are also slightly older and have fewer children at home. The proportion of retired persons in some districts is approximately one-third. The interesting thing about these dstricts in Minneapolis is not the fact that families with children live

in this zone—it is that proportionately fewer of these families live here than in the aging inner ring and turnaround zones. Almost all of the districts in this zone have recently been losing traditional families. This is not conclusive evidence that families reject this wholesome environment. Instead, it indicates that the youngest children in some families are now old enough to leave home. It may also be an indication that young families with children cannot afford to buy into these areas.

Residents of the suburban-in-city zone exhibit more diversity than we would expect to find in such areas. In Minneapolis, all districts have household incomes above the average, but none are at the highest level. Nor is this a stronghold of white-collar professions. The percentage of professionals and managers exceeds the city average in only one half of the Minneapolis portion of the zone. There are substantial numbers of well-paid skilled workers in many districts. Another surprising feature of the Minneapolis zone is that it holds the only district with a sizable minority population: Shingle Creek, on the northern city limits, whose black population in 1970 was equivalent to that in some sections of the Near Northside.

DISTRICTS OF THE SUBURBAN-IN-CITY ZONE

Each small area within the broad suburban-in-city zone has its unique personality and problems. Although we do not have enough space here to cover all districts, it is possible to illustrate some of the diversity (and similarity) in this zone by taking a closer look at four areas in Saint Paul: the Battle Creek area, or the southeast quadrant; Hayden Heights-Hazel Park, or the northeastern corner of the city; the core area of Highland Park; and the Stonebridge area in the western sector of Saint Paul near the Mississippi River Boulevard. We will also provide an overview of the districts in Minneapolis.

Battle Creek

The Battle Creek area is the largest of the residential districts and is representative of the newest building for upper middle-class households. It is triangular in shape, approximately four miles long, and one and one-half miles wide at the broadest point. Its topography is truly spectacular. Here sharp and rugged bluffs rise nearly two hundred feet from the marshy floor of the Mississippi Valley. Steep rocky ravines slice through the face of the cliff cut by streams with their headwaters in the small lakes and springs located in the rolling uplands. Dry in the summer, the coulees roar with raging torrents during the spring. One of these ravines is the park and recreation area known as Battle Creek Park. Its steep terrain has lured ski jumpers to it for several decades.

Although this district is still being developed, it was actually the location of the oldest settlement within the modern limits of Saint Paul, the winter village of the Kaposia Band of Dakota Indians. Their homes, located in the vicinity of Battle Creek on the valley floor, were relocated to present-day South Saint Paul in the 1830s when the Indians lost the title to the land east of the Mississippi.

White settlement did not occur in this area for many years because of transportation problems. The enormous swamp surrounding Pig's Eye Lake precluded the development of a steamboat landing. Although one of the oldest roads in the state runs along the foot of the cliff, only a handful of roads climbed from the valley floor to the upland. These roads are frequently described as "bobsled runs" by motorists first encountering them in winter. Therefore, even though the district is relatively close to the center of Saint Paul, it remained rather inaccessible until the 1950s when the Hudson Road, or Highway 12, was improved. A building boom in the northern part of the district soon followed.

Two stations in the old rail commuter system which ran along the foot of the cliff, Highwood and Highwood Park, are recorded as place-names on modern maps, but they did not provide an impetus for urbanization. On the contrary, development on the eastern edge has resulted essentially from the upgrading of McKnight Road, which also serves the land in the adjacent suburb of Maplewood. It is now almost impossible to see any striking differences between Maplewood and the southern portions of the district. Just as the upgrading of the route to Hudson has increased the accessibility of the northern edge of the district, the improvement of Lower Afton Road opened the central and southern sections.

The housing in this district can be placed in one of three categories. In the northern section, the area cored by Upper Afton Road, single-family, detached housing was built in the 1960s and early 1970s on a grid street pattern modified by cul de sacs. The second category consists of the houses on large lots in the southern section. One group of these line the bluff top along Burlington Road. The remainder are scattered through the area and are sometimes located as much as one-quarter mile off a public road. The third category are large apartment and condominium complexes built in the northern and central sections during the 1970s. These developments house two distinctive populations. One group are rather well-off, mature people who have adopted multiple-family units so they do not have to deal with home maintenance problems. The other is a more typical apartment population—younger, with incomes somewhat lower, and living in one- or two-person households. The large complexes, nearly megastructures in scale, are used as infill development in the portion of the district closest to Interstate 94.

The low density of housing and mobility of the population have prevented the development of an extensive pattern of commercial buildings. There are only fifty-three business establishments in the area, about one-half the number serving other districts. A convenience shopping center at Lower Afton and McKnight serves the southern section, whereas the freeway-oriented development along Ruth Street and the Interstate serves the northern areas. Residents think nothing of making five- or six-mile roundtrips to the grocery store, cleaners, or for other convenience goods and services.

This area contains about 3 percent of Saint Paul's housing units (3,126) and households (3,052). Although the city as a whole lost housing in the 1970s, this district has continued to grow. The only other areas in Saint Paul to add sizable numbers of new units were the apartment development on the city's northern fringe, the downtown area, and the districts undergoing urban renewal. There has been a chronic shortage of housing in Saint Paul in recent years. The city-wide vacancy rate hovers around 3 percent, whereas most observers of the housing market think that a 5 or even 6 percent vacancy rate is ideal. This latter rate provides enough flexibility to accommodate a wide variety of people. In the southeast quadrant there are essentially two vacancy rates. The single-family home rate is very low, around 1 percent, and the multiple-unit rate is close to 4 percent.

The Battle Creek district experienced the greatest increase in number of households and population within Saint Paul during the 1970s. Although the new housing units added in renewal areas replaced structures that had been razed, so that no great increase in households resulted, the new units in Battle Creek are in fact additional units.

Although the popular stereotype of the suburbs calls for landscapes covered with single-family houses, the economics of construction in recent years have dictated that an ever-increasing percentage of new housing starts are multiple-family units. Therefore, although the home ownership rate in Saint Paul is about 59 percent, in this district it is below 50 percent. Obviously the ownership rate is lowest in the area near the Interstate.

Perhaps the best indication of the special character of this district is the average number of people per household. The rate in the Battle Creek area ranges from 2.6 in the north to 3.0 in the south. No other part of the city has a higher average. This substantiates the image that the suburban-in-city zone, as well as the suburbs themselves, have been determined to be good places to raise children. One of the more interesting aspects of the population here is the sizable number of large households. In 1976 nearly 22 percent of all households had five or more members. The only area with a higher percentage was the largely Spanish-speaking renewal area along Concord Street on the West Side of Saint Paul. Fifty-five percent of the households living south of Upper Afton Road had children. No other part of Saint Paul even comes close to this rate. The city rate is about 34 percent.

Although the houses in the area are new and the residents can afford to travel long distances for convenience goods, the population is essentially middle-class. The average annual income of the area is high and increasing. In 1978 the average for the southern section of this district was $19,170, as compared with $16,095 for Saint Paul as a whole. Two other census tracts had a higher income — both are in the suburban-in-city zone. Even though this population has a high income, it does not have an especially high concentration of wage earners in the high-status occupations. In 1978, 27 percent of the household heads were in professional and managerial occupations. This is considerably higher than the city-wide rate, but well below the 41 percent figure for Highland Park and the River Boulevard district,

or the 38 percent of the Crocus Hill district within the protected genteel zone. Likewise, the concentration (30 percent) of households that might be considered low income, such as retired, jobless, unskilled, and service workers, is considerably below the city-wide average of 46 percent. Only the other suburban-in-city districts and the protected genteel district of Saint Anthony Park in Saint Paul have such low rates. Battle Creek has a very low concentration of retired heads of household. Thus a smaller fraction of the lower-income households in the southeastern quadrant are retired workers than in other districts with concentrations of low-income households.

Battle Creek does not have a stable population. Between 1976 and 1978, 52 percent of the housing units changed hands. This compares with a city-wide turnover rate of 38.99 percent. The suburban-in-city zone in general has a rather high turnover rate, but few districts are as transient as this. In Saint Paul only older areas near the city center have higher turnover rates. The factors producing the high rates in the Battle Creek area are, of course, the high job mobility rates in the middle class and the rather high percentage of renters living in the area. Although the large apartment complexes are not unpleasant places to live, they have not attracted long-term tenants. Most of the apartment dwellers expect to move up the socioeconomic hierarchy. These people tend to move to more private quarters as soon as their financial situation allows them. Another factor affecting turnover is the new construction within the district which attracts new households. The net result is an area with a large number of new people and with a dynamic social structure, but without the social organizations found in older communities. There are few churches and essentially no meeting halls or other places for the population to gather in informal settings. Many of the apartment complexes have party rooms for residents. The outdoor recreation facilities are also dispersed, although they appear to be adequate. The open spaces of the district encourage the active forms of recreation. Here residents pursue the vigorous life and individualized recreation.

The growth of the Minnesota Mining and Manufacturing Company has had an unalterable impact on Battle Creek. The company's world headquarters lies only a few minutes away, north of the district on McKnight Road, and has attracted employees from all over the city and world to this area. The result has been an ever-increasing amount of traffic. (One resident nostalgically recalled the time, only two decades ago, when "only seven cars came down Ruth and four were coming to my house." Land now vacant will soon hold large apartment complexes or commercial buildings, and the flow of traffic will continually increase. Residents will undoubtedly continue to appeal to the city to protect their residential districts from commercial "encroachment."

Hayden Heights-Hazel Park

The northeastern corner of Saint Paul is considerably different from the Battle Creek area. The areas known locally as Hazel Park and Hayden Heights have a distinctive history and character.

Streets in this part of the city were platted in the late nineteenth century in association with the building of the Saint Paul Harvestor Company factory in 1872 on the Chicago and Northwestern tracks just east of White Bear Avenue near the intersection of Case and Hazel Avenues. This area was developed as an industrial suburb connected to the central city by the Saint Paul and White Bear Electric Railway, which was completed in 1891. Early developers of the land included Governor Alexander Ramsey and his daughters. The area did not grow, however, and as late as 1940 most of the region outside the immediate vicinity of the route of the old interurban station at Hazel and Maryland was still vacant. Today the route of the old "Interurban" is marked by an unusual double street, called Curve Street, which runs diagonally through the northeasternmost section of the district.

This gently rolling land, platted with streets and accessible to city utilities, was most attractive to developers during the postwar boom. By 1965 the area was essentially built up, with most of the houses constructed during the period immediately after the war. The houses are sited on standard city lots and tend to be of the Cape Cod and small rambler variety. They are extremely well maintained. Except for the commercial strip along White Bear Avenue and the 3M distribution plant that occupies the site of the old Harvestor factory, the area is exclusively residential, with large areas of open land around playgrounds, Hillcrest Golf Course, and Beaver Lake.

Multiple-housing units are scattered throughout the older sections of the area, and four extensive apartment complexes were built on vacant land in the vicinity of Phalen Shopping Center during the late 1960s. These utilitarian structures are representative of the ubiquitous three-story brick veneer buildings surrounded by an asphalt parking lot that became an architectural cliché in the 1970s.

In spite of these buildings, the district is dominated by single-family homes. The district contains about 4 percent of Saint Paul's housing units. In the past few years there has been essentially no change in the number of units.

As might be expected in an area dominated by single-family housing, the vacancy rate is extremely low. In 1978 the northeast corner of the district had the lowest vacancy rate in the city, less than .6 percent. The vacancy rate in rental property is somewhat higher, around 1 percent, but this is still well below the city-wide rate of 3 percent.

The population in the district declined slowly during the 1970s as a result of two countervailing trends. In the eastern section, dominated by single-family housing, the maturation of families produced a slight outmigration of young adults whose parents have continued to occupy the family home. In addition, families moving into this section have fewer children than did the people who first lived in the district. Thus the area has the potential to house comfortably a population somewhat larger than the number living there today.

The number of homeowners in the area is very high. In the far northeast corner, east of White Bear Avenue and north of Maryland, some 96.6 percent of the households own their own home. The rate for the city of Saint Paul is 58.1 percent. Only in the portion of the district near the large apartment blocks does the home ownership rate approach the city-wide figure. Forty-four percent of the households are families with children, most of them with two parents. Like the Battle Creek district, this area is made up of middle-class families who do not hold high-status jobs. In fact, the percentage of household heads in professional and managerial positions is somewhat lower than the city's rate.

We see in this part of Saint Paul's east side a nearly perfect example of the stereotypical suburban landscape and social community: an area with single-family, detached houses, occupied by skilled laborers, craftspeople, and

One portion of the extremely prosperous Highland Village shopping district. It was built to accommodate shoppers who arrived by car.

Adath Israel Orthodox Synagogue. Built originally as a Christian Church with a parking lot and converted to a synagogue, it now serves an orthodox congregation that walks to services through a suburban landscape with few sidewalks.

white-collar workers, who are busy raising families, enjoying the recreation opportunities provided by nearby open spaces and the playgrounds. These people shop in the malls and along White Bear Avenue. Many work in the suburbs.

Residents love this area. As a result, it has one of the lowest rates of outmigration in Saint Paul. To be sure, there is some turnover of the apartment units, but that mobile population is not large enough to give the area a mobility rate that approaches the city-wide average. In the late 1970s the area of detached housing east of White Bear Avenue had the second-lowest turnover rate in the city.

For some families the only shortcoming of this district is that the Hill-Murray High School, a parochial school with an excellent hockey team, lies just across the city border in Maplewood. Many hockey players who might otherwise have played for one of the public schools on the east side go to Hill-Murray, much to the chagrin of die-hard boosters of hockey teams in the public schools.

Highland Park

Located within the southwestern sector of Saint Paul is an area of detached houses built in the 1950s and 1960s and occupied by upper-income families. This is the Highland Park district of Saint Paul. From its northern edge at Highland Parkway, it stretches south over the high bluff to Saint Paul Avenue, and is bounded on the east by Snelling Avenue and on the west by Cleveland Avenue. in a city notorious for confusing place-names, Highland Park ranks near the top of the list. Because most people like to think they live in prestigious areas, people as far north as Saint Clair Avenue—indeed, some who live on Grand Avenue—tell visitors they live in "Highland" or "Highland Park." In fact, the *Highland Villager*, a local shopper newspaper, is delivered to their doorstep. But it is also rather common for high-status people to attempt to disassociate themselves from lower-status families. Therefore, people who live south of Edgecumbe Parkway are known to refer to Montreal Avenue as the northern limits of "Highland Park." Yet people who live north of Montreal and south of Ford Parkway call Ford Parkway the northern edge. And so it goes.

The undeveloped southern section of Saint Paul must have intrigued real estate developers and promoters at the

136

end of World War I. The land was high but rather level. The bluff lines afforded fine views, and the district was well connected to the rest of the city. A streetcar line ran along Randolph Street just north of the district, and major streets had been developed running north toward the built-up areas. Indeed, Edgecumbe Parkway (née Summit Avenue South) was platted in the first decade of the twentieth century.

Most of the region was developed by the now defunct Highland Park Company, a real estate firm, led by Den E. Lane. The establishment of the Ford Assembly Plant on the riverbank above Lock and Dam #1 was expected to make this part of the city extremely desirable. The Depression and competition from developments across the bridge in Minneapolis retarded the area's growth. Thus, although the city installed and paved streets in the area during the 1920s and 1930s, little building actually took place until after World War II. Upper and lower Saint Denis Road and Colven Avenue were platted in 1953. Lots along these streets were developed one at a time for the following decade.

This two-phase platting results in a set of small-scale communities with housing of different vintages and a marked change in street patterns. The northern section has traditional grid-pattern streets lined with "midwestern tudor" and colonial style houses surrounded by lush hedges and mature trees. The southern section along Saint Denis Road is platted into large, irregularly shaped lots occupied by expansive ramblers set in the midst of lawns unmarred by sidewalks. Several of the ramblers along the edge of the bluff are sumptuous and give the term "postwar rambler" an entirely new connotation.

The core area of Highland Park contains a little less than 2 percent of Saint Paul's total housing units. During the late 1960s several apartment blocks were constructed along the southern edge of the area below the cliff. Therefore, only some 77 percent of the housing units are owner occupied.

The population has declined slightly in the past few years because many children have grown up and left their family homes and because families moving into Highland Park have fewer children than the households leaving the area. Families here are not especially large. Only 12 percent have five or more members.

Highland is clearly a high-status district. In 1978 the average annual income per household ($21,070) was higher than any other district, and 41 percent of the heads of households were employed as professionals and managers. This latter rate is almost three times as high as the rate in the Hazel Park district and significantly higher than the rate in Battle Creek.

This area is distinctive for another reason: the high concentration of Jewish people living here. Because this area was being developed during the years when the Jewish population was moving out of the old ghetto in the Summit-University area of Saint Paul, it was a natural area for resettlement. In addition, before the open-housing era, most other suburbs had restriction against home ownership by nongentiles. These regulations and other expressions of anti-Semitisim in the new communities made the voluntary community in Highland very attractive. As the center of the Jewish population shifted to Highland during the 1960s, their institutions and shops also relocated. Today Highland is not exclusively Jewish, but it is the only Jewish community within Saint Paul.

The special culture in the area, the high income and status of the households, together with the attractive and well-maintained landscape, make it a particularly interesting example of a suburban-in-city residential district. Note that we cannot find an analogue for Highland Park in Minneapolis. Only in the suburb of St. Louis Park do we find a similar landscape and culture.

The Stonebridge Estate

Although each of the small infill districts built throughout the Twin Cities during the postwar era has its own particular history, few are as intriguing as that of the area lying between the Mississippi Boulevard and Mount Curve Boulevard between Saint Clair and Jefferson Avenues. This thirty-two-acre site was first developed in 1915 as a lavish estate, Stonebridge, by Oliver Crosby (1856-1922), the founder of the American Hoist and Derrick Company. Surrounded by a high fence of green boards, the estate had a special system to provide water for a swimming pool, a series of trout ponds, and a stream. The stream flowed over a series of waterfalls, under two bridges—one on the estate and the other on the River Boulevard—on its way to the Mississippi. The granite paving stones that were used to

Suburban-style housing off River Road in South Minneapolis. Houses built in this zone after 1960 mimic the styles of outer suburban development of the same period.

line the stream bed can be easily seen from the River Boulevard today.

The brick mansion was an elaborate structure with colonnades and curved porches. The estate had several outbuildings including a greenhouse and a nine-car garage. Stonebridge Boulevard provided access to the grounds from Saint Clair, and a road wound through the estate from the River Boulevard, crossing a small but lovely stone bridge, which is still standing but barely visible from the boulevard.

After the death of Oliver Crosby, the estate was divided into large building lots. The riverward side was developed first, and a particularly beautiful stone house was built facing the old mansion on the circle at Standford Court and Woodlawn Avenue. The mansion was offered to the state to be used as a governor's mansion, but the legislature would not appropriate the required funds, and so the family let the house go for back taxes. It was razed in 1952, and the remainder of the estate subdivided.

Today this section of the city forms one of Saint Paul's finest microneighborhoods. The low ramblers here, occupied by physicians, industrialists, stockbrokers, and lawyers,

contrast sharply with the two-story houses built to the north of Saint Clair. Houses in the latter area, known as King's Maplewood, are also occupied by professional households, but this development is older, having been built in the late 1920s right before the crash of the stock market.

The Minneapolis Districts

The Minneapolis examples of the suburban-in-city zone are neither as varied nor as extensive as those in Saint Paul. There is nothing in Minneapolis even slightly comparable to the recent, rapid growth of Battle Creek. Most of the zone developed in the manner of early postwar suburbs, simply extended beyond the previously built-up area.

One Minneapolis section is a rough counterpart of the Stonebridge estate: the group of streets near West River Road at East 40th Street. A forty-four-acre section of land between Dowling and Breck schools was given to the University of Minnesota in 1923. It was a bequest from William Henry Eustis, whose will stipulated that proceeds of any sale provide facilities for crippled children. The

University held the land until 1959, when funds were needed to build a children's rehabilitation center. The land was then sold to the Marvin Anderson Company, an active builder of suburban housing. During the 1960s the site was subdivided, and the streets were named after the buildings on the University campus. It was then filled with interstingly designed modern houses that blend into the nearby pre-war amenity landscape.

A more typical example of this zone in Minneapolis is the Kenny area, which extends from Lyndale Avenue to Morgan Avenue and from West 54th Street to the Crosstown highway. This area had some houses as early as 1912, and more were built in the 1930s, especially along Aldrich Avenue. But most of the area was open field. It had once been part of the Bachman farm, and in the forties a large nursery remained, located south of 58th Street. The area became extensively built up during the early 1950s. Small contractors would buy a few lots and build three or four houses at a time. By the late fifties most of the area was filled in, except for some low-lying blocks and the marshy land around Grass Lake.

Many of the first residents in this area were Catholics, attracted by the presence of Annunciation Church and its school near 54th and Harriet South. They were soon joined by substantial numbers of Lutherans. The churches built by these two groups represent some of the most interesting architecture in the area. Most early residents were families with small children, second- or third-generation Americans, and many of them had relatives in the area. They were not professionals, but skilled workers wanting a little more open space than was available closer to the city center. Longtime residents maintain that an established mobility pattern functioned in this area. Families started out in Kenny. When they had more money and had outgrown the area's small houses, they moved north of Minnehaha Creek into more spacious homes. Kenny was a neighborly area where people knew one another and helped one another. It had most of the traits of classic postwar suburbia, but it also had a major shopping area (54th and Lyndale) within walking distance and good transportation to downtown.

Today this area remains much the same. The housing is in good repair, and trees have grown tall around it. Some residents who moved in during the 1950s are still here, though most of their children have left. In recent years younger families have moved in, filling some of the houses with children once again. Kenny is a stable area that offers good access to both the city and the suburbs. It has few problems currently, and seems unlikely to acquire any substantial problems in the near future.

CONCLUSION

As can be seen from the few examples presented here, the suburban-in-city zone contains a wide range of landscapes and people—just like the range that exists among suburban municipalities. However, all the suburban-in-city districts have some fundamental characteristics in common. They were designed for a life-style based on the automobile and are intended to be occupied by families, the majority living in detached houses. Like most postwar developments, these districts were scorned by writers popularizing social science in the early 1960s. The style of houses now receives the disdain once applied to Victorian buildings. The "ticky-tacky" label still brings knowing smiles from strangers who happen to stumble into one of these middle-class districts. Be that as it may, the zone still has not become a slum as early critics assured us it would. It still provides homes for the majority of Saint Paul's elite and stable communities for the large middle class for which the Twin Cities is duly famous. It appears that the very wealthy have neither the time nor the inclination to restore houses. If they continue to live within the city limits, they will probably prefer to occupy the newer housing, either in the suburban-in-city zone or the new buildings downtown.

Conclusion

The most obvious conclusion to be drawn from the foregoing description of the residential zones of the Twin Cities is that Minneapolis and Saint Paul do not have two completely different sets of residential districts. As we have seen, the patterns of residential communities show little regard for the city boundaries. For example, people living in the suburban-in-city zone of Saint Paul have more problems and experiences in common with residents of the Minneapolis part of the zone than they do with residents of Saint Paul's aging inner ring or turnaround zones. Thus it is possible, we would argue it is necessary, to consider both municipalities as one unit.

Each of these eight zones, or categories of residential districts, has its own peculiar set of traits that distinguish it from the others. Because the factors that combined over the past century and one-half to produce our present configuration of housing have been diverse, it is not possible to define residential districts in terms of measurements of variation in a single characteristic or attribute. Therefore, we have used a range of attributes including age, social and economic status of residents, presence of major building programs, and likelihood of dramatic changes. Like all abstract classifications, these zones and their component districts are not completely uniform. They all contain structures and blocks of houses that are out of character. Fortunately, such occurrences are rare, and the careful observer will have no difficulty recognizing them.

Five of the zones, the aging inner ring, the protected genteel zone, the rebuilt zone, the settled mid-city, and the turnaround zone, were developed at about the same time — the last portion of the nineteenth century and the first decades of the twentieth. These places have come down to us in varying degrees of maintenance. They are characterized by striking differences in building type and architecture style. Today the five zones are occupied by people who are quite different from each other. The lower-income households are concentrated in the aging inner ring, turnaround, and rebuilt zones. The protected genteel zone houses the upper middle class. In the turnaround zone, the middle class is gradually replacing the other residents as these districts are redeveloped.

The prewar grid and prewar amenity zones were also developed before World War II and are distinguished today by the number of amenities they contain. Today they house people from the wide range of middle-class households in the Twin Cities. For the most part, they provide ideal living conditions for their inhabitants.

The newest zone contains the most surprises. Although

many commentators on the urban scene imply that Saint Paul is much older than Minneapolis, we have seen that most of the suburban-in-city zone lies in Saint Paul. In addition, this zone covers more territory than any other zone in Saint Paul. Because the city's landmarks and cultural institutions are not found in this zone, few outsiders have any degree of familiarity with it.

The protected genteel, prewar amenity, and suburban-in-city zones appear to be in the most enviable position. These places are considered desirable residential environments by almost everyone. Houses in these zones are of high quality and sell quickly; households that move out of these zones are replaced by others of equivalent status and economic achievement. People who live here are generally quite pleased with their situation. The settled mid-city and prewar grid zones seem only slightly less fortunate. Although houses in these zones are not pretentious, most of them are large enough to shelter the middle-class families who have always lived here.

The "issues" that arise in most of the zones indicate their essential security. In portions of the settled mid-city and prewar grid zones home maintenance is a problem, largely because elderly homeowners are not as able to care for their homes as they once were. Economic issues are the key to the future of these zones, as they are for both cities generally. These are the places that have to remain affordable for middle-class families if Minneapolis and Saint Paul are to remain healthy. Even the rebuilt zone, which may not look especially attractive to many people, has passed through its period of rapid decline and is now generally improving. This zone has "bottomed out" in a sense; some districts were as deteriorated as they could possibly be, and even these have been redeemed. It is unlikely that any of the rebuilt districts will ever again decline as precipitously as they once did. Of the eight zones, only two—the aging inner ring and the turnaround zones—seem likely to change significantly in the near future. All the zones appear to be well established, and changes, when they occur, will be positive and unthreatening.

Because so much of what is being noticed and written about cities today focuses on "turnaround" activities, it is quite tempting to believe that the future of urban America rests on such activities. Although we do not believe that turnaround activities alone will determine the future

residential character of Minneapolis and Saint Paul, it is useful to consider the overall impact of turnaround activities on any city.

The rewards and costs of turnaround activity can be viewed straightforwardly. The first people who move into and rehabilitate these districts get spacious living conditions for relatively little money. They may even gain a sense of community by sharing their work on and hopes for their houses with others like themselves. In time, the housing is greatly improved, as are public services and facilities. For the city, the tax base of the districts increases, generating more revenue. The people who move into these districts either to rehabilitate houses or to buy houses that have already been improved are generally more affluent than former residents. Many of the new residents are also more stable, and thus in need of fewer social services. As the number of apartments decreases as a result of demolition or condominium conversion, the proportion of owner-occupants increases. This may indicate even higher levels of stability.

On the cost side for the city is the need to provide these districts with services that had been discontinued or diminished. For example, most of the turnaround districts in Minneapolis lost their neighborhood schools many years ago; in some areas it may eventually become necessary to provide schools once again. The new residents may also clamor for public services, like police protection, garbage collection, and street cleaning, which may not have been consistently provided to former residents.

Perhaps the major cost generated by turnaround activity is the displacement of longtime residents from these districts. In order for an area to "turn around," the population of the area has to change substantially. The shift is usually from low- and moderate-income residents (who tend to be elderly or minorities) to middle- and upper-income residents (who are likely to be young and white). In recent years neighborhood activists and social critics have rallied around the displacement issue and have taken public officials to task for promoting it.

Cities are obviously caught in a bind here. On the one hand, city officials want to increase the tax base and attract residents who are able to pay their own way. On the other hand, no one wants to be accused of throwing old or poor people out of their homes. The fact that most of those being displaced are renters, and that the recent flood of condominium conversions has probably reduced the supply of rental housing, only worsens this situation. The alternatives for those forced to move out of turnaround areas, especially for those with children, are extremely limited. Recently programs for housing displaced people have either disappeared or have become less accessible. The federal government has tried to get out of the housing construction business, and rent subsidy programs have been increasingly directed away from the central city, where most people who are displaced might prefer to remain.

So the Twin Cities are faced with a difficult choice: whether to continue encouraging middle-class migration into turnaround districts and accept the responsibility for displacement; or whether to limit economic development in favor of addressing the needs of people already in these areas. There is no easy solution to this problem. Activist resident groups will not allow any city official simply to choose in favor of economic development. And in a time of decreasing federal and state aid, cities will be hard pressed to resist increasing their own tax bases, regardless of the social costs. American cities and their neediest residents can no longer look to another level of government for resources that once flowed freely. In the coming decade city governments will have to fund themselves, and less fortunate urban dwellers may suffer in the process.

The Minneapolis city government has determined that one way of saving money, while encouraging desegregation, is to close a number of public schools. This past year (1981) the School Board proposed a major restructuring of the Minneapolis public school system by closing eighteen schools at once, including three high schools. Parental and student opposition to this policy has been strong, but the decision has been made to implement it. No one is quite sure what the outcome of this decision will be. It is likely that some children will be transferred to private schools. It is certain that many fewer children will be able to attend schools near their homes. The demise of "neighborhood" schools in Minneapolis will certainly have an impact on all residential districts in the city. It remains to be seen whether this impact is negative or positive.

In general, the future looks promising for residents of Minneapolis and Saint Paul. The tax bases of these two cities are sound, and seem likely to remain so. Both cities have inaugurated policies designed to retain and expand the middle-class population base which each possesses. Efforts to reduce property taxes and to encourage both industrial and office development are among these policies. As our review of the eight zones shows, the problems associated with living in Minneapolis and Saint Paul are minimal for most people. It seems clear that many residents of the Twin Cities have fled more harried urban environments for a variety of reasons. Most say that they would not be very willing to trade their lives in Minneapolis and Saint Paul for the more hectic pace of New York or Chicago, and this is a positive sign for both cities. The residential opportunities within the two cities are many and varied, as we have seen. There is a sufficient range of choice to provide for a wide social spectrum, and to provide some choice within each economic level. The challenge for the leadership of Minneapolis and Saint Paul in the coming years will be to gain a working knowledge of this range of residential options and to ensure that it is not diminished.

Appendix

Bibliography

and Index

Appendix

All the tables are composed of composite figures based on census-tract data from the R. L. Polk Directory Company, Urban Statistical Division, Cincinnati, Ohio, and the Minneapolis "State of the City" report for 1978, published by the Minneapolis Planning Department.

Table 1. The Aging Inner Ring: Households and Dwelling Units in 1978

| | General | | | | Households | | | | | | | | |
Residential Area	Number	Change[a]	Mobility[b]	Av. Annual Income	Single-Person	With Children %	With Children Change[a]	Female-Headed	Prof.-Managerial %	Prof.-Managerial Change[a]	Retired	Jobless	Lower Incor
Minneapolis	155,932	+682	47.0%	$15,246	33.4%	26.7%	−940	5.9%	16.3%	+217	24.1%	17.5	48.3
Bryant	1,042	. . .	36.4	15,120	31.5	35.0	−21	10.5	16.0	+9	19.8	20.8	50.5
Corcoran	1,786	−58	39.4	15,220	28.0	29.3	−48	6.5	10.5	. . .	27.4	14.5	51.4
Eastern Phillips	2,388	−233	59.7	13,060	42.2	33.3	−113	13.7	10.4	−9	19.5	23.9	56.8
Harrison	956	−24	54.7	14,180	32.0	32.5	+13	10.9	10.0	−1	23.0	18.2	48.3
Hawthorne	2,521	+41	52.0	13,445	46.2	33.3	+39	9.6	6.0	+7	34.5	18.5	66.0
Holmes	1,514	+147	87.1	12,245	38.8	11.5	+4	2.6	14.0	+2	10.0	28.1	43.0
Logan Park	1,125	−40	39.6	13,880	39.8	26.8	−38	5.3	7.2	−4	32.4	13.7	55.6
Sheridan	960	−30	48.4	13,650	35.2	26.6	+6	7.7	9.2	+3	26.7	18.1	52.5
Saint Paul	103,163	+983	39.0%	$16,095	29.7%	33.8%	+251	6.5%	16.9%	+452	26.1%	12.5%	45.8%
Frogtown	1,679	−39	44.0	14,600	29.8	36.0	−30	9.0	7.5	+21	29.0	15.0	55.0
North End	3,629	−17	35.0	15,300	28.0	36.4	−4	7.5	7.0	+18	29.0	12.0	51.0
Swede Hollow	746	+34	60.8	12,743	42.1	31.9	+18	9.6	6.8	−6	33.9	161.	58.3
West Seventh	558	+12	51.4	12,500	38.0	34.0	−9	15.9	9.5	+9	27.0	20.0	57.9
West Side	3,752	+96	36.0	14,700	29.0	38.0	+70	8.0	7.0	+11	31.0	13.7	53.5

[a]From 1977 to 1978.　[b]Percentage of dwelling units with a change in occupancy.　[c]Percentage of all dwelling units.　[d]Data for the specific communities are not availabl

Table 2. Protected Genteel Zone: Households and Dwelling Units in 1978

| | General | | | | Households | | | | | | | | |
Residential Area	Number	Change[a]	Mobility[b]	Av. Annual Income	Single-Person	With Children %	With Children Change[a]	Female-Headed	Prof.-Managerial %	Prof.-Managerial Change[a]	Retired	Jobless	Lowe Incor
Minneapolis	155,932	+682	47.0%	$15,246	33.4%	26.7%	−940	5.9%	16.3%	+217	24.1%	17.5%	48.3%
Kenwood	840	−23	32.4	21,687	23.6	33.7	−6	3.5	47.4	−7	16.9	9.7	29.2
Lowry Hill	1,775	+25	62.5	15.746	41.5	22.1	+45	4.7	29.0	+17	15.0	21.3	41.3
Prospect Park	1,148	+21	44.3	17,858	34.1	25.3	+3	4.2	40.6	+13	12.3	11.7	27.2
Saint Paul	103,163	+983	39.0%	$16,095	29.7%	33.8%	+251	6.5%	16.9%	+452	26.1%	12.5%	45.8%
Crocus Hill	1,113	+18	37.2	19,566	28.9	34.5	−23	4.6	37.7	+16	16.3	10.6	30.2
Saint Anthony Park	1,814	+51	51.5	17,381	23.9	29.9	. . .	3.5	30.2	+17	16.2	13.4	32.2

[a]From 1977 to 1978.　[b]Percentage of dwelling units with a change in occupancy.　[c]Percentage of all dwelling units.

Table 1—*Continued*

Residential Area	Number	Change[a]	Vacancy Rate[c]	Single-Family	Multi-Units	Owner-Occupied %	Change
Minneapolis	162,784	−1,055	4.2%	53.6%	46.4%	52.6%	+527
Bryant	1,154	−5	9.6	71.6	28.4	65.1	−1
Corcoran	2,067	−25	3.6	68.6	31.4	67.0	−25
Eastern Phillips	2,983	−119	10.4	43.5	56.5	32.3	−22
Harrison	1,009	−25	5.2	52.4	47.6	48.3	−23
Hawthorne	2,653	. . .	5.9	36.5	63.5	33.2	+20
Holmes	1,593	+132	5.0	13.6	86.4	12.8	+26
Logan Park	1,210	−23	5.7	31.3	68.7	46.4	+26
Sheridan	995	−20	5.1	39.5	60.5	45.6	. . .
Saint Paul	106,273	−432	2.9%	58.1%[d]	41.9%[d]	58.8%[d]	+277
Frogtown	1,763	−71	4.7				+12
North End	3,765	−21	3.2				+19
Swede Hollow	774	−12	3.6				+13
West Seventh	598	−11	6.7				−12
West Side	3,892	+31	3.5				−5

Table 2—*Continued*

Residential Area	Number	Change[a]	Vacancy Rate[c]	Single-Family	Multi-Units	Owner-Occupied %	Change
Minneapolis	162,784	−1,055	4.2%	53.6%	46.4%	52.6%	+527
Kenwood	874	−10	3.4	66.6	33.4	67.5	−1
Lowry Hill	1,822	+14	2.6	24.1	75.9	33.2	+55
Prospect Park	1,163	−7	1.3	56.5	43.5	53.4	+4
Saint Paul	106,273	−432	2.9%	58.1%	41.9%	58.8%	+277
Crocus Hill	1,133	+9	1.8	58.3	41.7	63.0	+4
Saint Anthony Park	1,830	+28	0.9	57.8	42.2	55.0	+5

145

View of downtown Minneapolis from the East Bank of the Mississippi above St. Anthony Falls.

Table 3. The Rebuilt Zone: Households and Dwelling Units in 1978

Residential Area	Number	Change[a]	Mobility[b]	Av. Annual Income	Single-Person	With Children %	With Children Change[a]	Female-Headed	Prof.-Managerial %	Prof.-Managerial Change[a]	Retired	Jobless	Lower Income[c]
Minneapolis	155,932	+682	47.0%	$15,246	33.4%	26.7%	−940	5.9%	16.3%	+217	24.1%	17.5%	48.3%
Cedar-Riverside	1,836	+194	80.5	9,480	67.6	8.4	−2	4.5	6.8	−7	28.1	37.2	70.7
Gateway	742	−5	34.7	13,387	65.6	3.1	−12	0.4	25.8	+19	41.5	15.4	59.7
St. Anthony East	1,037	−13	39.1	12,740	45.0	20.9	−10	4.3	8.0	−3	40.1	10.9	60.9
St. Anthony West	929	+15	43.0	13,294	39.8	22.3	+6	4.6	13.5	+4	30.7	14.1	52.9
Sumner-Glenwood	1,303	−122	78.8	10,613	38.3	41.8	−47	25.9	7.0	−4	20.1	39.1	65.8
Saint Paul	103,163	+983	39.0%	$16,095	29.7%	33.8%	+251	6.5%	16.9%	+452	26.1%	12.5%	45.8%
West Side	471	+14	34.0	11,790	40.5	44.8	+12	15.3	5.5	+1	40.0	19.7	73.7

[a]From 1977 to 1978. [b]Percentage of dwelling units with a change in occupancy. [c]Percentage of all dwelling units.

Table 4. The Turnaround Zone: Households and Dwelling Units in 1978

Residential Area	Number	Change[a]	Mobility[b]	Av. Annual Income	Single-Person	With Children %	With Children Change[a]	Female-Headed	Prof.-Managerial %	Prof.-Managerial Change[a]	Retired	Jobless	Lower Income[c]
Minneapolis	155,932	+682	47.0%	$15,246	33.4%	26.7%	−940	5.9%	16.3%	+217	24.1%	17.5%	48.3%
Loring Park-Stevens Square	5,984	+144	79.7	11,494	54.1	9.4	+65	3.0	12.6	−64	20.6	24.9	54.7
Wedge	3,677	+102	80.5	12,646	41.9	17.7	+93	6.2	14.9	+11	9.5	32.5	50.5
Whittier	2,735	+51	45.3	16,302	23.3	47.1	+28	16.0	13.2	−6	16.3	21.8	48.1
Saint Paul	103,163	+983	39.0%	$16,095	29.7%	33.8%	+251	6.5%	16.9%	+452	26.1%	12.5%	45.8%
Ramsey Hill	1,568	+35	71.2	14,476	48.0	18.2	−20	5.0	26.9	+40	15.6	15.4	36.4

[a]From 1977 to 1978. [b]Percentage of dwelling units with a change in occupancy. [c]Percentage of all dwelling units.

Table 5. Settled Mid-City Zone: Households and Dwelling Units in 1978

Residential Area	Number	Change[a]	Mobility[b]	Av. Annual Income	Single-Person	With Children %	With Children Change[a]	Female-Headed	Prof.-Managerial %	Prof.-Managerial Change[a]	Retired	Jobless	Lower Income[c]
Minneapolis	155,932	+682	47.0%	$15,246	33.4%	26.7%	−940	5.9%	16.3%	+217	24.1%	17.5%	48.3%
Bancroft Powderhorn Park	4,177	+6	51.7	14,912	33.2	27.6	+1	6.6	14.5	+42	22.6	19.9	50.4
Camden-McKinley	2,757	−31	39.3	16,643	23.2	38.1	+4	8.2	10.4	+15	26.9	12.3	48.8
East Isles-East Calhoun-Harriet	5,217	−53	53.8	15,629	37.5	23.3	−61	4.4	24.2	−19	17.5	20.1	43.5
East Seward	2,098	. . .	36.7	13,475	42.0	23.7	−10	4.0	13.0	−5	37.5	11.3	55.3
Holland-Windom Park	4,756	−47	42.4	15,702	29.2	31.3	−52	7.1	13.2	+46	27.6	13.1	48.8
Saint Paul	103,163	+983	39.0%	$16,095	29.7%	33.8%	+251	6.5%	16.9%	+452	26.1%	12.5%	45.8%
Macalester Park	1,015	−2	44.4	16,680	37.7	30.6	−3	3.1	26.5	+10	24.0	11.1	39.0
Middle Ground	1,923	+11	33.0	15,300	30.5	33.0	−6	6.0	11.0	+2	34.0	10.0	51.0

[a]From 1977 to 1978. [b]Percentage of dwelling units with a change in occupancy. [c]Percentage of all dwelling units.

Table 3—*Continued*

Residential Area	General Number	General Change[a]	General Vacancy Rate[c]	Single-Family	Multi-Units	Owner-Occupied %	Owner-Occupied Change
Minneapolis	162,784	−1,055	4.2%	53.6%	46.4%	52.6%	+527
Cedar-Riverside	1,968	+7	6.7	1.9	98.1	6.9	−36
Gateway	832	+17	10.8	1.6	98.4	47.9	+91
St. Anthony East	1,071	−13	3.2	32.3	67.7	39.6	+22
St. Anthony West	947	+5	2.0	39.4	60.6	39.4	+12
Sumner-Glenwood	1,642	−155	20.5	49.6	50.4	12.9	+2
Saint Paul	106,273	−432	2.9%	58.1%	41.9%	58.8%	+277
West Side	484	+12	2.7	60.0	40.0	56.0	−8

Table 4—*Continued*

Residential Area	General Number	General Change[a]	General Vacancy Rate[c]	Single-Family	Multi-Units	Owner-Occupied %	Owner-Occupied Change
Minneapolis	162,784	−1,055	4.2%	53.6%	46.4%	52.6%	+527
Loring Park-Stevens Square	6,604	+57	9.3	1.2	98.8	6.3	+5.1
Wedge	3,881	−2	5.3	12.2	87.8	14.8	+10.5
Whittier	6,216	−27	6.3	11.7	88.3	13.3	+125
Willard-Homewood	2,917	−8	6.4	74.6	25.4	66.6	−7
Saint Paul	106,273	−432	2.9%	58.1%	41.9%	58.8%	+277
Ramsey Hill	1,643	−13	4.6	18.0	82.0	25.8	. . .

Table 5—*Continued*

Residential Area	General Number	General Change[a]	General Vacancy Rate[c]	Single-Family	Multi-Units	Owner-Occupied %	Owner-Occupied Change
Minneapolis	162,784	−1,055	4.2%	53.6%	46.4%	52.6%	+527
Bancroft-Powderhorn Park	4,292	+5	2.7	52.4	47.6	51.5	−20
Camden-McKinley	2,845	−94	4.2	79.4	20.6	76.9	+12
East Isles-East Calhoun-Harriet	5,494	−101	3.2	39.6	60.4	43.6	+50
East Seward	2,135	−33	1.7	49.0	51.0	47.2	+13
Holland-Windom Park	4,769	−99	2.4	60.2	39.8	63.7	+5
Saint Paul	106,273	−432	2.9%	58.1%	41.9%	58.8%	+277
Macalester Park	1,034	−7	1.4	60.0	40.0	54.0	+12
Middle Ground	1,800	−4	1.8	77.0	33.0	69.0	−4

Table 6. Pre-war Grid Zone: Households and Dwelling Units in 1978

Residential Area	General Number	General Change[a]	General Mobility[b]	Av. Annual Income	Households Single-Person	Households With Children %	Households With Children Change[a]	Households Female-Headed	Households Prof.-Managerial %	Households Prof.-Managerial Change[a]	Retired	Jobless	Lower Income[c]
Minneapolis	155,932	+682	47.0%	$15,246	33.4%	26.7%	−940	5.9%	16.3%	+217	24.1%	17.5%	48.3%
Cleveland-Victory	4,362	+43	31.0	16,974	24.4	35.0	−27	5.0	13.2	+27	34.3	9.0	50.5
Linden Hills	1,594	+8	28.3	18,788	25.8	33.2	−5	5.1	26.9	+10	24.1	12.4	39.9
Longfellow	3,880	+3	29.0	16,923	25.3	34.4	−41	4.7	13.3	+32	30.5	12.5	49.1
Minnehaha	1,659	−4	26.6	17,351	22.3	34.9	−10	4.8	14.8	−22	30.0	11.9	47.8
Northrop	1,524	−1	26.9	17,428	25.4	27.9	−15	3.4	17.8	+2	31.4	11.4	47.9
Standish	2,674	+22	29.5	15,921	28.9	28.9	+5	5.6	12.0	+15	32.0	11.6	50.4
Saint Paul	103,163	+983	39.0%	$16,095	29.7%	33.8%	+251	6.5%	16.9%	+452	26.1%	12.5%	45.8%
Central Fairview	1,679	+10	22.2	18,507	25.1	34.3	+7	3.3	26.1	+1	32.8	6.3	41.0
South Phalen	1,429	−2	24.4	17,013	26.0	34.5	−8	4.3	14.3	−2	33.4	7.1	48.2

[a]From 1977 to 1978. [b]Percentage of dwelling units with a change in occupancy. [c]Percentage of all dwelling units.

Table 7. Prewar Amenity Zone: Households and Dwelling Units in 1978

Residential Area	General Number	General Change[a]	General Mobility[b]	Av. Annual Income	Households Single-Person	Households With Children %	Households With Children Change[a]	Households Female-Headed	Households Prof.-Managerial %	Households Prof.-Managerial Change[a]	Retired	Jobless	Lower Income[c]
Minneapolis	155,932	+682	47.0%	$15,246	33.4%	26.7%	−940	5.9%	16.3%	+217	24.1%	17.5%	48.3%
Cedar Lake-West Calhoun	2,981	−40	40.9	18,605	31.2	26.1	−1	3.0	37.0	−4	19.1	14.9	37.1
Diamond Lake	1,806	−6	27.3	18,528	26.9	33.1	−18	3.4	27.5	−11	28.1	11.0	42.5
Lynnhurst	1,440	−10	20.2	21,898	17.4	40.5	−39	3.5	37.1	+18	21.2	8.9	32.6
Nokomis	2,606	−6	23.6	18,735	21.5	32.6	−18	3.6	23.9	−4	27.6	11.1	42.7
Saint Paul[d]	103,163	+983	39.0%	$16,095	29.7%	33.8%	+251	6.5%	16.9%	+452	26.1%	12.5%	45.8%

[a]From 1977 to 1978. [b]Percentage of dwelling units with a change in occupancy. [c]Percentage of all dwelling units.
[d]The small size of the specific communities (smaller than census tracts) made data collection impracticable.

Table 8. Suburban-In-City Zone: Households and Dwelling Units in 1978

Residential Area	General Number	General Change[a]	General Mobility[b]	Av. Annual Income	Households Single-Person	Households With Children %	Households With Children Change[a]	Households Female-Headed	Households Prof.-Managerial %	Households Prof.-Managerial Change[a]	Retired	Jobless	Lower Income[c]
Minneapolis	155,932	+682	47.0%	$15,246	33.4%	26.7%	−940	5.9%	16.3%	+217	24.1%	17.5%	48.3%
Armitage-Kenny	3,943	−11	20.2	21,389	16.3	37.9	−63	3.4	33.3	−1	21.9	8.6	33.6
Diamond Lake	1,419	−21	18.5	19,453	18.9	30.8	−8	3.1	27.1	−12	30.0	10.0	44.3
Shingle Creek	1,165	−4	22.4	19,778	13.7	42.3	−4	6.3	13.6	−5	16.4	12.4	35.3
Waite Park	2,354	−3	20.4	18,637	17.7	33.2	−29	4.3	17.1	+8	29.3	6.7	42.8
Saint Paul	103,163	+983	39.0%	$16,095	29.7%	33.8%	+251	6.5%	16.9%	+452	26.1%	12.5%	45.8%
Battle Creek	3,052	+159	52.0	18,750	20.0	38.5	+57	5.0	27.0	+13	12.0	12.0	29.5
Hazel Park	1,819	+9	15.6	19,947	14.6	44.1	+1	3.2	16.0	+13	22.1	6.6	36.0
Highland Park	2,048	−10	21.7	21,070	20.7	31.4	−1	2.9	41.0	+12	22.7	7.5	32.2

[a]From 1977 to 1978. [b]Percentage of dwelling units with a change in occupancy. [c]Percentage of all dwelling units.

Table 6—*Continued*

Residential Area	Dwelling Units General Number	Change[a]	Vacancy Rate[c]	Single-Family	Multi-Units	Owner-Occupied %	Change
Minneapolis	162,784	−1,055	4.2%	53.6%	46.4%	52.6%	+527
Cleveland-Victory	4,436	−1	1.6	87.7	12.3	87.2	+30
Linden Hills	1,630	+22	2.2	75.7	24.3	72.6	+4
Longfellow	3,958	−3	1.9	88.4	11.6	84.4	. . .
Minnehaha	1,683	−19	1.4	89.7	10.3	84.0	−8
Northrop	1,558	. . .	2.2	91.9	8.1	84.2	−15
Standish	2,715	+12	1.5	81.3	18.7	76.9	−26
Saint Paul	106,273	−432	2.9%	58.1%	41.9%	58.8%	+277
Central Fairview	1,690	−10	0.6	82.3	17.7	81.0	−7
South Phalen	1,445	−13	1.1	57.4	02.6	81.0	−9

Table 7—*Continued*

Residential Area	Dwelling Units General Number	Change[a]	Vacancy Rate[c]	Single-Family	Multi-Units	Owner-Occupied %	Change
Minneapolis	162,784	−1,055	4.2%	53.6%	46.4%	52.6%	+527
Cedar Lake-West							
Calhoun	3,082	+2	3.6	48.6	51.4	51.8	+45
Diamond Lake	1,837	−5	1.7	86.8	13.2	81.3	−6
Lynnhurst	1,499	−17	1.1	93.0	7.0	90.9	−10
Nokomis	2,655	. . .	1.7	91.8	8.2	87.4	−30
Saint Paul	106,273	−432	2.9%	58.1%	41.9%	58.8%	+277

Table 8—*Continued*

Residential Area	Dwelling Units General Number	Change[a]	Vacancy Rate[c]	Single-Family	Multi-Units	Owner-Occupied %	Change
Minneapolis	162,784	−1,055	4.2%	53.6%	46.4%	52.6%	+527
Armitage-Kenny	4,006	. . .	1.3	93.7	6.3	90.7	−27
Diamond Lake	1,444	−6	1.7	97.7	2.3	93.4	−19
Shingle Creek	1,189	+1	2.0	94.1	5.9	92.4	+3
Waite Park	2,381	−8	1.2	91.2	8.8	89.8	−10
Saint Paul	106,273	−432	2.9%	58.1%	41.9%	58.8%	+277
Battle Creek	3,126	+99	2.5	55.0	45.0	48.0	+26
Hazel Park	1,830	−6	0.6	96.0	4.0	96.0	+26
Highland Park	2,083	-4	1.7	79.0	21.0	77.0	−7

Unusual form of lawn-mowing on pastoral Nicollet Island.

Bibliography

BOOKS AND JOURNAL ARTICLES

Abler, Ronald, John Adams, and John Borchert. *The Twin Cities of St. Paul-Minneapolis*. Cambridge, Mass.: Ballinger Press, 1976.

Anderson, Chester G., ed. *Growing Up in Minnesota: Ten Writers Remember Their Childhoods*. Minneapolis, Minn.: University of Minnesota Press, 1976.

Atwater, Isaac, ed. *History of the City of Minneapolis Minnesota*. New York: Munsell & Co., 1893.

Borchert, John R. "The Twin Cities Urbanized Area: Past, Present, Future." *Geographical Review* 51(1961):47-70.

Empson, Donald. "Highland-Groveland-Macalester Park: The Old Reserve Township." *Ramsey County History* 10(1973):13-19.

_____. *The Street Where You Live: A Guide to the Street Names of St. Paul*. Saint Paul: Witsend Press, 1975.

Gebhard, David, and Thomas Martinson. *A Guide to the Architecture of Minnesota*. Minneapolis: University of Minnesota Press, 1977.

Kunz, Virginia. *St. Paul, Saga of an American City*. Woodland Hills, Calif.: Winsor Publications, 1977.

Lanegran, David A. "Swedes in the Twin Cities." In *Swedes in Minnesota*, ed. Byron Nordstrom. Minneapolis: Denison Press, 1976.

_____. *Urban Dynamics in St. Paul: A Study of Neighborhood and Center City Interaction*. Saint Paul: Old Town Restorations Press, 1977.

_____. "Urban Neighbor: Macalester's Role in the Development of St. Paul." *MAC Today* 6(1977):1-4.

_____. "Neighborhood Conservation in the Twin Cities." *Architecture Minnesota* 4(1978):14-20.

_____, and Ernest R. Sandeen. *The Lake District of Minneapolis*. Saint Paul: Living Historical Museum Press, 1979.

Lentz, Ted. *Selby Avenue: Future of the Street*. Saint Paul: Old Town Restorations Press, 1978.

_____. *Selby Avenue: Status of the Street*. Saint Paul: Old Town Restorations Press, 1978.

Martin, Judith. *Recycling the Central City*. Minneapolis: Center for Urban and Regional Affairs, 1978.

Richter, Bonnie. *St. Paul Omnibus: Images of the Changing City*. Saint Paul: Old Town Restorations Press, 1979.

Sandeen, Ernest R. *St. Paul's Historic Summit Avenue*. Saint Paul: Living Historical Museum Press, 1978.

Schmidt, Calvin F. *Social Saga of Two Cities*. Minneapolis: W.P.A., 1937.

Shutter, Marion D. *History of Minneapolis*. Chicago and Minneapolis: St. Charles Publishing, 1923.

Smith, Rebecca Lou. *Postwar Housing in National and Local Perspective: A Twin Cities Case Study*. Minneapolis: Center for Urban and Regional Affairs, 1978.

Steinhauser, Frederic. "St. Anthony Park: The History of a 'Small Town' within a city." *Ramsey County History* 7(1970):3-11.

Wirth, Theodore. *Minneapolis Park System, 1883-1944*. Minneapolis: Board of Park Commissioners of Minneapolis, 1945.

Wolneiwicz, Richard. "Ethnic Persistence in Northeast Minneapolis." Unpublished masters thesis, University of Minnesota, Minneapolis, 1973.

Women's Cooperative Alliance (publisher). *Study of Community Conditions: North District*. Minneapolis, 1925.

PLANNING REPORTS AND RELATED PUBLICATIONS

Minneapolis Planning Department (publisher). "Community Improvement Program Reports, 1965-1966." 1966.

_____. "Urban Renewal Plans for Neighborhoods, 1962-1968." 1968.

_____. "State of the City, 1977." 2 vols. 1977.

_____. "State of the City, 1978." 1978.

_____. "State of the City, 1979." 1979.

_____. "State of the City, 1980." 1980.

NEWSPAPERS

Altrowitz, Abe. Neighborhoods of Minneapolis series in the *Minneapolis Star*, Feburary 13 to February 28, 1958.

There are a large number of neighborhood newspapers published in the Twin Cities. Several have provided valuable background information about their local communities. Among them are the *East Minneapolis Argus*, the *Loring Community Crier*, the *North Minneapolis Post*, the *Highland Villager*, the *Grand Gazette*, and the *Frog Town Forum*.

Index

Judith Martin is coordinator of the urban studies program and research associate at the Center for Urban and Regional Affairs at the University of Minnesota. She is the author of *Recycling the Center City*. **David Lanegran**, a professor of geography at Macalester College in St. Paul, has written several books and articles on the Twin Cities, including *Urban Dynamics in St. Paul: A Study of Urban and Center City Interaction* and *The Lake District of Minneapolis* (with Ernest R. Sandeen).